WHEN I GROW UP
A Memoir

Juliana Hatfield

WILEY

John Wiley & Sons, Inc.

Published by John Wiley & Sons, Inc., Hoboken, New Jersey
Published simultaneously in Canada

The names of some characters and locations have been changed.

For general information about our other products and services, please contact our Customer Care Department within the United States at (800) 762-2974, outside the United States at (317) 572-3993 or fax (317) 572-4002.

Wiley also publishes its books in a variety of electronic formats. Some content that appears in print may not be available in electronic books. For more information about Wiley products, visit our web site at www.wiley.com.

Library of Congress Cataloging-in-Publication Data:

Hatfield, Juliana.
    When I grow up : a memoir / Juliana Hatfield.
        p.   cm.
    ISBN 978-0-470-18959-7 (cloth)
    1. Hatfield, Juliana. 2. Singers—United States—Biography. 3. Guitarists—United States—Biography. I. Title.
    ML420.H19
    [A3   2008]
    782.42164092—dc22
    [B]

                                                                    2008027940

Printed in the United States of America

10 9 8 7 6 5 4 3 2 1

Contents

Acknowledgments

Thank you: Jeff Kellogg at Pavilion Literary Management, Eric Nelson at Wiley, Grub Street, Gary Smith, Tom Johnston, Bobbie Gale, Jennifer Trynin, and Dinny Roberts, without whose encouragement and counsel this book might not have been written.

Prologue

Some club owners and promoters opt to give the band drink tickets, good for complimentary beverages at the bar, instead of setting up a spread backstage. A long strip of those little generic "admit one" tear-off tickets is given to the tour manager, who then distributes them to his charges. Usually we'd get about four tickets each, which was normally enough. I'd only need one of mine—one drink per night was generally all I ever had—and I'd give the rest to the others, and everyone was happy. And if one of them ran out of tickets before the night was over, before he was done drinking, he could always find a girl to buy him a drink. (People always want to buy drinks for the band.)

The dressing rooms in these small rock clubs are often unwelcoming and unpleasant. The drink tickets make sense because bands would rather be out in the club hanging out at the bar, mingling with the people, watching the opening act. The tickets are better for the club, too, than schlepping a big cooler with ice, and a bunch of beers, sodas, and waters into the dressing room.

An up-and-coming band commands bigger guarantees, and the rider is nonnegotiable. They get the bottles and the ice backstage, no discussion. But when you're in my position, you go along with the drink ticket compromise. And you try to be grateful that you are being given anything at all, for free. You can usually find what you want at the bar.

On one particular night, on a headlining solo tour in 2004—no band, no crew; just me with one guitar and one little Fender Champ amp—I had just finished my soundcheck and was looking forward to relaxing in the basement dressing room, reading the *New Yorker* in the quiet before the doors opened and the people came, and the house music system was turned up really loud, and started pounding on the walls of the dressing room.

After I'd settled down on the the dirty, beer-scented, cigarette-burnt couch and tucked my feet under me Indian-style, Ike, the big bald bouncer and club owner's right-hand guy, walked in. He'd been assigned drink ticket distribution duty. He ripped off four from the ticket roll in his hand, handed them to me, and said, "These are good for well drinks and beer at the bar." ("Well liquor" is the cheap, generic stuff clubs use when you order a mixed drink without specifying a brand of liquor.)

I said, "Okay. But how about if I want to get, say, a shot of good tequila? Will two tickets get me that?"

Ike looked at me skeptically and said, "Well, tell me exactly what you want and maybe I can work something out, but these tickets here are just for well alcohol and beer. But, like I said, I can probably arrange it beforehand with the bartender and the owner if you want something else."

It was still early and I didn't know exactly what I was going to want to drink, if anything, later in the night. So I said to Ike, "Forget it. Never mind. Thanks."

I didn't want to get into an argument with Ike. He was quite tall and muscular. Mean-looking. He obviously considered this drink ticket business a very serious matter. I didn't. In monetary terms, the difference between one performer having one good free drink and not having any drink was negligible. Either way, the night's bar take would be pretty much the same.

Did they think I would try to deplete their inventory of expensive tequila? Did I *look* like a lush, sitting quietly, reading my *New Yorker*?

Did they think that if they let me have that one shot, it would be like opening the floodgates? That I would think, "Hey, I figured out a way to scam these suckers into giving me top-shelf liquor with the drink tickets! I'm going to run to the bar and drink them into bankruptcy!"

About an hour and a half later, I decided I wanted a shot of Patrón. I went to the bar, money in hand, fully prepared to pay for it. Otherwise it was much too complicated. (Prearrange it with the owner, the bartender, *and* the bouncer, and still only the promise of "maybe"? Were they kidding me?)

The handsome young blond bartender poured me a shot. The bar was empty, except for the bar staff, since the doors hadn't opened yet. I had my wad of cash in my hand and said to the bartender, "How much?"

He said, "You're playing, right? It's on the house," and he smiled.

I said, "You sure?"

He said, "Yeah." ("Ah, how nice," I thought. "A sensible human being.")

So I said thanks, tipped him two dollars, and went back to the dressing room to sip my shot in peace.

About two minutes later, Mark, the owner of the club, walked in, looked disapprovingly at my shot glass sitting innocently on the low table in front of me, and started to explain to me how the drink tickets were supposed to work. It was the exact same spiel Ike had given me: "I just wanted to let you know that the drink tickets are good for just well liq—"

"Yeah," I interrupted. "I know. Ike told me. But I wanted a shot of Patrón."

Was Mark *spying* on me? Did someone rat me out? How did Mark even know I'd gotten a drink? I hadn't seen him in the bar area.

"Well," Mark continued, "these tickets don't get you Patrón."

"Well, I *wanted* to pay for it. I really did."

"*Believe* me," I thought, "I *really* wanted to avoid this. I didn't want you coming after me to lecture me and scold me like I was a misbehaving eight-year-old. It's not my fault the bartender wouldn't take my money. Not my fault the bartender was just being cool."

Then Mark said, accusingly, almost hatefully, "Yeah, the bartender's cute, huh?"

Mark seemed to be implying that since the bartender was studly, I must have flirted and sweet-talked him into giving me a free shot. Of course, nothing could've been further from the truth, but I wasn't going to waste my time trying to explain myself. I just wanted to play my show and get out of there.

I had been playing in these kinds of places for so many years that the novelty had worn off. Rock clubs were fun and exciting when I was a teenager, but I wasn't a kid anymore. And I was still being treated as if I were. The clubs all stayed the same but I had changed.

This wasn't what I thought my life was going to be. I thought that by now, in my thirties, I'd have reached a certain level of success and comfort and respectability. I thought that if I put in the time and the work, it would eventually take me to a nicer, better place than where I was now. And I *had* put in the time. I'd worked *so* hard.

Why was I still doing this? Why didn't I quit while I was ahead? The truth was, I'd lost my chance to quit while I was ahead. At this point, quitting would be cutting my losses. The returns were diminishing— had been for a while—and this truth was hitting me hard down there in that cold basement dressing room.

Sometimes I almost wished someone would just end it for me— force me out—because I couldn't seem to pull myself out of it and move on to some life more becoming to a grown-up woman. There never seemed to be a definite point at which I should throw in the towel. What if I didn't *want* it to be over? What if I just wanted it to be—and still believed it could be—better?

Maybe it was time for me to get a real job. But what would I do? The question "What am I going to be when I grow up?" had suddenly become very pertinent. I had never needed to ask that question when I was younger, because I *knew*. It was always going to be music. That was what I thought then. But I learned that it's not that simple. There's more to a career in music than music. And all those other complications had caught up to me, and led me to question everything that had been certain for so long.

How could I ease out of this with some of my dignity intact? What was keeping me here in this kid's game?

I'd bet my whole life and my future on playing it, and winning. And it *had* paid off, for a good chunk of time, in my twenties. More importantly, it had saved me. Many times. When I was falling apart, an emotional mess, it held me together. When I didn't know who I was or what the hell to do with my life or how to do it, music gave me a purpose. When I felt small and insignificant and worthless and totally confused about almost everything else, music gave me pride and self-esteem. I was a shy, quiet, doubtful girl. Only music brought me out of my shell. On good days, it made me feel ten feet tall. Even on bad days, it was a reason to endure. It made me feel like I had value, like I mattered, like all the broken pieces of me fit together. All my faults and problems even made my music *better*; they gave it its power. The sum of my damaged parts was whole great songs and albums.

My music was my religion. It grounded me *and* opened the door to the heavens. From the age of about sixteen I had absolutely no doubt that this was what I was meant to do. Born to do. But then, right around the time of the drink tickets, my God seemed to have abandoned his post in my wheelhouse. He seemed not to be guiding me anymore through the fog of life's confusions and pains. I felt lost, like a ship drifting at night with the stars and moon all gone from the sky.

Everything started to fall away. My audience, my listeners, record buyers, my confidence, my conviction. My belief in what I was doing—in what had always seemed so necessary, so important, so certain, so closed to debate—wavered. It was scary as hell.

I would have quit right then in that basement dressing room (or after the show, anyway). I would have quit for good and retreated into a life of dignified anonymity, if not for two things: I didn't know what else to do, and I wasn't quite done yet. I still had more to say with my music, if only: "You haven't seen the best of me yet." I could feel it—some spark still deep in me and dying to burn. That little bit of me that I'd always been holding in reserve, for a time like now, perhaps. I still needed to prove—to myself and to the world—that I mattered. I'd never felt that I had fulfilled my potential as an artist. I still had to make something great happen before I could quit. I didn't want to go out with a whimper. I would retire with a blast of beauty. I knew I had a great, untapped album in me. I was always a late bloomer and I knew from the beginning that my best wouldn't show itself right away. But unfortunately the entertainment business does not wait for slow growers like me to ripen.

This book is a chronicle of that idea, and where it led me. When I was a young girl, I thought I wanted to be a rock star when I grew up. But what happens when a rock star starts to wonder if maybe it's time to grow up? Maybe I never became a household name, but I have made a living with my music. I've heard my songs on the radio, I've seen myself on TV and in magazines, and I've played in front of tens of thousands of people.

You could say this story began the first time I picked up a guitar, or heard the Replacements for the first time.

You could say it began when I was on the cover of *Spin* magazine, or when I first performed on *The Tonight Show*.

You could say it all started when I signed my first record deal with an independent label, or when I was dropped from Atlantic Records. You could say it started when I canceled a whole string of European shows due to severe depression.

Or you could say that it really began in earnest when I set out on yet another cross-country tour of small clubs, a few years back, and came face-to-face with my growing inability to play this role any longer; that it took me a whole decades-spanning career in music to realize that maybe I wasn't really cut out for the job of rock star.

1

August 1

Hoboken

There was a trail of garbage all along the road that led from the highway exit to the Palace Hotel. I looked out the window at the ground and watched it all whizz by—candy wrappers, stray newspaper pages, Styrofoam cups, chicken bones. Poking up from between pieces of trash were anemic bunches of weeds, wilted by the heat wave and the soot.

"How sad," I thought. "Those poor plants born here, right by the New Jersey Turnpike, in a perpetual exhaust-fume haze." In place of clean water, there were dousings of coffee from cups tossed out of passing cars. Instead of wispy summer breezes, there were intermittent blasts of hot air knocking the plants violently around and bending them back and over until their uppermost parts almost touched the ground. But they kept springing back up again.

I know exactly how that feels.

The Palace was a hulking gray blocklike structure built into the side of a hill next to the turnpike, just a few miles outside of Manhattan in North Bergen, New Jersey. The building's face loomed south over an unsightly highway vista of smog and power lines and clouds of black smoke belched out of big trucks that lumbered, dangerously and loudly, at high speeds.

The Palace was to be our home for the next three nights. It was convenient to Hoboken (the scene of our first gig, that night) and also to Philadelphia and New York City (the following two gigs, respectively). And it was cheap.

A large crowd of mostly blond, Teutonic-looking young men and women were gathered outside the front entrance of the hotel when we pulled up. There must have been a hundred of them. They looked remarkably hearty and hale, for the most part, with a collective rosy, wide-cheekboned glow. Some were sitting on the curb and others were standing in groups of two or three, chatting. It sounded like German. Many of them held backpacks. They appeared to be poised to go somewhere, en masse. Sightseeing, probably: Empire State Building, Statue of Liberty, Ground Zero, Macy's.

The band, the merch guy, and I waited outside for Tim to check us in and get our room keys. Soon two big charter buses arrived and all the foreigners loaded themselves and their rucksacks in and were whisked away.

Tim was my soundman and tour manager. He ran a recording studio out of his loft in South Boston, doing engineering and production, and he was also a live front-of-house and monitor mixer. He took his job very seriously, and he was seriously good at his job. I never got as many compliments after my shows ("You sounded great! Who does your sound? He's good.") as I did when Tim was behind the sound board. The fact that Tim could do double duty as a tour manager—handling all the logistics of having a band on the road—was a big plus for me since it effectively eliminated one whole employee. It kept costs slightly down and made for more room in the van.

I tended to be booked in a lot of small, grungy rock clubs whose sound systems were kind of old and clunky. Tim—who often worked in nice theaters with the likes of Aimee Mann, Richard Thompson, and Marc Cohn (some of Tim's other clients)—could get a bit huffy when a club's PA was not well maintained. He'd scurry around the club trying to recalibrate and rewire things that had been neglected, muttering to himself about the unprofessionalism of his slacker colleagues in the live sound trade—the ones who had left the sound system in such an egregious state of subfunctionality.

I liked the fact that Tim cared so much about his work. I knew that he could extract the very best out of a crappy old sound system, and that was why I had hired him. If he tended to get emotionally involved in his work, well, I was glad for it, frankly. His job was to make me sound great, whatever it took.

As for me, I'd learned to make do with whatever I had to work with on my part of the stage by wearing earplugs during gigs. My voice wasn't a naturally loud instrument and often the ancient, grime-encrusted vocal monitors in front of my feet didn't have the power to boost my voice above the din of the drums and amps. Earplugs made my voice louder in my head, while blocking out some of the harshness of the other noises. And with Tim out front, I was confident that my voice would shine through loud and clear for the crowd.

When Tim came out from the lobby he handed us our keys and we all headed inside and up to the second floor, where our rooms were. The corridor leading from the elevator to the rooms resembled a hallway on a ship, with a thick rope railing hanging horizontally at hip level all the way along the middle of the walls on either side. The lower half of the walls was dark wood and the upper half was a strange mirrorlike material. The effect of the shiny wall coupled with the nautical rope was disorienting. It was like being on a cruise for swingers.

When I entered my room, I saw that the same silvery stuff was covering the ceiling of the bathroom, and the mirror was also made of this material. It was like a combination of reflective glass and aluminum foil; like metallic wallpaper. This paper, however, was not uniformly flat; there were bumps and bubbles dotting its surface, as if it had been sloppily applied, or the humidity from countless steamy showers had loosened and unstuck its glue in spots, leaving it partially rumpled.

At any rate, I wasn't able to see a clear, accurate reflection of my face when I stood in front of the sink. What I could see was blurry. I was an amorphous blob.

"What am I doing?" I wondered. "What am I trying to prove, starting a new band, after all this time on my own? It's just gonna confuse people."

After many years releasing albums under my own name, I had recently begun a creative musical collaboration with Freda Love and Heidi Gluck, calling the group "Some Girls." We had written and recorded an album together, which was going to be released sometime in the coming year. This tour was my way of introducing my fans to the idea of Some Girls, and to the songs. I was still the main attraction—the shows were billed as "Juliana Hatfield and Some Girls" (or were supposed to be; some promoters neglected to add on the "and Some Girls" part). I was afraid that if we called ourselves simply "Some Girls" right out of the gate, before the record was out, no one would show up at the gigs, because no one knew yet who or what "Some Girls" was. I hoped people would warm to the concept. Maybe Some Girls would even surpass my solo accomplishments, and go on to be bigger and more of a name brand than I ever was on my own.

I had known Freda, the drummer in Some Girls, for about fifteen years, since we were both teenagers. We'd met in the late 1980s and formed a band together—my first, the Blake Babies—and then we'd gone our separate ways after the band's breakup four years later. Freda had secured a place forever in my top five favorite people of all time. She was a warm, funny, smart, direct, patient, and empathetic companion, the kind of wholeheartedly cool person that other people aspire to be more like. She was a great drummer, too, with a distinctive style—simple, driving, sparing with the fills. Freda was like a smiling, sexier Mo Tucker (of the Velvet Underground).

Freda had a calming, grounding effect on me. Whereas normally I felt I was in danger of coming apart, pieces of me flying off in all different directions, Freda's presence made me instinctively want to pull myself together; to try my best to follow her example.

Heidi was more of an enigma. I had only just met her that past year when Freda and I had decided to embark on this new project and we needed a bass player. Freda, who lived in Bloomington, Indiana, suggested an acquaintance of hers, a twenty-three-year-old, good-looking, supertalented multi-instrumentalist and singer from Indianapolis by way of Winnipeg, Canada, named Heidi Gluck. We invited her into the studio for a sort of, casual audition. Low-key, low-maintenance, dryly funny, quietly intelligent, Heidi fit right in. She learned the songs quickly and had good creative ideas.

Since making *Feel It*, that first Some Girls album, I had spent a total of only about two weeks with Heidi—ten days in the studio and a few days of rehearsal for the road. As a result, I didn't know her very well when we embarked on this tour. Still, being aligned with her and Freda, I felt I was part of something again. After more than ten years of shouldering a solo career and being in that spotlight, with all the pressure and criticism solely on me, it was a relief to step back into the safety and comfort of the symbolic gang (of sisters, in our case): the rock band. We would all carry equal weight—we'd share songwriting and singing, and all earnings and expenses would be split equally, three ways.

Although my name was more well-known than the others', and I would most likely be singled out as the front woman in the press and promotion, I just wanted to be one of the Girls.

We had some time before we needed to be at Maxwell's, the club we were booked to play, so I decided to take a shower and wash off some of the clammy heat-wave grime that had accumulated on the four-hour drive from Boston.

The sliding shower door had been painted an opaque gray. This door went all the way up from the tub to the ceiling, so that when I got in and closed the door, I couldn't see anything. The soap and the washcloth and the hot and cold controls were all shrouded in darkness, and I had to slide open the shower door a few inches to let some light in.

During the course of my hair-washing, water spilled out all over the bathroom floor, because the shower door was open. When I was done rinsing, I put one of the only two thin polyester towels on the floor (there was no bath mat) and the rag was instantly soaked. The one flimsy towel remaining was used trying to dry off my long hair and my body and then there was nothing left to put on the wet floor. I really wanted to avoid stepping on the floor, because this wasn't the nicest hotel. I couldn't *not* put my feet down at *all*, so I ended up stepping around the bathroom on tiptoe, to be safe.

I decided not to take any more showers until we got to the next hotel, four days from now. Showering was just much too complicated.

I walked through the room—it was done up in muted pink and purple tones, like salmon and black raspberry ice cream—to the balcony and looked out at the highway. Just south, I knew, was the oil refinery belching sulfurous toxins into the air and whose nauseating egg

11

odor I could smell from here, miles away. I had driven by it many times on past tours. It was like a deserted, postapocalyptic machine city, with its industrial flames dancing malevolently on the tops of impenetrable steely towers. It always scared me, especially at night when the flames were brightest, and made me want to drive faster, away from it.

The phone rang. It was Tim, reminding me that it was time for all of us to go to the club for soundcheck.

Maxwell's was a well-known, well-loved indie rock club in the heart of Hoboken, New Jersey, a tunnel away from Manhattan. It was just down the street from the Maxwell House coffee factory and the air around Maxwell's always smelled strongly, pleasantly, of coffee. I always looked forward to playing Maxwell's. Gigs there usually had a looser, more fun vibe than ones in New York City, where artists (including me) are often anxious about putting on a good, streamlined show for the discerning, uber-hip, hard-to-impress, trendmaking New York critics and audiences. Maxwell's was almost like a rest stop—a welcome, much-needed break on the way to or following bigger, more pressurized gigs. A band could loosen up, get drunk, play a ridiculously long and/or sloppy set, and the crowd would love it.

One side of Maxwell's was the club—the small room, with a small bar, in which bands played. The other side—through a narrow hallway—was a restaurant, serving good, simple, nutritious, comforting fare (soups, pastas, salads) to the night's featured bands (bands ate for free) and to regular restaurantgoers who'd stroll in from the street.

I liked Maxwell's because of the relaxed atmosphere and the good, free food, but also because the room the bands played in was so small that every artist was virtually guaranteed a full or seemingly full house. So that even if you were a brand-new band, just starting out, you felt important, like your music mattered.

At Maxwell's there were two bouquets of flowers waiting for me at the bar. One was from my friend Metcalf. The card read, "Happy opening night. Have a great tour." Metcalf's flowers were pretty pinkish-purple Gerber daisies—they would coordinate perfectly with my pink and purple hotel room. I could put them in water and enjoy them for a while, since we'd be in the same place for three nights.

The other bouquet came with belated birthday greetings from a guy named Skeet. I knew Skeet from the countless shows of mine that he had attended. He was a dedicated live music fan and a postman by trade. He used to follow the Grateful Dead around on tour, when Jerry Garcia was alive, and record their shows and trade the tapes with a network of fans around the country. I guess you could call him a Deadhead. A harmless old hippie in sandals and a tie-dyed T-shirt. Somewhere along the line someone turned him on to my music, and that was when he started coming to as many shows of mine as he could, sometimes traveling quite far from his home in upstate New York, and recording most of them. He had established himself as my de facto, if unofficial, archivist. He traded Juliana Hatfield bootlegs just as he'd done with the Dead. He would most likely be at Maxwell's tonight, documenting this historical first-ever Some Girls show on tape.

The dressing room was down a steep flight of gnarly, old, uneven wooden stairs. As I descended them, I thought, "I wouldn't want to be drunk and in high heels going down these stairs. A girl could really hurt herself."

The stairs led to the cellar. The basement often doubles, in these little rock clubs/bars, as both a storage area and a holding room for the band. Put the talent down with the canned goods and the cobwebs and the mouse droppings, is how the thinking goes. A tiny room to the right of the bottom step was for us. It was the size of a narrow walk-in closet, about ten feet long and five feet across, with a built-in wooden bench running along one wall and taking up about half the already cramped space. It was extremely cozy, and very warm, in the dressing room. A stuffy heat trap, some might say.

I was excited and nervous when I stepped onstage at showtime. It had been about a year since I'd played my last show. Although I had done this hundreds of times before, this time was different. There were new tunes that no one had ever heard before, and a new band, with a new name, and I wasn't sure how people would react. Right away, though, the crowd made me feel welcome, surging warmly and clapping. Someone yelled, "I love you, Juliana!"

It felt natural and unnatural at the same time to be up there in front of the people again.

"Aah, yes," my physical self remembered. "Left hand around the guitar neck, right hand holding the pick, mouth on the microphone, feet planted firmly. This is what I *do*."

But it took my brain a few seconds longer to adjust to the sudden shift into this alternate reality. It struggled, for a moment, to reacclimate: "Wait a second. What is happening? Why am I standing exposed, in bright lights, in front of a bunch of strangers who are clapping and yelling and staring, at *me*. Whoa. Oh yeah, I remember. Oh yeah. Oh . . . *yeah.*"

And then we kicked into the first song. After that, I don't remember anything.

The first show on a tour is like kissing someone for the first time. It's a kind of wonderful blur. It happens in a flash of blinding light as if time has no weight or meaning and then, suddenly, it's over. After the initial thrilling, terrifying dive into it, the experience never again has the same intensity. Some of the magic, wired energy slips from your hands—maybe because your nerves have settled—and though you strive to reclaim it every night thereafter, you do settle into a workaday routine of gig after gig.

All of us—Freda, Heidi, and I—were smiling and kind of giddy when we got down to the dressing room after the encore. The one hundred and fifty people that constituted a packed house (Maxwell's was *really* small) were still applauding.

"That was so fun!" said Freda.

"Yeah," I said. "I think the people dug it."

But part of me was thinking, "It's all downhill from here."

It was really hot and hard to breathe in our little closet area, so we moved out into the main room of the cellar and stood among the shelves of canned tomatoes, industrial-sized plastic containers of yellow mustard, and cases of beer.

Heidi's boyfriend, Jesse, came down to the basement with a couple of his friends, one of whom was a really cute guy with a mohawk. They were sweaty from being packed in like sardines upstairs, and we girls were sweaty from rocking, so all of us got in the meat locker to cool down. Normally I don't go for guys who put a lot of thought into their hairdos, but the mohawked guy really was handsome and I was kind of lonely and I started wishing it was just me and him in the meat locker, making out. I tried to transmit a message to him telepathically: "Like me. Like me. Like me," I commanded, really concentrating, and then "I like you. I like you. I like you," and I think it worked 'cause then Mr.

Mohawk invited me and Freda to go to a party in the city with him and Jesse and Heidi and the rest of them.

But I declined. I was tired. And I knew it wouldn't have worked out with me and the trendy haircut guy anyway. He and I were just a fantasy that could never be real. I was too old to make out with strangers with silly roosterlike crests on their heads. Mohawks, like drugs and cigarettes and hooking-up, are for kids. And I wouldn't have had any fun at that party. Parties are almost never fun for me. My idea of fun was to go back to the hotel and get into bed and fall asleep. Now, *that* would be a good time.

Freda thought so, too. We two older girls both stayed behind and the kids went off to Manhattan.

A little later, after most of the crowd had gone home and all of our equipment had been loaded into the van, Freda and Brian, our merch guy, and I went outside while Tim and the promoter tallied up our money inside.

There were a few stragglers on the sidewalk by the side door waiting for us to come out.

One was a heavyset, bearded, bespectacled man in his thirties and one was a younger, thinner guy who looked like he couldn't have grown a beard even if he had wanted to. They were an incongruous pair but they appeared to be together. The older man greeted me enthusiastically with a handshake. "Hi, I'm Charlie. I'm a big fan. And this is my friend Nigel. Nigel came all the way from England to see you play."

I said hello to Charlie and the English boy. Nigel said, smiling, "Wow. It's brilliant to meet you. That was a brilliant show."

I said, "You came all the way from England just to see me? That's insane."

He didn't really seem insane, though. He seemed completely normal; unthreatening and genuinely nice.

"Yeah, I did! Well, you never come to England and I thought, why not? Go over and see you play in the States, make a holiday of it."

"Wow. That's amazing that you flew here just for one show."

"Actually, I'm coming to the show in New York City, too. I thought I'd get in two shows while I'm here. Do the tour of the New York area, you know?"

"How do you know Charlie here?"

"We met on the Internet. We're both big fans of yours and Charlie helped me get the tickets to the shows. He's sort of showing me around."

"Is that where you're staying? With Charlie?"

"Yeah. He's putting me up."

Charlie and Nigel didn't appear to want anything from me except to just say hello. They didn't want autographs or hugs or anything. To see the shows and maybe meet me was all Nigel had hoped to accomplish when he got on that plane and jetted across the ocean. The simplicity and sincerity of the goal, and Charlie's seemingly innocent desire to help his new friend achieve it, were sweet. It humbled me and disarmed me while at the same time it gave me a sense of the importance of this whole undertaking. I was suddenly reminded of the fact that I needed to be responsible, by staying honest and dedicated to what I was doing with my music. Because it was having some effect on the world. It still meant something to somebody. Small pockets of humanity were inspired by my music to do fantastic things like leave their country. And this gave *my* life meaning.

Tim came out of the side door of the club, all ready to go, backpack in hand, and got in the driver's seat of the van. I said good-bye to Charlie and Nigel. Nigel said, with a warm smile on his face, "I'll see you at the New York show the day after tomorrow."

I offered, "I'll put you on the guest list."

"Oh, no, I already bought a ticket. But thanks! I'll see you Saturday night! Bye!"

I waved as they walked away.

2

Vision

I came home from school one afternoon during my junior year in high school to an empty house. My mother was at work at the *Boston Globe*. Dad had moved away after my parents' divorce five years earlier. My younger brother was off somewhere, probably at a friend's house, and my older brother was at boot camp in Texas.

When all of us were together, the house was often filled with turbulence and fighting and yelling and weighty objects hurtling through the air, so it was always a relief whenever I had the place to myself. I could let out a deep breath and relax. The solitude worked like medicine.

I lay down on the white shag rug in the living room, soaking in the delicious quiet and calm. The afternoon sun streamed in onto me through the sliding glass doors that led out to the brick patio. It was a chilly October afternoon. All the leaves outside were starting to turn— yellow, orange, rust, gold. It was almost three o'clock, when I would turn on the television to *General Hospital* like I did every day. I lay there on my side, my head on my arm that was extended upward, my mind lazily blank, just enjoying the wonderful warming sun on my back and the silence as dust motes floated down in slow motion in front of my eyes.

Suddenly my attention was drawn diagonally, toward the far corner of the room, over near the wall where the wood-burning stove stood. I looked, and I saw something. It was a vision of me, standing, singing, alone on a big stage in front of an audience partially obscured from me by the light shining on the stage; an audience so vast that its individual members' features and forms were blurred into a nebulous sea of love and happiness. This mass of humanity was singing along as one with me like a rumbling tidal wave, its unified spirit breaking over me, and I was answering them with my perfect, beautiful music. Everything was just as it should be.

I wasn't dreaming. This was a waking vision, like a crystal ball telling me some important personal truth. I knew at that moment that I had to pursue music seriously as a calling. It was foreordained. I no longer had any real fear or doubt about it, deep down. I'd seen my future across the room, playing like a movie meant for my eyes and no one else's.

It was a secret between me and the universe.

3

August 2

Philadelphia

We left for Philadelphia at around one in the afternoon, taking the Jersey Turnpike south. It was still very hot and excessively humid after three straight days of the temperature being in the nineties, and the road was a mass of unpleasant noises and smells. Engines revved angrily as cars darted across lanes, tailpipes retching, in temper tantrum–like displays of machismo.

In a couple of hours we arrived at the North Star Bar. I sat for a minute in the parked van while everyone else got out and stretched their legs; I wanted to delay my immersion into the scorching late-afternoon fire bath at least until the door of the club had been unlocked and I could run for cover. When Tim poked his head out from the side entrance and gave the signal for us to start bringing stuff inside, I stepped out onto the sidewalk, winced, and jogged around to the open back doors of the van, eager to get the load-in process over and done with as soon as possible.

There's a Ray Bradbury short story, "The Long Rain," in which a group of astronauts crash-lands on Venus, where it never stops raining. The astronauts search and search but can't find any shelter of any kind, and they gradually go insane from the effect of the water pounding and pounding and pounding down on them.

I felt like one of those astronauts, but with sunlight instead of rain. Is it possible for a person to develop an allergy to the sun? I didn't remember it being so painful as a child, or even five years ago. Maybe I had thicker skin when I was younger. Maybe the sun had gotten hotter.

Once all the equipment and merch had been loaded in, we began to set up camp in the wonderful coolness of the dark, empty, air-conditioned club. All of us methodically unpacked our gear from the piles of stuff that had been placed randomly on the stage and on the floor in front of it. This was the routine. Haul it in (and do it fast so you can move the van before you get a parking ticket, if the van is parked illegally in front of the club during load-in, which it sometimes is) and then start putting it all together. Drums had to be taken out of roadcases and assembled with their hardware and cymbals; amps had to be taken out of *their* roadcases, and set in their proper places, and plugged in; worn guitar strings had to be replaced with fresh ones (I generally did this string-changing every other night on tour) and then stretched and tuned (old strings break more easily and are harder to keep in tune than new ones). Tim placed microphones strategically, according to his method—not just vocal mikes (for my lead and Freda and Heidi's background vocals) but also in front of drums and amplifier speakers, and Brian arranged his mobile CD and T-shirt store in some highly visible area of the room that would most likely get a lot of foot traffic (and hopefully, a lot of business).

Unpacking and setting up is simultaneously boring and exciting. Imagine a country doctor on a late-night house call arriving at a patient's home, taking off his coat, rolling up his sleeves, and opening his black bag containing the tools of his trade. The tools themselves—stethoscope, tongue depressor, thermometer, needle, bandages (or in my case guitar, pick, capo, microphone)—are lifeless and thoroughly unromantic objects made of metal, wood, rubber, and such. However, in the right hands they are the tools that can help heal. Preparing to do my job, like the doc preparing to attend to his sick patient, I feel a tingling buzz of anticipation as I think of the potential power of what my equipment can do in my skilled and practiced hands.

Touring in winter, a guitar, first taken from the back of the van, may be cold to the touch. Once it is held for a few minutes in your hands—with your hot blood pulsing through them—and plugged into the amp, everything comes to life. Speakers buzz, shaking off their silence; volume knobs are turned up; electricity hums. The first chord you play is like a brilliant blinding sunrise or like a giant bear emerging from hibernation, and you feel its power, in your hands, in your body, all over.

Soundcheck also acclimates you to a new space. You get comfortable with the feel and layout and sound of each new and different stage. No one stage size is standard stage size. Same for width or length or height or shape or even placement in a room. To maintain some sense of consistency and normalcy, we three Girls positioned ourselves and our rigs in the same way every night: I stage right, Heidi stage left, and Freda in the middle, slightly behind Heidi and me. We made our temporary home feel as comfortable and familiar as possible, like it was *our* stage, like we *owned* it, so that when showtime rolled around we were feeling confident that we belonged, and were ready to put on a good show.

When we had run through a few songs, and Tim had set levels and tweaked his machinery and got a good mix, then the traveling circus was ready to open for business.

After soundcheck, the five of us—Freda, Heidi, Tim, Brian, and I—headed away from the club on foot, and toward the Italian restaurant the promoter had recommended for dinner. ("Go as a group," he had warned us. "This isn't the best neighborhood.") We took in the local color—derelict brick tenements and vacant storefronts—at a brisk pace, trying not to make eye contact with the crackheads and winos sitting on the crumbling stoops.

We made a right turn onto the side street the restaurant was on, and it was like stepping into a completely different town; we had crossed the gentrification line. I had no problem with that. I didn't want to solve society's problems tonight; I just wanted a warm meal in a safe place and to not have to worry about anything else for the next hour. There were lovely old brownstones and an interesting multi-cultural mix of people, adults and children, strolling on sidewalks in a comfortable, purposeful way that made it seem like this was *their* neighborhood, which they had claimed for themselves, and rehabilitated, with pride. As if they had changed not just the face of this once neglected street, but the heart, too, into something a bit more hopeful and energetic. Like I said, I had no problem with that.

After dinner we all, for lack of any better ideas, hung out in the dressing room down the stairs below the main floor of the club. Freda practiced drumming beats on her portable practice pad, Tim did some tour manager business on his laptop, and I browsed through Freda's copy of *Yoga Journal.* Heidi smoked a cigarette. Brian opened a beer and then went upstairs to man the merch stand. And thus we passed the hour and a half until showtime.

A few minutes before we were supposed to go on, I suddenly had to pee (preperformance jitters) but there was no toilet in the basement where we were stuck. The only restroom was up the stairs that led to the stage at the front, then all the way through the crowd and to the back of the club, and then into an adjoining room that housed the bar. And then clear across *this* room was the one tiny ladies' room that I was sure had a line of women waiting to get in by now, as it was the only toilet in the entire place, which happened to be full of people.

I didn't have time to wait in line. And there was no way I was going to hold it for our whole seventy-five-minute set, so I picked up a plastic cup from the hospitality table and I warned Freda and Heidi, who were the only ones in the room with me (Tim had gone up behind the soundboard) that I was going to "pee in this cup so don't look."

I found a semi-hidden spot under the stairs and next to some stacked cases of beer, pulled my pants down to my ankles, held the cup under me, and let it out.

This maneuver is performed more frequently on tour than the layman might realize. Often the makeshift backstage areas of these small clubs do not contain their own private bathrooms. (Why would they? Why put a toilet in a storage closet?) And when you are on the road on the cheap, with no commode-equipped tour bus to escape to, and you gotta go but there is nowhere convenient and nearby to do it and you have to be onstage in two minutes, pissing in a cup is the only practical solution.

But sometimes there are complications; sometimes, like tonight, not only is there no toilet in the room but there is no sink and there isn't even a wastebasket. So tonight I had no choice but to leave my full cup somewhere in the room when I was done doing my business. I tried to find a place where no one would accidentally knock it over or pick it up and take a sip out of it. The choices seemed to be either way up high on top of a stack of boxes or down on the floor in an out-of-the-way place like a corner of the room behind the couch. I chose the former. That way, it seemed, at least the cup would be found and discarded and not left to grow rank and moldy in some hidden dark nook.

I don't particularly enjoy the fact that cups full of my bodily fluids are sitting, uncovered, in various backstage rooms across the country, but what is the alternative? The alternative would be, I guess, to pee on the floor. And I really don't want to do that. That would be rude. If the venue doesn't have an accessible bathroom for the band, the least they could do would be to provide us with entrée to a sink with a drain. Or if that isn't possible, a plastic bag–lined trash can or bin for us to dump our waste, liquid or otherwise, would be nice.

Besides, what about the banana peels and beer bottle caps and snot-filled napkins—all the other stuff that the bands might need to throw away? What about the used condoms, candy wrappers, cigarette butts, spent syringes, bongwater, bullet shell casings—what are we supposed to do with *them*? And what if somebody had to vomit? Where would she go to do it?

Freda wasn't fazed at all when I peed in the cup. She'd seen me do it before. She'd had to resort to it herself a few times. But young Heidi was horrified. She nearly threw up at the sound of it. I felt bad for her, but, like I said, what was I supposed to do? Pee in my pants?

4

In the Woodshed

The Berklee College of Music in Boston is a place for young musicians who are interested in establishing careers in jazz or rock or
pop or R&B rather than classical music. At Berklee the curriculum is
more free-form and not so narrowly focused on old European guys as
at a typical conservatory. Students are taught both jazz theory and traditional theory—horn chart arranging and Bachian counterpoint—as
part of a comprehensive, practical musical education. Extensive ear
training (learning to identify chords and individual notes, and the
intervals between notes, by ear) is required, and electives are offered
from a vast range of contemporary courses of study such as electronic
music, pop songwriting, recording studio production and engineering,
and the business part of the music industry. The hope is that each student will leave school with the tools to communicate in various musical
situations.

Although some percentage of Berklee alumni probably go on to
productive careers in the opera or the symphony, the majority of grad-
uates (and dropouts, of which there are many) enter, or attempt to
enter, the modern music industry upon leaving school.

I transferred to Berklee after having spent one very unhappy semester at Boston University right after high school. I had initially planned on simultaneously furthering my academic education and getting a band going, but at BU at the end of 1985, I had realized with a kind of desperate clarity that I needed more than anything to be playing my songs, right now, and concentrating all my energies on that, and not wasting my time with a safe, wide-ranging, vaguely defined "liberal arts" curriculum that was going to get me nowhere in particular while my band dream languished.

I had attempted to get a band together at BU by putting a "seeking musicians" ad in the student newspaper, but I'd had no luck. I met with a couple of guys who seemed all wrong and then I gave up. I wasn't going to find my dream band at BU, so I needed to get out of there.

At BU, I couldn't figure out how people lived normal, everyday lives so effortlessly or why they seemed so content living these lives. Getting up, going to classes, doing homework, eating and sleeping, going to parties and bars and movies and football games, having boyfriends, and a job—was that enough? It seemed like a boring, repetitive, pointless game with no ending and no way to win. Normal life seemed so impossible to me, unimportant everyday interactions so tricky to navigate. Where had my fellow students learned to flirt and make small talk? Why didn't I know how? Who taught them to navigate a conversation so expertly? How did they acquire the confidence to throw in their two cents even when they had nothing, really, very interesting to say? Who showed the girls how to put on their makeup so flawlessly and to blow-dry their hair? (At eighteen, my first year in college, I had never worn makeup, never touched a blow dryer. No one ever told me I needed to know how to do these things.)

The pull for me toward music—toward a life focused on it and built around it—became so strong during my semester at BU that it blinded me to anything else, leaving me lame in all other areas. I felt completely bewildered by the thought of any other kind of existence. Some young women, at college, are focused on finding suitable husbands. The pull that these women feel toward traditional family and security and domestic stability, and a mate who has a steady, well-paying job with opportunity for promotion, is just as strong and just as fierce for them as mine was toward music. Mine was just a different

25

color of ambition. Some girls needed to land a future doctor or lawyer or banker to make them feel like their life was on the right track. I needed to get a record deal. And first, I needed to get myself into a band. And to make that happen, I needed to be among fellow rock obsessives and away from frat boys and sorority girls and keg parties.

When I made the decision to go to music school, I was sure I was doing the right thing, but part of me still thought it was a terrifying, reckless, and stupid thing to do. A bachelor of arts degree, if I got that far, does not guarantee a successful, or even rent-paying, career in the arts. Fortunately, however, in my particular field, technical mastery was not a prerequisite for success. Originality, confidence, emotional honesty, charisma, a hook, luck, timing—all this was just as important, if not more important, than technique or schooling. You don't need to be the best singer or the best player to make great pop music. I armed myself with this knowledge and took the plunge, although at this point it didn't really seem like a choice anymore; I had to do it, and no one could stop me. I was half-blind, maybe crazy; it was like falling in love with a dangerous guy. I knew that it would be fun and exciting and passionate and difficult and long and torturous and that he would be a real bastard sometimes. That the relationship would kick my ass and test my strength, and that I could easily lose myself in it.

From the start I knew it would probably end badly, but I didn't care.

My mother had started out as a music major at the University of Michigan, studying to become a concert pianist. After a couple of years, though, she changed her major to journalism. She decided that the life of a concert pianist would be too difficult, too lonely, too competitive, too stressful for her, and she didn't really believe she would make it. To succeed as a classical solo pianist, one must be among the very best of her peers, and must make a lot of sacrifices in order to stay on top of her game: practicing all the time, traveling, suffering through the terror-laced nerves of high-pressure performances in which any and every single wrong or misplayed note is noticed, and scrutinized, and frowned upon. My mother made the choice to have a more normal, manageable, secure life. After college, she married a medical student (my father) and went on to have a long and fruitful career writing for various newspapers and magazines. She continued to play piano for fun, and gave lessons in our home in her free time, and also volunteered as accompanist for the local church choir, throughout my childhood.

Like my mom, I knew I wasn't the best, and that I probably never would be. I've never been the best at anything. I ranked seventh in my high school graduating class; I came in third in my middle school talent show; I got an honorable mention in a writing competition. I got red ribbons and white ribbons and gold ribbons but never any blues. I was always competing, and I did all right, but I was never number one. I knew I wasn't the best singer, either, but unlike my mother with her piano dreams, I knew that I didn't have to be the best. My intense, almost pathological compulsion to write and sing my songs, along with my persistence and dedication, would carry me when I got bogged down in doubt and fear. And my imperfections would distinguish me. However they tortured me sometimes, my imperfections were what made me unique.

Besides, once a standard of perfection has been set, how tedious and, ultimately, impossible it must be to maintain it throughout a lifetime or a career! Perfection is banal, anyway, and even boring. It cancels itself out. The beautiful and interesting face with the slightly skewed nose, or the smile with the funky crooked tooth, or the eyes a little too close together or a little too far apart, is more alluring and holds one's interest longer than the one with the perfectly aligned features and geometrically correct dimensions.

I was voted "Most Individual" in my high school graduating class. My photograph (me standing against a brick wall with a Mona Lisa smile, next to the male choice, both of us facing away from each other) was featured in the yearbook alongside the choices for "Best Looking" and "Best Dressed" and "Most Likely to Succeed." I was so happy, and proud, to have been singled out for this distinction. Though one could say that "Most Individual" is a euphemism for "Biggest Loner" or "Person Who Spends the Most Time off in the Corner by Herself" or "Weirdest" or "#1 Freak," to me it meant that I wasn't like everyone else, and that was good. My classmates couldn't categorize me as any particular "type," and that made me at least interesting. I stood out just for being myself. Maybe my music would stand out, too.

I wanted to learn how to strengthen my voice, which had always been technically weak and thin. I had great natural pitch and could carry a tune as well as anyone, but my instrument was not powerful in volume or heft or tone, especially up above the break line, up in the falsetto range, and because of this I lacked confidence as a vocalist.

I had had no formal voice training and knew just the basic stuff on guitar (though I planned on playing guitar and singing in my band); when I was a preteen, I'd had a few sessions with a neighborhood guitar teacher who explained open chords to me and how to read them, and made me play rudimentary folk/pop songs like "Leavin' on a Jet Plane." Then, a few years later, a high school friend gave me a barre chord tutorial one afternoon.

I had studied classical piano starting at a young age, continuing into high school. Upon discovering punk rock, though, I suddenly lost all interest in piano and started playing guitar in earnest. That meant learning to play songs off of records, and making up weird, pretty chords with odd tensions and droning high notes, chords that were sort of a combination between the open As and Es and such, and the barre chords that I had been taught. Once I had strung together some chords, I would begin transforming my teenage poetry into songs.

I applied to Berklee as a piano student, thinking that if I got in, I would at least be there, among kindred struggling musicians, and I could then figure out a way to transfer to the voice department and become a vocal student. I chose voice over guitar because my voice needed more work than my guitar playing. Almost anyone can learn to play the guitar well enough to play along with others. All anyone really needs to know is the two barre chord hand positions. Then she can move her hand up and down the neck, and then she can write simple chord progressions, and then she can start a band. (This is what the Ramones taught us.) I was, however, going to be the lead vocalist in my band; my voice was going to be out front, so I needed to learn how to boost my vocal strength.

I was accepted into Berklee as a piano player, and I began my studies, running scale after scale on the keyboard and learning how to "comp" from a lead sheet.

But first they had to explain to me what a lead sheet was and how to read it.

A lead sheet is a kind of shorthand version of a song's notation.

Usually it's printed on stave paper featuring just one stave instead of the usual two (the treble and bass clefs), with the melody written in the five parallel lines of the paper's staves and the chord names written like this—G, Amaj7, C#, or whatever the chords happened to be—above the corresponding melody notes. The lyrics—if there are any—are placed below the staff.

Comping was forming chord voicings of my choosing with the left hand while improvising upon the melody with my right. I was used to reading the clear, definitively notated staves of Bach and Brahms and Beethoven and Schumann, playing the piece as it was written, knowing exactly where I stood. We worked on jazz standards taken out of a fake book (a photocopied, cheaply bound homemade-looking, often hand-written collection of lead sheets of jazz standards).

It was a strange new world with an unfamiliar language. Measures were now referred to as bars. The treble clef was now simply the G clef. A trumpet was a horn in jazz slang. Practicing an instrument was called "shedding," or "hitting the woodshed"—the symbolic woodshed, one's private, often isolated rehearsal space where one went to do his scales and exercises and chip away at his craft.

I was in the woodshed every day, attempting to forge new bonds with my piano, to enter a new phase in our relationship, to force open doors to new ways of looking at each other so I could gain some mastery of it and show the teachers I was teachable, and making progress (and so I could pass my regularly scheduled piano proficiency tests). But my heart wasn't in it. I wanted to be on a stage playing guitar and singing in a rock band, not running scale after scale alone on an upright piano in a broom closet–sized practice room with only a tiny vertical sliver of a door window and the muffled sounds of other fingers on other pianos down the narrow hall full of occupied practice rooms to remind me that outside there was a world, and life, and other people, forming original bands. I wanted to be one of those people forming one of those bands, playing my songs, not attempting to improvise jazz badly, uncomfortably, ineptly, with an instructor looking over my shoulder and coaching me in the rudiments and subtleties and philosophy of a form of music I had no interest in, really, at that time.

My tuition at Berklee covered classes, rehearsal facilities, housing, and meals. The plan was to live in the main Massachusetts Avenue building in a shared dorm room, and to eat my meals in the basement cafeteria. But I was incredibly shy; I was so petrified to go to the cafeteria by myself that I never once ate a meal there, even though all my meals had already been paid for in my meal and housing plan. I did venture down there, gingerly, one time, at the beginning of the semester, at the dinner hour, to have a look. When I saw the food line and all the students in it and beyond, sitting and eating and talking and laughing at all the tables under the bright overhead lights, I felt a sudden extreme, uncomfortable self-consciousness and a tightness in my stomach, like there was a fist around my guts, squeezing, and I wasn't hungry anymore. I turned around and went straight back up to my room.

So for the rest of the school year, instead of going to the cafeteria I would buy a take-out hummus or falafel sandwich from Café Bouquet across the street from the dorm and eat it in my room alone. Or I'd grab an egg and pepper sub from Supreme Pizza, a block and a half down Mass. Ave., and bring it back to my room. Breakfast would be a muffin and a small bottle of orange juice from the little Au Bon Pain stall next to the entrance of the Auditorium subway stop across Boylston Street, on the way to class. Sometimes I would buy a loaf of sliced bread and a package of American cheese (individually wrapped single slices) and I would dine on dry cheese-and-bread sandwiches, storing the cheese in the space between the windowsill and screen, hoping the cold winter air from outside would refrigerate the cheese and keep it fresh enough to last me for a few days.

Since I was so withdrawn, I was relieved that I had my own space— my own little room, really—in which I could close myself off from my two roommates without having to subject them (or me) to the unpleasantness of my interpersonal awkwardness. We were housed in a three-person suite, and my roommates shared the bigger room with the bunk beds and the bathroom just off of it, and my little single-bed space had a door that closed my area off from the two other girls'. I would always wait until I knew they were out of their room—until I heard no sound coming through the wall and I knew they had both gone—before I went in to use the bathroom. They were both into jazz (I heard them talking enthusiastically, sometimes, through the wall, about Bird and 'Trane and Monk) and I was into rock (I was sure they'd never heard of Paul Westerberg or Ian MacKaye or even John Fogerty), so we probably didn't have anything to talk about anyway.

I would close myself off from them and the world and I would sit on my single bed and eat my pathetic stale, stiff, cold, dry cheese sandwich and wish someone would come and knock on my door and save me from a future of more lonely dry cheese sandwich dinners and no band of my own. I needed to make some friends with the same likes and dreams and hopes and ambitions and abilities as mine, but I didn't know how on earth I was going to make it happen if I couldn't even manage to say hello to anyone without breaking into a stammering, heart-pounding sweat.

5

August 3

New York City

These sheets feel like fiberglass," I said to myself as I awoke, feeling not at all rested and a little ill with the sting of a burgeoning cold in my throat. The Palace Hotel had spared every expense, including soft cotton bedding, to ensure its guests' discomfort.

My insomnia was raging. My internal alarm clock was going off every hour. I calculated that, with all the starts and stops in my sleep, I'd been averaging about three hours a night.

I had sleeping pills in my bag, but I wanted to avoid them for as long as I could; I didn't want to get myself strung out on them here, now, at the very beginning of the tour, like an idiot. They would be a last resort. So even if I didn't act very rock and roll, I would at least look the part: haggard. From a lack of sleep. And haggard is cool. I would embrace it. Haggard is rock and roll.

I wanted to make the most of this tour, no matter what; no matter how sick I got or how little I slept or how uncomfortable the beds were. I wanted to honor this thing; this job; this compulsion to play my music in front of people that had always felt like some kind of destiny which I was too self-critical and ill-equipped and ambivalent to fulfill.

I just wanted to rise to the occasion and not fuck it up or slack off or fail to have a good time, as I had so many times in the past.

I had always believed that touring—playing my songs in front of people—was an integral part of my musical expression. You can't fully appreciate or understand a singer or a player until you've seen him or her live. There is a crackling energy in the live arena that is very difficult to capture in the recording studio. My voice in the studio is more controlled, more disciplined, more consciously and painstakingly manipulated by my will and intellect than it is onstage, where my singing is louder, rawer, more uninhibited and animal. I had to go out on the road to prove myself; to show people this side of me—the daring, confident, fun Juliana.

The stage—the lights, the heat, the adrenaline, the electricity, the energy in the air, the intense give and take between me and the audience, all of us in various and heightened states of consciousness—drew something out of me, something that needed to be freed. It was a thrill to to be purged like this every night. It felt so healthy, physically and emotionally, like a kind of meditation or renewing ritual.

In early shows, sometimes I would be so carried away by the experience of being onstage, playing my music, loud, electrified, in front of a crowd, that I would experience a kind of natural high. Thought and consciousness would leave my body and drift away, over and through and beyond the temporal shackles of everyday life. My physical self kept on working, doing its thing, down on the stage, like a perfect, efficient machine. It was a wonderful feeling. People do drugs to get that feeling. It was ecstasy. And it was contagious.

To be able to see, right in front of me, that my music was having some dramatic, positive effect on people became crucial. Playing live gave fans a chance to commune with me (or with my musical persona) in a way that they couldn't just listening to my records. It was a kind of conversation: They would clap, I would sing. They would cheer, I would bang out some chords or a solo.

Plus, it's downright fun to turn an amp up really loud and make a lot of guitar noise, and yell and scream and jump up and down and fling my sweaty hair around and, once in a while, spit—brazenly, gratuitously; like a guy—on the stage, in a show of coarse, delicious, carnal, joyful freedom and strength. I held on to my guitar like it was a weapon, protecting me and mowing down naysayers with volume and distortion; if anyone had anything bad to say about me, I'd just turn my amp up louder and drown him out.

It was power. Being onstage enabled me to recognize that I had power. My music had a palpable transformative effect on people. On good nights, when everything was going well, no one could touch me. I felt important. Like a king, ruling this little piece of the world that I reigned over. I felt I was doing what I was born to do.

Over the years, some of the thrill and novelty had gone out of the enterprise—the out-of-body experiences were fewer and farther between. The more I did my job, the more I thought of it as a job, and job grievances began to accumulate, same as for anyone else who has worked the same job for a number of years. But it was still possible to achieve something like transcendence, on a really really good night, when everything fell into place just right. And I was always chasing that feeling.

At the Knitting Factory that evening, we set about lugging the equipment out of the back of the van and into the club and onto the stage. I used to be able to lift my SVT bass head (the one Heidi had borrowed to use as her main amp on this tour) by myself, back in the early days, when I was playing bass for a time. But today I needed help carrying it. It seemed so heavy, like it had gained a bunch of weight.

After soundcheck Freda and Tim went on a mission to find some sushi. Brian went to the front of the club, near the entrance, to set up his merchandise table. I stayed behind in the dressing room with Heidi and her boyfriend, Jesse. I was putting on makeup in the long skinny wall mirror when I suddenly decided that my hair was too long and that I needed to cut it, right now. I went and found some scissors in the production office and brought them back up to the dressing room, above and to the side of the stage. I started chopping, trying to take a few inches off the bottom.

Jesse, who was watching me, said, "Hey, do you want some help with the back?"

"Okay, yeah," I answered.

He took the scissors and approached from behind.

"Have you done this before?" I asked.

"No."

"Oh. Ha ha. Well, how hard can it be to trim the back, right?"

"Right."

Jesse did his best, but neither of us is much of a hairdresser, so my haircut ended up looking kind of uneven.

"I don't care. It's just hair," I said to Jesse as we surveyed the slightly botched results in the mirror.

No one that I knew came to the show, but Nigel, the young Englishman who'd been at the Maxwell's gig, was there afterward. He was set to fly back home to England in the morning and he just wanted to tell me hello and, "Thanks, again, for being so great," with warm appreciation.

Again, like the first time I'd met him, I was gratified, and amazed to have made someone feel good, without even trying. It's a strange feeling to be sort of loved, unconditionally, by a stranger. It had required absolutely no sacrifice on my part to bring a smile to Nigel's face. I was just doing what came naturally. Playing my songs.

I know what it feels like to be Nigel. Once in a while someone— some singer or songwriter or guitar player—will articulate, with his music, something about myself and my life that I cannot, and for that I instantly love him. I go all soft and mushy inside. I think, "Someone understands."

I fall for it every time. It never gets old because the relationship is never consummated; the music-maker is just a tease. He holds out something beautiful and tantalizing and sublime: the possibility of impossible things like love, happiness, or a true, lasting connection between people. This is the promise of a song. And the music-maker holds it out to us when the curtain comes up, only to close his hand back around it and draw it in at the end of the show. The tease is never intentional or mean-spirited; it's just the nature of the job. He's just say-ing what he feels, and it just so happens that I feel it, too.

In the van, as we were pulling away from the Knitting Factory at the end of the night, I announced, "None of my friends showed up tonight."

Freda said, "Aww," sympathetically.

Brian said, "Well, we sold a ton of stuff. I think it was the best night so far."

"How much?" I asked.

"Like forty CDs and twenty-five T-shirts."

"Right on, Brian. Excellent work."

And so, although no one came that I was hoping would come to see me play, it was a really good night. For merchandise.

6

Angel Girl

There was a girl, about my age, whom I'd been noticing around the Berklee campus and on the streets in the neighborhood since I enrolled. She was a quietly luminous, dreamlike presence who, whenever she crossed my path, would invariably brighten that brief moment for me. Like a fresh, sweet breeze, she would glide past and then she would be gone and I would forget about her until the next time I saw her. Was there a dimly glowing, gold-white aura around her (like when you get out of a chlorine-filled pool after swimming laps for a long time and your eyes are burning and itchy and there's a hazy ring around everything you try to focus on—every light fixture and every person and even the sun) or did I imagine this? I had never spoken to this girl, of course, on account of my debilitating shyness, but it seemed as if she was very much aware of my presence anyway. She would smile and make eye contact, as if to say, "Hi," whenever we passed each other on the street or in the hallways at school, as if we had a delicious but wholesome secret in common. And I would feel a little spike in my pulse, as if a spark had jumped off her onto me. And then I would quickly look down, or away, and keep walking, as if I might burn up if

I lingered in her presence. I didn't know her name and I didn't know how I would ever learn it; making friends seemed such an impossible, insurmountable task.

I don't know why I didn't think of this girl as someone I could start a band with. That would have given me the strength to break my silence; making friends was too hard but making music with people was something I knew I could do; in a band no one has to really talk or explain himself. The music can be a voice, saying all that needs to be said. I guess I assumed that all my bandmates would be men, because all of my instrument-playing role models were men.

The girl was very pretty, and didn't wear any makeup—a scruffy rock-and-roll nature-girl with wavy dirty-blond hair mussed by the wind. Some days she wore a plain cotton thrift-store dress, like a dust-bowl Depression-era mother in a Dorothea Lange photograph, with combat boots. Some days she wore a T-shirt, jeans—a bit loose on her (the same way I wore my Levi's) and with holes in the knees, scuffed black army-navy store lace-up shoes (just like mine!), and a too-big hand-me-down black leather motorcycle jacket.

I wondered who she was and where she came from. She kept turning up, appearing out of nowhere, in my path, so I couldn't deny her presence. I began to think she was an angel sent by God to remind me of my mission.

After a few weeks of keyboard studies, I did the switcheroo and became an official student of the vocal department. I waited just long enough to make it seem as if I hadn't *planned* on duping the admissions staff into letting me in as a piano student and then switching instruments but had rather made the decision to switch after weeks of careful consideration. It was surprisingly easy to transfer my "principal instrument" status. It seemed almost criminal, like I was getting away with something illegal, or at least really sneaky.

Now I was one step closer to my goal of singing in a band. But how to make that happen? I had almost no contact with anyone outside of classes and my part-time job at the Erewhon natural food store over on Newbury Street. Part of the problem was the fact that I was surrounded by experienced musicians with impressive chops, and their skills and confidence intimidated me. They were accomplished before they'd even gotten here—they were the ones voted "most musical" in their high school graduating class; the stars in their school jazz bands, the singers who'd played the leads in their school musicals. They were the prodigies who had spent their teen years holed up in their bedrooms practicing their scales and learning the whole Yngwie Malmsteen catalog note for note, guitar-speed freaks who could make smoke come off the fretboard with the velocity of their fingers. *My* strengths were in the realm of melody rather than power or agility, and having a gift for melody isn't a very impressive claim, so I had an inferiority complex, and felt I would never catch up. I'd thrown myself into this foreign environment that people around me had seemingly grown up in, and *fit* in, and I was scrambling to learn their lexicon and techniques.

The other vocal majors all seemed so comfortable in the Berklee milieu, and familiar and self-assured and strong-voiced—everything that I wasn't. All of them seemed proficient in the art of scatting, for example, and seemed willing to gladly do so (scat) at the drop of a hat, while I wouldn't be caught dead trying to scat. (Thank God scatting proficiency was not required). Cole Porter and George Gershwin standards were second nature to many of them. Well, except for that one girl whom I witnessed singing "Let's Call the Whole Thing Off" in front of a class. She'd been instructed to sight-read the song and I guess she had never heard the song before, because when she jumped up out of her chair, bounded onto the little stage, and began earnestly singing "You say tomato, I say tomato/You say potato, I say potato" along with the piano accompanist, she pronounced "tomato" the same way—with a long "A"—each time the word appeared. Same with "potato": "Po*tay*to, po*tay*to, to*may*to, to*may*to," the girl sang. Even *I* knew that it was supposed to go like this: "po*tay*to, po*tah*to, to*may*to, to*mah*to." Obviously. The whole point of the song is that the guy and the gal in it don't see eye-to-eye. Duh.

This incident taught me that a person with confidence doesn't necessarily *know* more than an insecure person. It just means that she has confidence. It doesn't even necessarily mean that she is especially skilled. Or maybe she *does* have certain impressive qualities, and is justifiably confident about them, but that doesn't mean that she doesn't lack *other* qualities. In fact, this girl's voice was nothing to write home about. She did have a rich tone, but her phrasing was stiff, and didn't swing. And from then on I felt a little less insecure about my place in

Berklee. But I still felt silly singing those old-fashioned tunes; I always thought "My Funny Valentine" was *so* dumb.

The singers at Berklee seemed to be of a different species than I was. They even *looked* confident, well-groomed, and put-together and nicely dressed, like professionals. Like they were always on their way to an important Broadway audition, or a job interview. I was an amateur and I looked the part in loose, faded, ripped jeans and T-shirts and an old leather jacket and unbrushed hair and no makeup. Other singing students called themselves "vocalists." I thought of myself as just a singer. They seemed Amazonian to me, towering over me, louder than me, taking up more space than me, with bigger personas, bigger voices. Future Beyoncés and Linda Ronstadts and Whitney Houstons and Janis Joplins and Ellas and Arethas. I felt like a mouse. Quiet, tiny. Even my voice was small, thin, weak. Mousy.

"I don't belong here," I thought every day. "I didn't belong at BU and I don't belong here. What am I going to do? How am I going to make my vision come to life? Isn't there anyone here who thinks like me and wants what I want and feels like I do?"

I kept my eyes open all the time to see if anyone struck me as future bandmate material, but I felt like a mutt, or a stray—shaggy, scrappy, kind of pathetic and lost—among purebreds. I felt separate from everybody else, like an oddball. If I had taken the time to talk to people, gotten to know some of them, I would probably have seen that we all had similar hopes and goals, with minor variations in the details. There was much common ground. It was a music school, after all, and we were all there for the same reason—we all wanted to live lives of music. I wasn't as separate from all the other students as I believed myself to be. I separated *myself* by believing—insisting—that I was different. All I wanted to do was make some melodious, heartfelt, unpolished do-it-yourself guitar pop-rock. What was so weird about that?

The first time I sang alone in front of a Berklee vocal instructor, for my first vocal assessment, she stopped me after a few bars and said, "Whoa. You're going to hurt your voice. You need a lot more breath support. Use your diaphragm. And you need to open your mouth wider." My technique was *all wrong*. Or nonexistent. Breath support? What was that? And . . . my *diaphragm*? Wasn't that a birth control device? I had a "diaphragm"? Where was it? What was I supposed to do with it? I had no idea what she was talking about. I only knew that I had a long way to go before I would be getting any gold stars from this teacher. I was going to have to start from square one learning the basics, while most of the other vocal students at the school were way past that point.

It was March 1986, the second semester of the year, and I had been at Berklee since the end of the Christmas break. I had been out walking around one night and I made my way back through the chilly air to the Berklee dorm at about nine o'clock. I went in the main double doors and down the stairs into the near-empty lobby just below street level and over to the elevator, contemplating the absurdity and the frustration of being at music school and having no one to play music with. Wondering, as usual, how long I could go on like this. Putting an ad in the paper and a notice on the bulletin board wasn't going to work for me. It hadn't worked at BU and I didn't want to waste anyone's time trying it here and failing again. Besides, auditions were too artificial; too forced and uncomfortable. I needed it to happen on its own, organically, as naturally and effortlessly as possible. My future bandmates and I needed to bump into one another and lock eyes in a mutual connection and understanding; we needed to just happen upon one another. I was staking everything—my future, my happiness, my sanity—on that happening. I'd done my part and put myself in an environment in which there were hundreds of young, eager musicians all around me and where my chances of finding comrades were statistically higher than in other environments. Now all I had to do was wait for fate to bring me my future to me.

When I reached my floor, I walked slowly to my door, put the key in, and entered my room. I went over to the window, which was slightly open, with an opened package of American cheese propped up against the screen. I picked the cheese up so I could close the window, because it was nighttime in March in Boston, and it was cold in the room. The cheese was hard, semi-frozen. It wouldn't be any good to eat any more. I dropped it into the trash can next to the desk in front of the window. As I gazed outside at the big elevated Citgo sign flashing its red and white neon on and off in nearby Kenmore Square, and I contemplated how I would eat tomorrow, there was a knock on my door. I flinched—

no one ever knocked on my door—and I got up to see who it was.

When I opened the door, two people were standing there side by side, facing me. A guy and a girl. It was the girl from the street. The angel girl. I don't think it had registered that she was a real person—and not an apparition or my imagination—until this moment when she stood in front of me, in the flesh. Suddenly it all flashed back to me, the memory of her, as she stood there in front of my open dorm room door in the seconds before any of us said anything.

Her companion was tall, about six-foot-one, and attractive in a skinny, brainy-looking way—a handsome nerd—with thick medium-length brown hair and a long crooked nose and a sardonic but not unfriendly look on his face, like you were in on the joke with him. The girl was about six inches shorter than him, and thin, exactly my height and size (we could have been sisters), with big sparkling blue eyes and a healthy pink flush on her cheeks that shined like two spit-polished apples when she smiled the sweetest, warmest, sincerest, most generous, and comforting smile I had ever seen.

"Hi," she said, still smiling, glowing. "I'm Freda. And this is John."

"Hi," I said.

"Do you want to be in our band?"

Freda was John's girlfriend. She had come with him to Boston from their hometown in Indiana so the two of them could be together and start a band (she played drums, he played guitar) while John studied music production and engineering at Berklee. They'd followed me up to my dorm room; it turned out they'd been staking me out, watching me, investigating me, over the past few weeks. They needed another person for their band—someone to be the lead singer—and after observing me, they had come to the conclusion that I was the one. (They told me later, after I'd gotten to know them, that up until then they had referred to me between themselves as the "dream girl," just as I had referred to Freda in my thoughts as the "angel girl.") They knew I was a singer, but they didn't know what I sounded like, or if I was any good. But they were certain—they knew just by looking at me—that I'd be perfect as the front person in their band. And if I played guitar, too, that would be gravy.

They said they even had a name for the band, already. "Blake Babies." They had gone to a recent Allen Ginsberg poetry reading at

Harvard and during the postreading Q&A session, John and Freda had stood up and gone to the mike, into which John said simply, "What should we name our band?" Ginsberg looked at them for a second and then replied, "Blake Babies." (Ginsberg famously loved William Blake.)

They explained all this to me while I half listened, half tried to focus on reminding myself to keep breathing. And then they asked me if I wanted to jam with them.

My heart sped up even more. Everything was happening. Right now. My destiny had arrived, had come right to my door, and actually *knocked* on it.

"Jam?" I asked. "You mean, like, right now?"

Yeah, right now.

They lived in an apartment right around the corner on Hemenway Street, where they had a small drum kit, a couple of amps, and a microphone set up.

I was terrified. I had never jammed with strangers before. I sang in a cover band in high school, but that was with guys I had known forever, and none of us took it very seriously because there was nothing much at stake. This was different. No one like John and Freda existed anywhere in my past, in my hometown, nor had I met or even seen anyone like them these past few months at Berklee. And now all of a sudden these two held all the promise and I needed to not screw it up.

"Um, okay, yeah."

I would have to wing it, with no safety net. I assumed that mikes and amps meant we would be jamming electric. I had never played an electric guitar, only an acoustic one.

"Do you have an extra guitar that I can play?" I asked John.

He did.

We took the elevator down and walked out to Mass. Ave. and we crossed it together and went down the little side street, turning left onto Hemenway. We entered the first building on the corner, climbed four flights of stairs and, with a turn of John's key, we were in his and Freda's studio apartment. It had worn wood floors and there was a small alcove off to the left side, presumably for sleeping (there was a little single mattress on the floor there). There was a narrow kitchen space on the opposite side of the room, with no door and no room for a table and chairs—only to stand and assemble, on the small counter, and then cook, on the small stove, a meal—and a small bathroom next to it, with a claw-foot tub with a shower curtain on rings going around it. Bay windows looked out over Hemenway Street, and across to the Boston Conservatory of Music. (This was music school territory.) The apartment was barely furnished. Just the mattress, a small gray foam love seat sitting on the floor in front of the window, and a lightweight wooden coffee table, both of which had probably been scavenged from someone's discarded moving day stuff in front of a building. There was a black cat, Jessup. And a small, sparkling gold drum kit, a mike on a wobbly-looking stand, two small guitar amplifiers, and a couple of guitars. And John and Freda.

It was perfect. Everything I wanted and needed. John picked up a Fender Stratocaster and handed me the other guitar—I think it was a Japanese Fender copy—and a pick, and he plugged us both into one of the amps, which had two inputs. The vocal mike went into the other amp.

"I've never actually played electric guitar before," I said. "Is it really different than playing acoustic?"

John said that it was easier, actually, to play electric guitar; you don't need to press down as hard on the strings.

I put the guitar strap around my neck, and it felt really good. I felt suddenly strong, tough, and totally cool—it was a new, thrilling, empowering rock-and-roll sensation. John leaned toward me, holding his guitar against his body with one hand while he turned the volume knob up on my guitar so sound would come out, and then he fiddled with the amp's treble and bass and volume a bit until he was satisfied with the sound and we were both set to go.

Freda was already ready, sitting on her drum stool, back straight, smiling and holding her drumsticks, one in each hand.

"What should we play?" I asked nervously.

John suggested the Velvet Underground.

"How about 'Femme Fatale'?" I asked. "Do you guys want to do that one?" I prayed they would say yes. It was the only Velvets song I knew how to play. I had just recently learned it. The words and the chords were simple and easy to remember, and I knew I could manage the song and not embarrass myself too much.

Freda enthusiastically approved of my song choice. John, too.

44

And so we began. Freda tapped lightly on her drums—not shy, just careful and steady as she could. John, who was a more accomplished musician (he was studying guitar at Berklee but he also played drums), had just recently begun giving Freda drum lessons so they could be in this band together. John seemed patient, gentle, encouraging, and nonjudgmental. I sensed that he, as a more technically proficient instrumentalist, wasn't going to hold my lack of training and chops against me, just as he obviously didn't with Freda. He took us both completely seriously. He welcomed me and whatever I had to offer right from the beginning, just as he believed Freda could play drums in a band, and do it in her own uniquely Freda-esque style, despite the fact that she had only been playing for a few months. I, like Freda, was unsteady on my instrument(s), but excited and eager to learn. Our enthusiasm and drive to play was paramount.

I put my mouth on the microphone and sang, "Here she comes . . ."

Freda kept the beat, smiling the whole time, and John strummed patiently, and I got used to the feel of the light electric strings and the thin body of the guitar and the strap around my shoulder. The three of us proceeded at a slow pace, creating a tentative, innocent, charming version of the menacing Velvet Underground song; it was someone else's song but almost immediately it became our own. Playing with John and Freda was like putting on a brand-new pair of beautiful Italian leather shoes; it was a little uncomfortable at first, but I knew that once we settled in to one another, the fit would be perfect, and would last a long time.

Relief. Relief, more than anything, was what I felt. Relief and *joy.* This was it. This was what I had been waiting for, living for, dying to find. They found me and so I found them. I wasn't alone anymore.

We were the Blake Babies. We were allied, unified. We all three had the same idea and wanted the same thing. We wanted to create our own music, with no real blueprint. We would let it be what it wanted to be, organically, naturally, and my and Freda's lack of formal training would not hinder us in discovering, unearthing, and then releasing our own original sound, a sound that had never been made before. This was the beginning of tomorrow and beyond. Great things were ahead of us, I was sure of it.

7

August 4

North Bergen to Boston

We were finally leaving the Palace Hotel, to head back north to Boston. I gathered my things—backpack, bag full of clothes, bag full of shoes, and my SG guitar in its gig bag—and then paused to look at my flowers in their vase on the bureau, next to the TV. They were still vibrant after three days. I hated to think of these pretty things being dumped in the trash, so I made an attempt to prolong their survival with a note to the housekeeper. It read: "I'm checking out today. Please take these flowers home with you, if you like. I can't carry them with me." I put the note so that it was sticking part of the way out from under the vase.

Tim settled our bill and went to get the van. He drove up in front of the lobby and the rest of us went to load our bags and guitars into the back. Someone had written the words "www.washme.com" in the dirt on one of the rear windows with a finger.

Once we were settled in and had been cruising for a while on the Merritt Parkway, Freda asked me, "Hey, Juliana, do you have any good books at home? I need a book to read on tour."

I lived in Boston, and we were on our way there for a night off and then a gig the following night.

I answered, "Yeah. I've got lots of books. What kind are you looking for?"

"I'm not sure. Something good. Do you have any Proust? I've been wanting to read some Proust."

I had just finished reading *Swann's Way*, as a matter of fact.

"How was it? Was it good?"

"Oh my God. It was so bad. I hated it."

"Really?" said Freda, chuckling.

"Yes! But I wasn't expecting it to be like that, 'cause everyone's always saying how great Proust is."

"Yeah, I know. That's why I wanted to check him out."

"Me too. That's what I was thinking. He's so in the public consciousness. You know, like the madeleine. I had to see what that was all about."

"Yeah."

"So I finally decided to read it. To see what the big deal was. And it was such a letdown. It was horrible. Just, really bad."

"Did you read the whole thing?"

"Yeah. Well, *Swann's Way* is one part of a bigger thing called *Remembrance of Things Past*. I can tell you, though, that there's no fucking way I'm reading the rest of it. It nearly killed me trying to get through this one. And the only reason I suffered through the whole thing was that I have to finish every book I start. Even if I hate it. It's like a weird compulsion."

"What didn't you like about it? What was it like?"

"It was just interminable. He took so long to say what he was trying to say, which wasn't anything. It took him ten pages to describe a cookie. No, to describe the memory of the cookie. First he had to talk about, in detail, how the cookie used to make him feel when he was younger and then he talked about all the new feelings stirred up by remembering how the cookie used to make him feel."

"My God," said Freda. "It sounds really boring."

"There was just nothing going on. But you should read it anyway, maybe. Just so you can say you did. So you can have an opinion about it. And, hey, maybe you'll like it."

"Yeah," said Freda, serious, pensive, appearing to be formulating a decision in her head. "I think I'd still like to read it. Just to see for myself. It's been on my list of things to read."

"Okay. I'll bring it for you to the gig tomorrow. Don't say I didn't warn you."

"Okay," Freda said, smiling.

"My dad used to say that he hated Proust. I should have listened to him. But I just always figured my dad didn't really know what he was talking about because he's the only person I've ever heard say a bad word about Proust."

As we drove on toward Boston, I thought of the guy who was always standing in front of me when I played. He had been at every show so far and he was at almost every show on my last tour. He seemed harmless but you never know. He looked almost cartoonishly normal, like a caricature of a "normal" person: glasses, polo shirt underneath a windbreaker, blue jeans, average haircut, average height, average weight, early thirties. He would stand there with a slight smile on his face, alone, looking completely benign and almost willfully, happily ineffectual, like he was content to just exist, in one spot, unacknowledged by me or anyone around him, for about five hours nightly—from the time the doors open to the last note of the last song of the encore—gently spectating. The expression on his face never changed—it was the definition of mildness. Who was this guy? What did he do for a living? Where did he live? Did he have a family, and if so what did they think of his going to so many of my shows? I kind of wanted to know but I didn't want to start a conversation with him because he might be crazy. (Ted Bundy looked normal, too, remember.)

Everything about him was very consistent from night to night. His unassuming behavior, his clothing, his position in front of the stage, were always the same. I could picture him continuing to smile if I punched him in the stomach—he'd grunt, maybe, and pitch forward a bit, just for a second, and then straighten up and continue standing there, quietly, with the same mild-mannered expression on his face. But I just left him alone. I would nod at him or say hey when I saw him on my way back from dinner, out in front of the club waiting for the doors to open so he could get in and claim his usual spot directly in front of my perch at the microphone, but I wouldn't make a big deal out of the fact that he was there every night, and following me around the country, and spending his hard-earned money on tickets to my shows, because I didn't want to draw attention to what he was doing.

I didn't want to expose him; I didn't want to embarrass him.

Because I think it would be embarrassing to be the guy who follows Juliana Hatfield around the country. I mean, it would be one thing if I were Led Zeppelin circa 1972 or something, I guess; if I were one of the best rock-and-roll bands in the world at the height of their fame. But I was just me, post–commercial heyday, doing my little pop-rock thing that I'd been doing for the past fifteen years. When I would see him standing there I couldn't help but wonder, "Isn't he bored of me yet? Isn't he sick of the songs? Sick of looking at the same black nylon guitar strap I wear every night?" There was some variation in the set list from night to night but still, I'd be bored at this point, if I were him. No one is that interesting, after a while.

Christ, I wouldn't want to see even Led Zeppelin circa 1972, ten nights in a row.

8

The *Interview* Interview

The Blake Babies broke up in 1991. I instigated the break. I had been feeling increasingly constricted by the limitations of the lineup of John and Freda and me. And I wanted more control over the sound and the direction of the band, rather than to continue sharing and collaborating in everything. John and Freda and I were beginning to drift apart, anyway, and beginning to disagree about more and more.

In 1990 we'd recorded a demo with David Kahne, a legendary producer and, at the time, a big cheese at Columbia Records. He was interested in possibly signing the Blake Babies to a deal with Columbia and wanted to see what would happen when we were put in the studio with a big-time L.A. hit-making producer (him). Would we rise to the occasion or were we slacker indie kids content to go on living in relative obscurity? Could we let ourselves be molded and polished (for the greater good of the song, of course)?

Kahne chose a new song of mine called "I'm Not Your Mother"—which we had already recorded once for our album *Sunburn*—to record in his Hollywood studio. The end result was a tight, punchy, radio-ready version of my song, and I loved it, loved where Kahne had steered us, how he had pushed us to become a better, more accessible, and, I thought, more exciting version of ourselves. A bigger, more fabulous mainstream Blake Babies who somehow sang and played better. He'd made the song sound like a top-40 hit, like a radio song—I wanted to be on the radio! I wanted a hit!—with that invisible sparkle that a good producer can magically sprinkle over a song/band/session by paying close attention to detail and by eliciting good perfomances.

But John and Freda didn't share my enthusiam. They thought the finished song was too slick and that Kahne had bent and shaped us into something too Hollywood. They felt that Kahne had taken us, unecessarily, out of our comfort zone and imposed an uncool aesthetic on us, and that he had an unpleasantly dictatorial way of controlling the session. Kahne had produced hits by the Bangles and Romeo Void and lots of others, and I thought we should let the expert run the show. I *wanted* someone to drag me out of my comfort zone and away from the same old musical habits that I kept repeating. I simply disagreed with John and Freda. To me, the David Kahne experience was a step up and forward from where we were.

Then again, I had always loved sleek, gleaming, gushy, gooey, big-chorus top-40 radio songs and John and Freda generally just, well, didn't. At the time of the David Kahne session, Wilson Phillips—the pop group made up of the daughters of Brian Wilson (of the Beach Boys) and John and Michelle Phillips (of the Mamas and the Papas)—was all over the radio. I'd bought that first album and was eating it up. I adored their syrupy three-part harmonies and sunshiny gloss but John and Freda scoffed at it, didn't get it, thought it was a joke, ridiculous. They didn't understand why or how I (or anyone) could enjoy that sort of shamelessly commercialized pop product.

But I did. I loved it, even though it didn't make any rational sense, and if I listened too closely to the lyrics even I had to admit that they were for the most part terrible, high school diary entry–type pabulum. But their voices together, and the clean, twinkling, soothing, icy/warm production, connected with some pleasure center in my brain. Sure, I loved the Stooges and Blue Cheer and Squirrel Bait, but I loved Wilson Phillips, too. Why couldn't I? But John and Freda insisted that Wilson Phillips were just awful, dreadful, totally uncool, with absolutely no redeeming value and that they were, from an intellectual and analytical standpoint, reprehensible in their shameless pandering to the mainstream. I didn't think that just because something was cynically and ruthlessly designed for and marketed to the idiot philistine masses didn't mean it was necessarily not fun to listen to.

I needed to move on, though I never stopped loving John and Freda. I had grown frustrated. I wanted more. I wanted bigger and better things, new and different things. I wanted to realize unseen, unknown potential. I wanted to set out on my own.

In 1991 my first solo album, *Hey Babe*, was released on Mammoth Records. It was my first work since the Blake Babies had broken up. Mammoth was a relatively new label, based in Chapel Hill, North Carolina, and they were the only record company who had made an offer for the Blake Babies. Mammoth had retained me as per the "leaving member" clause in the Blake Babies recording contract and now the label was putting a lot into the promotion of my new album. It generated a lot of press attention, especially for an independent release. I was selling more as a solo artist than the Blake Babies had sold.

The head of Mammoth, Jay Faires, had designs on being a big player in the industry, with ambitions of one day selling his label to one of the major ones, and so he was really pushing me, gambling on me. Faires wanted to prove that he could succeed at building a viable, profitable record company from the ground up; and I, along with some of the many varied acts on the roster such as the Melvins, Victoria Williams, Seven Mary Three, Squirrel Nut Zippers, and Fu Manchu, seemed like a good bet to help make that happen. (Seven Mary Three and Squirrel Nut Zippers went on to sell a million albums each.)

When *Hey Babe* came out, Mammoth hadn't yet established itself as a serious player in the record business. By the time Seven Mary Three exploded onto the charts with "Cumbersome," Mammoth had aligned with Atlantic Records and was much better equipped to break a band in a big way. I did sell 60,000 copies of my *Hey Babe*, which was much more than the Blake Babies ever sold. At that time, 60,000 was considered very respectable for an emerging artist on an independent label. To me those numbers were astonishing—a definite success. The Blake

Babies' first, self-released album sold fewer than 1,000 copies—the copies that were manufactured, on vinyl.

Faires seemed pleased with my numbers, and was reasonably convinced that this was the first stage of my ascent to bona fide commercial success. Mammoth did, as I said, soon join with a major label (Atlantic Records) and was ultimately sold in 1998—to Disney (officially known as the Walt Disney Company)—for a huge amount of money. Jay Faires went on to be president of music and publishing at Lions Gate Films in Los Angeles.

It was new for me, and kind of exciting, to be all of a sudden featured in national magazines, because it meant that my music was being introduced into more people's lives. I wanted so much for my music— for my voice, and my words, and my feelings—to be heard, because I had been so desperately shy and so hidden and so mute and ineffectual in my personal relations for so long.

Music was the one way I could communicate, and one way to open more ears to my music was through the press. Of course the press was a big, complicated truth- and personality-distorting monster, but I hadn't learned that yet.

While promoting *Hey Babe*, I did an interview with a journalist from *Interview* magazine.

Our talk turned toward love and relationships since a lot of *Hey Babe* (and Blake Babies) songs seemed to explore this subject matter in tortured, obsessed depth, and the interviewer thought readers might appreciate some more detailed, specific insight into who, if anyone, was breaking my heart, and how, in all of these songs. I could tell from the way he was posing some of his "boyfriend" questions that the journalist seemed to have some preconceived erroneous ideas about me and whom I was or was not dating. It was making me uncomfortable; I was becoming concerned that he might misrepresent me in his article if I didn't clarify something. And that was when I let slip, casually, that "I've never gone all the way."

It was a true statement. I was twenty-three years old.

When the article hit the newsstands, I was shocked by the amount of attention generated by that one little six-word declaration of virginity. It was my first real taste of the "flies-on-a-discarded-piece-of-meat" aspect of the media. People jumped on the quote, tripping over one another to get to it, like what I had tossed out flippantly was something really important, or scandalous. Almost every subsequent article written about me referenced the quote. I couldn't shake it; my recorded words were like an incurable disease. The fact of my admitted advanced-age virginity was restated and reprinted all over the place, again and again, reverberating for months and months and even years (even now people refer to that article) afterward, whenever anyone mentioned me or my music. It was the go-to Juliana Hatfield quote of note, which helped define me and my public image for many years, for better or for worse.

I could be disingenuous and say that by admitting my virginity I was just being honest, just going with the flow of the talk, and that I had no reason not to tell the truth, and, well, what's the big deal with being a twenty-three-year-old virgin, anyway? But I must have known that saying what I said, publicly, would have some effect, even if it wasn't one hundred percent consciously calculated to do so.

My intention had been to make a statement about my individuality, my independence. I was proud of the fact that I was still a virgin. To me, not giving away that part of myself before I felt I was ready was an assertion of my strength and my freedom and my ability to trust my instincts and to think for myself. It meant that I would not compromise my integrity and that I was impervious to outside pressure or influence when it came to making the important decisions in my life. Rather than being a cheap grab for attention, "I've never gone all the way" meant that I was in control of my body. It meant that I didn't need to be half of a couple to be interesting; I was interesting on my own, I thought, regardless of all the constant speculating and rumor-mongering that went on. People were always trying to link me to whatever guy I happened to be hanging out with on any given day, and that annoyed me.

I'd hoped this would also clear up the misconception that I was Evan Dando's girlfriend.

I did an interview with a man from *GQ* a year or two later, and the conversation veered toward the subject of Evan, my friend and music collaborator, as interview conversations often did in those days. (Everyone was eager to hear any details pertaining to our assumed "relationship." The Lemonheads—Evan's band—and the Blake Babies had bonded early on in Boston, when both of our bands first started gigging. As Evan and I gained fame, we stayed connected to each other and to each other's music, and this connection was somehow a fascination for some people.) At one point, mid-talk, the journalist threw out a seemingly innocent, randomly curious question about Evan, who had recently dyed his hair very blond: "So, what is Evan's natural hair color?"

I answered, innocently, "Mmm, it's kind of dirty blond."

Later, after the interview wrapped up and the man had gone, I realized that he had tried to get me to divulge some particular intimate detail of my and Evan's so-called private life. "What is Evan's real hair color?" was code for "What color is Evan's pubic hair?" It didn't dawn on me until later how incredibly rude and obnoxious the man's question really was. How had that gotten past me? I had been tricked into a false confession. Evan's real hair color was dirty blond, but I only knew this because I had spent enough time with him to know that the hair on his head was naturally dirty blond.

I thought that by admitting my virginity I was being subversive, declaring my right to choose how to live. I thought feminists and anarchists and freethinkers and outsiders and late bloomers everywhere would cheer when they read the interview. Maybe people misunderstood me and were unable to decipher my motives simply because there is no archetype of a female loner-by-choice, especially in the pop-rock music world. The strong, silent, individualistic, solitary outsider—the lone wolf—is historically always male. But that is how I saw myself: standing alone, off to the side, with a tight grip on my own original, quixotic ideas, and not as a pathetic waif, desperate for some record executive to make me a star; not as a delicate shrinking violet waiting eagerly to be swept up in the arms of my future husband who would ravish me in a dramatic, yearned-for defloration. I thought everyone would understand where I was coming from. But that's not what happened.

Some people thought I was lying about my virginity and that my words were cynically and strategically chosen and placed in order to shock, to grab people's attention—to build on my fame—or possibly to reinforce the kind of particular vulnerable, delicate, little-girl, coy image that had attached itself to me, an image that I hated and considered a grave misrepresentation of who I believed myself to be.

I was honestly pretty clueless about the big bad world of the publicity machine. I never had any media training like young bands do today. I never practiced or mastered the art of the well-crafted, well-timed, well-placed sound bite. If I had, I would have realized that my admission of virginity would be the sensationalistic shot heard round the alternative rock world that it turned out to be, and not what I intended.

I wanted to tell the truth about myself, to be understood. I believed honesty was not a bad thing, and was even a good thing, and honorable, and sensible, and much more interesting and entertaining than the made-up stories many celebrities and their publicists issue to the press to gloss over the more unconventional details and untidy truths of their complicated real lives. I didn't have many stories to tell, yet; no scandalous love affairs to recount. Sure, Evan and I had fooled around a little, but I wasn't ready for a real boyfriend. Music came first. And that's not a very interesting story, is it?

9

August 5
Cambridge

At the Middle East Cafe, where we were scheduled to play tonight, the load-in was from the back and down a treacherous, steep flight of stairs. I showed up late, accidentally on purpose, to avoid having to schlep my heavy equipment down those stairs. I felt kind of guilty about not helping but I knew there were plenty of beefy guys on staff at the Middle East who would pick up my slack, and get paid for it. "I'm entitled to one night of laziness in my hometown," I rationalized.

My career had begun in the late 1980s, back while I was still a student at the Berklee College of Music. The Blake Babies held band practice in the Berklee rehearsal rooms. At early gigs the audiences were made up largely of friends and family members. Gradually we became more known. Boston was home to many colleges and was full of young students, and there were lots of small clubs to play in—the Rat, Bunratty's, T.T. the Bear's, Green Street Station. It was a fun, supportive, inspiring environment. And it was an especially exciting time to be in an indie rock band because all around us great original music was being created by bands like Dinosaur, Throwing Muses, Volcano Suns, the Pixies, the Lemonheads, Galaxie 500. All around the country—and the world—people were taking notice. (The English music press was always fawning over our latest musical export, asking, "What do they put in the water in Boston to produce all these incredible groundbreaking bands?") The Blake Babies got some of this attention, but not quite as much as those other bands (we were more a local phenomenon, and to some extent a national one). Bands like the Pixies and Dinosaur were technically my peers, but I never felt I was in their league.

J Mascis, singer, guitarist, and main songwriter of Dinosaur—they later changed their name to "Dinosaur Jr." after an old California group called "The Dinosaurs" issued a cease and desist order over the name—was one of the most naturally talented, interesting, original, innovative guitar players of my generation. I was in awe of his gorgeous, superloud, overdriven guitar solos as well as his twisted, tender, tortured, pretty/heavy songs. He walked our streets and he was our age and he was one of us. A rock prodigy in our midst. It was inspiring.

The Blake Babies took the Orange Line subway train out to Jamaica Plain to see our first Dinosaur show at a small bar called Green Street Station, which no longer exists. Though there were only about twelve people in the audience, including us, J played as hard and as fast and as loud and as possessed as if he were playing in a stadium to a full house of ten thousand screaming, worshipful girls. He could've been anywhere, the way his long hair covered his face and the way he lurched and swayed to the beat of whatever was inside him, and never acknowledged the audience. When he broke a string, he walked to the side of the stage and got a new string out of a pack in his guitar case, and proceeded to change the string right there on the side of the stage, never hurrying, as if he was at band practice, while the audience and the two other guys in the band—Lou Barlow, the bass player, and Murph, the drummer—waited patiently in the awkward silence for more music.

The early Dinosaur shows were some of the loudest shows I'd ever witnessed. The extreme volume was part of the thrill (and I imagine it was part of how J got his righteous guitar tone). It was so loud that I couldn't swallow. So loud, I felt the guitar sounds hitting my body like gusts of wind in a tunnel. To forgo earplugs was to invite possible permanent hearing damage, or at the very least a postconcert ringing in the ears.

In 1988 the Blake Babies were recording at Fort Apache Studios in North Cambridge. Dinosaur recorded their third album, *Bug*, during the daytime and we worked the cheaper overnight studio shift.

At some point I went into the big tracking room to sing a vocal. On a music stand next to the microphone that had been set up for me to sing into were two pieces of notebook paper torn out of a ringed binder. I picked the papers up and saw that they had words on them, handwritten in a distinctive boyish hand. I recognized it as the same handwriting as in the credits on the back of *You're Living All Over Me*, Dinosaur's 1987 masterpiece and my obsession at the time. As I read the words, I deduced that J must have written the credits on the back of *You're Living All Over Me*, and that I was looking at the lyrics to a new Dinosaur song-in-progress called "Freak Scene," which I had just heard. One of the Fort Apache engineers had played part of it for us on the big speakers in the control room as he was breaking down that day's Dinosaur session.

I had in front of me something that no one else had—words to a song so new that even its composer didn't know them well enough to sing them without looking at them. I'd lucked out.

As soon as I found myself alone in the tracking room, I took the two pages from the music stand, folded them carefully, and put them surreptitiously in my backpack. I rationalized the theft to myself by thinking, "J obviously doesn't need or want these anymore, or he wouldn't have left them here." After all, hadn't we just heard the song, with his lead vocal right there in the mix? He was done with the lyrics, done singing.

I took the two notebook pages home and stashed them in a secret hiding place like they were a special lottery prize I had won, like they were very valuable and I had to protect them. They *were* worth a lot, to me. They were a piece of a genius, left behind.

The Middle East Cafe, in Cambridge's Central Square neighborhood, on Mass. Ave. between Harvard and MIT, was originally just a bar and restaurant serving Middle Eastern food. A small room in the back was used for belly-dancing shows. In 1987 a local Cambridge scenester came up with the idea of putting on a night of rock-type music in that back room. He booked the Blake Babies, and that is how we came to be part of the inauguration of the Middle East Rock Club.

The show was a success, and the Middle East's back room quickly morphed into a full-time rock club. Years later the dark, cavernous basement of the building, which had at one time been a bowling alley but was then neglected, languishing in disrepair, was remade into another wing of the Middle East rock venue called, logically, the Middle East Downstairs. That was where Some Girls were playing tonight. The smaller, original back room of the restaurant became known as the Middle East Upstairs. (It was actually street level, but was called "upstairs" to distinguish it from the larger basement venue.) Both rooms host local, national, and international acts most nights.

I had played in these two rooms many times over the years. It was always nice to play in the Boston area because audiences there knew me and had known me for a while; had grown up with me, in a way. There was comfort in playing to people who had followed my music so closely over the years, and who were very generous—they kept coming back to my shows and making me feel that all the time I'd been away, away from the stage, I had been missed. A hometown crowd loves a hometown girl.

I walked in the entrance of the club, down the wide front stairs, and across the empty club floor and up onto the stage, where Heidi and Freda were setting their things up for soundcheck. I took *Swann's Way* out of my backpack and handed it to Freda.

"Here. Good luck," I said.

Freda smiled and said, "Thanks."

I went and threw my backpack backstage. The backstage area was a tiny room next to and a few steps down from the stage. A closet-sized hole in the wall that all the bands on the bill were meant to share. It had a door that opened in and no ventilation. The only way in or out of this firetrap was to go onto and across the stage, so that if you found yourself in the dressing room while a band was playing, and you wanted to get out, you had to walk behind the band, in view of the crowd, and embarrass yourself.

I'd played here numerous times before and the dressing room had always been kind of squalid. It never failed to astonish me, though, that so many band holding rooms were so consistently foul. At the same time I couldn't really blame the clubs for not wanting to spruce these places up; bands can be such pigs. They write on the walls, puke on the floors, spit in the ashtrays, spill beer on every available surface. They put their dumb bands' dumb stickers all over the one mirror in the room so that no others can ever again see how they look before they go on. They burn holes in the couches with their cigarettes, which they then snuff out in the cold cuts. Why would any club owner bother to put the time and money it takes into fixing up a filthy backstage room and making it nice when it is only going to be trashed again the next night when it's taken over by a new gang of infantile ne'er-do-wells?

The club had filled up when we returned from dinner.

If it wasn't sold out yet, it would be soon. Dave Pirner and his band were just coming onstage. Pirner had originally been scheduled to headline somewhere else in town tonight, but when that other place was shut down suddenly because of alcohol violations, Pirner was added on to our bill at the last minute.

This was part of the reason I was nervous about tonight; I was worried that the whole audience would go home as soon as Pirner finished his set, leaving me to play to an empty house.

Pirner was, you see, a big rock star, or at least had been at one point not too long ago. His band Soul Asylum had a bunch of radio hits in the 1990s and their videos were all over MTV for a while. They were always a pretty good live act, too, so not only was I afraid the whole audience had come to see Pirner and not me; I was afraid that he and his band might actually rock, and leave me looking like a lightweight.

And to add to my anxiety, the sheer scale of Pirner's whole production seemed designed to intimidate, especially in a relatively small club like this. Every inch of the stage was full of his band's gear.

Further aggravating my sense of inferiority was the fact that there was a big fancy spread on the table backstage, including a large hunk of fresh ginger. What was Pirner going to do with all that ginger? Chop it up and make dinner? Aromatherapize? Gnaw on it? It clearly was meant for him and his people and not me and mine. I rarely got this kind of layout, containing every obscure request I'd made, like fresh ginger root.

That stuff—food, drink, or any other needs a performer or band can specify in a clause in their contract—is called the rider. Even at the highest peak of my commercial viability I'd never made a practice of demanding things that were particularly odd or difficult to procure, though a bass player of mine once dared me to put "one warm brick" on the rider, just to see if any of the promoters would actually come through with it. Instead, I asked for stuff that my crew and I could and would really use: water, booze (readily available, mass-produced brands), nine-volt batteries (for our distortion pedals), cigarettes, towels, maybe a couple of postshow pizzas. But now, these days, I considered myself extremely lucky if I was given a bottle of water. And I just assumed that requesting something like fresh ginger would be ignored.

I watched Pirner and his band play from an incognito position in the dark in the back of the room, behind most of the crowd. The first song sounded kind of all right, a quasi-soul sort of thing. Pirner had moved to New Orleans and hooked up with some local musicians down there, and he was now integrating more black, southern, rootsy elements into his music in his own scruffy, white, midwestern, guitar-slinging way.

As the set wore on, my interest waned. Pirner seemed to have given us his best song first. The rest of the set was all kind of samey: midtempo, middle-of-the-road adult-contemporary R&B. Bland. I had the sense that Pirner was aiming for something but not quite hitting it. He was trying on a style of music that he clearly loved and revered as a fan but which did not naturally, instinctively, or all that authentically emanate from him. It was more like he was paying homage to a style of music. Almost like karaoke. But with songs he had written.

The audience appeared to be as uninspired by Pirner's new sound as I was. After the initial collective rapt first-song curiosity, people just weren't paying all that much attention. It was more like they were tolerating his new (Orleans) experiment with polite applause and a kind of good-natured but subdued respect.

I felt relief.

"Aah, okay," I thought. "I can go on after this. I'm all right. I can do this."

I walked over to the merch table to see how Brian was doing.

Brian was a friend of mine whom I had known for about six years. I met him on Martha's Vineyard, at an informal gathering at a house Evan Dando was renting on Moshup Trail in Gay Head. Brian, a born itinerant, was crashing in a shedlike guest house on the island that summer, when he wasn't sleeping on the beach. Somehow Brian and I had ended up living in the same funky old semi-rundown apartment building in Cambridge. We had a lot of the same interests: literature, obscure films, rock music, good food, skiing, the Red Sox. We would lend each other books and CDs and vegetarian recipes, and he would take care of my dog when I was away.

He had worked a lot in the restaurant and catering industries and had ideas about opening a restaurant some day and maybe writing a book. He liked doing outdoorsy things like hiking, wandering, and swimming in the ocean, but he was well educated and very intelligent. He was a bit of an underachiever, someone who hadn't yet found his way and was still searching. He seemed the perfect sort to bring on tour as crew—he was available, flexible, adventurous, and adaptable to new environments. He was generally pretty laid-back, took things as they came, liked to live in the moment. He liked to play hard, sometimes harder than he worked. And when he had a few drinks in him, his dark, combative, self-destructive side could flare up. Though this worried me some in terms of being cooped up in a van with him for a month, I found the fact that he was somewhat troubled to be a nice counterpoint to his easygoing side. Made him a more well-rounded, interesting person.

There was a bit of the old-fashioned, chivalrous, manly man in Brian. I knew that he would defend me and protect me—would maybe even throw a punch—if anyone ever tried to mess with me or harm me or get too close, and this was definitely a plus when considering whether or not to take him on tour. (It had actually happened before: Brian and I were out at a club and one of my loony, frighteningly over-enthused fans stepped over my personal space boundary line with a crazy look in his eyes. Brian stepped in and told the guy to back off.) He could double as my de facto bodyguard.

Like me, Brian was always struggling to keep his personal demons submerged and out of the way of a healthy life. There was anger and confusion and resentment simmering below his surface and this was part of what I liked about Brian. It made him relatable. Without this underlying tension, Brian might have been just another annoyingly mellow beach/ski bum.

Brian had casually offered to come on tour and help, in whatever way I wanted to use him. I told him I could use someone to sell merch, which meant setting up a table and displaying our Juliana/Some Girls tour T-shirts and CDs near the entrance to the club, where all the concertgoers would pass, and standing there selling during and after the show. At the end of each night, he would count and record how much money came in in sales and how many pieces of merchandise were sold. CD and shirt sales were a significant supplement to my sort of meager touring income, so I wanted to bring someone to sell, but there wasn't much room in the tour budget. I didn't know how I would afford it.

Brian offered to do the job, and offered to do it for nothing, for the fun and adventure of it. He had nothing else planned for the immediate future. I thought, "Sure! Yeah! Sounds like an excellent deal to me."

Our friendship was not without the occasional discord (like any friendship) but he *was* my friend, and his price was so right. It would be nice to have someone I knew fairly well on the road with me, rather than hiring some stranger who could turn out to be mean/dishonest/irritating/incompetent/stupid/crazy. Brian had never done the merch job before but it wasn't rocket science. All he had to do was carry, count, and sell stuff. I thought anyone could do it, if minimally motivated. Brian thought of it as a vacation, a free trip around the country, so whatever I paid him, he would probably be happy, and a good worker; any money would be like gravy to him.

I offered him $300 a week plus his own hotel room each night. He seemed genuinely excited, raring to go. Business was booming. There was a swarm of people crowding around Brian with money in their hands and hungry eyes, wanting to buy CDs and T-shirts. Brian looked kind of overwhelmed. I asked him, "Do you need anything?"

He answered, "Do you think you could get me a beer?"

"Yeah. Sure. What kind?"

"A Bass?"

"Okay. I'll be right back."

I went over to the bar that ran along the wall and asked for a Bass. The bartender wouldn't let me pay for it. I guess he knew who I was. I brought the beer back to Brian and I stood beside the merch table observing the action. Someone grabbed me and introduced me to Peter Wolf. This was, I think, about the third time I'd met him. I'm not sure he realized we had met (twice) before, but he did seem to be vaguely aware of who I was and that we were allied, sort of, in some very loose association of semi- or once- or quasi-famous Bostonians. But still I figured he must have come to check out Pirner's band, not me.

Why would Mr. J. Geils Band come out to see me? I'm small potatoes. I'm nothing compared to Dave Pirner and those New Orleans cats up there onstage. Pirner's a genuine, legitimate former rock star. I'm just a little alterna-waif manqué with negligible talents, in most people's eyes, if they've heard of me at all. I may be a medium-sized fish in this small New England pond, but Soul Asylum sold millions out there in the world. That has real cachet, not least of all in the eyes of other former rock stars. Pirner and Wolf belong to the same club, but I was never in their league.

After a quick hello and good-bye to Peter, I went and stood next to the sound board. In a matter of seconds Skeet, my middle-aged Deadhead postman friend, approached. "Hi, Juliana," he said with a smile.

"Hey, Skeet," I said. "How are you doing? Hey, thanks for the flowers in New Jersey."

"Oh, you're welcome, Hey, can I record the show tonight? I have a new mike that's really good and I think I can get a really great sounding recording with it."

"Skeet, why do you do this to me? You know how I feel about it; I don't wanna know about that stuff. Just don't even tell me about it. Can't we talk about something else?"

"Okay, okay. But, okay, so, I have your permission, in case anyone tries to shut me down?"

"Aarghh. Nnnnn . . . I guess so. I don't know. I just don't want to get involved. Don't involve me. Go ask Tim. I mean, I can't stop you, right? You're gonna do it no matter what I say, right?"

"Well, yeah, maybe," he said, smiling a mischievous smile. "But no. No. If you tell me not to record, I won't. But. I can get a really good sounding tape from this DAT machine, with this new mike! And don't you want to document these historic first Some Girls shows? You'll be glad I did it, later."

"Aargh! Stop! You're torturing me, Skeet. If it's a bad show, do you promise you won't make copies for anyone? You have to swear you won't send it around to people if it's bad."

"It's not gonna be a bad show! Come on, you're great."

"Well, I'll be the judge of that. It's quite possible that this will be a shitty show and if it is, I don't want anyone to hear that tape, okay?"

"Okay. How about this—I'll send the tape to you and you can listen to it and tell me if you think it's okay. And then if you do, I'll make copies and send it around. But not until you approve it."

"Okay. *Okay*. I have to go get ready to play."

And I fled to another corner of the room.

When Pirner's band was done playing, his crew went to work clearing their equipment off the stage. I waited ten or fifteen minutes and then went backstage to say hello to Pirner, whom I had never met before. He seemed real nice and he asked after a mutual friend of ours.

I noticed the ginger still sitting on the table and I asked Pirner, "What do you do with the ginger?"

He answered, "I make tea out of it."

It was getting close to the Some Girls set time, so Pirner and his people graciously vacated the band room to give us some private preparation time that I spent, or rather, wasted, trying on a bunch of different outfits that I had brought with me from home. I was feeling extra-insecure and unsure of myself. So many people I knew would be watching me tonight; scrutinizing me, making judgments and critiquing, and I would have to face them later, in the streets and in the bars and in the supermarkets—wherever I might run into them. I wanted so badly to be good for them, to deliver. And for myself, too, so that I could hold my head proudly high when I came home from the tour.

My nervousness was translating into an inability to feel comfortable in any of the clothes I had to choose from. I was too tense to put anything together. To dress well, one must trust, without thinking, in her powers of improvisation. It's the same with playing music; if you put too much conscious effort into it, it will look like you are trying too hard. The pressure was starting to overwhelm me.

I did a series of quick changes in front of Heidi and Freda. First I pulled a miniskirt on over my jeans and then yanked the jeans out from under the skirt. Then I tried on about three shirts and three pairs of shoes in quick frustrated succession, in various combinations with either the skirt or the jeans. Nothing was working. Every single mix felt wrong. I felt as if I had woken up in someone else's body. I wanted to

66

crawl out of my skin and escape this horrible drama—this horrible wardrobe calamity.

At a loss, I looked toward Freda and Heidi and asked, "What would Jesus wear?"

They assured me that what I had on looked fine. But I just couldn't let myself believe it.

Tim poked his head in the door and said, "Are you guys ready to rock?" I answered, "Not really," and he responded, matter-of-factly and, I thought, somewhat unsympathetically, "Well, you have five minutes." Then, suddenly cheerful, he added, "Have a great show!" and was off to the sound board.

I laced up my black Doc Martens boots frantically and decided, because it was time to make a decision, right or wrong, that this outfit I had on (pink Petit Bateau tank top, denim X-Girl stretch miniskirt, tall boots) would have to do.

We went onstage and as all eyes in the full house hit us I knew, instantly and definitively, that I had chosen the stupidest of all possible costumes.

"What am I doing? This isn't me," I thought, of the liberal amount of skin I was showing. Not only my arms but my legs, too, were on display, for all the world to see. How did I expect people to take me seriously as an artist when I was showing so much leg?

Not only was the miniskirt calling into question my artistic integrity, it was inhibiting my physical mobility. When I knelt down to plug in my pedals, I had to squeeze my legs together and sort of turn to the side and carefully maneuver my position so that my underwear wouldn't show. It was all much too complicated, already.

We started with "Feel It." We always started with "Feel It." It's a good one to play first because its groove is easy to grab onto and lock into. It has simple chords, a simple melody, and a cool, easy, driving beat. It sets a positive tone and it's hard to screw it up.

Unfortunately, it was all downhill from there. Like Pirner, I'd played my best song first. For the rest of the hour and fifteen minutes that I was contractually obligated to play, I struggled with every aspect of my performance. I was just too tense to lose myself in the music.

On a good night the band feels like an organism thriving in its natural environment—like an octopus whose multiple arms are working interdependently. On a bad night all the parts feel separated and unable to rely on one another or to find their way to doing what they are supposed to be doing, like the organism's nerve center is diseased, causing the whole thing to malfunction. But when it's working, the band is one whole living, breathing, propelling motion. The drummer is doing her thing, the bassist is doing hers, I'm doing mine, and it's all connected, somehow, by some invisible, ineffable, organic, cellular and metaphysical je ne sais quoi. We are like pistons in an engine, helping to push the machine forward, all chugging along, all directed toward the common, ultimate goal: songs, music, uplift.

But for the machine to be able to do its job, all the parts outside of us need to be in sync, too. Monitors and amps need to be loud enough and situated correctly so that everyone can hear what she needs to hear on the stage. And instruments need to be in tune—on their own and with each other.

I had often experienced problems with the stage and monitor sound when playing at the Middle East. It was never *just right*. I never felt that I'd put on a *great* show there. Maybe it was the way the room was constructed or maybe its feng shui was messed up or maybe the building had been erected on a sacred Indian burial ground and angry spirits haunted the place. Who knows? The energy and love coming from the crowds had always been hearty and effusive at the Middle East, but the stage situation was never optimum, and despite my hopes, tonight was no different.

I wasn't alone in my discomfort; every time I looked over at Heidi or back at Freda, they had concerned looks on their faces. At least I wasn't completely alone in my misery. Through the entire set, all three of us were laboring to come together, to make it all work, to unite. It just was not feeling quite right. It sounded weird onstage. Nothing was connecting to anything.

And then there was the terrifying ever present consciousness that my solo playing was not up to par. In fact, it had been deteriorating since the first show. Like a toothache or a tumor, my inadequacy was becoming harder to ignore; the awful fact of my shortcomings grew more painful as it gathered strength.

Something was happening to me. Some kind of physical or mental or maybe even moral degeneration? I was dropping the ball at the crucial, critical moments. It was as if my hands just suddenly stopped working, when I needed them most. Like a machine breaking down or a car tire blowing out during the sprint to the finish line.

In the lead section of "The Prettiest Girl" I stumbled all over in one of the most pathetic displays of incompetence that I had ever unleashed on an audience. As it was happening, I felt myself falling into a hole that I knew I wasn't going to be able to get out of.

When the song was finally over, I turned my back on the crowd in order to hide my shame, and I walked back to my amp and pretended to make an adjustment by fake-fiddling with its knobs. I tried to gather myself together, with egg all over my face, in my head, and muster some composure and courage so that I could continue.

"I am an embarrassment to my profession," I thought. "And to my gender. What kind of example am I, as a Woman in Rock, farting out crappy solos like that? They should kick me out of the musicians' union."

I raised my head and turned to face the audience. I started the next song, because I had to. I couldn't stop now; couldn't give up now. I couldn't walk off stage in the middle of a set. I would look like an ass-hole if I did that. No, I would *be* an asshole if I did that. The audience paid money to see me play. They didn't need to be burdened with my neuroses. They just wanted to have a good time. And they were having a good time. "Look at them," I thought. "They're smiling, and clapping, for me. For more. These generous, forgiving, warmhearted folks. I can do this. I can. I think I can. Anyway, I have to."

But I wanted so badly to run off the stage and go bury my head in the sand forever, or at least go lock myself in a room somewhere where no one would ever find me.

"Necessito" came up in the set list. Immediately I thought, "The solo on this one is so simple—it should be a piece of cake." It was a bad sign; why was I thinking about the solo, already, at the beginning of the song? Why was I thinking at all?

Thinking, on a concert stage, as on any competitive playing field, is a prelude to choking. There should be little or no conscious thought at this performance stage of the game. Your mind and body should be on cruise control; they should be in sync, doing what they have been trained to do. If they are not, it's probably because your head is getting in the way of your body, confusing things, throwing your body's balance off with the head's nagging interference: "Don't fuck it up, come on, come on, get ready, here it comes, look alive." Your brain, in this situation, is like the home crowd at a basketball game during a visiting opponent's free throw, shouting and hollering and frantically waving those plastic bat things, in an effort to distract the shooter and make him screw up so he can't get the extra point.

That's exactly what I was doing: pulling my Self out of the Zone; not trusting my fingers to do what they had practiced and rehearsed, over and over again. And in so doing, my fear of fucking up became a self-fulfilling prophecy.

When I got to the solo in "Necessito," again my fingers didn't do what I wanted them to do. Not exactly. They had some idea; some memory imprinted onto them of what they had practiced. They were making the right formations, but on the wrong frets and in the wrong key so the sounds coming out of the guitar were askew, nasty, atonal.

It was like one of those classic anxiety dreams in which you find yourself on a stage in front of an audience and you suddenly can't remember the song or the words or how to play your instrument.

Everything was crumbling and I couldn't control it. I felt brain-damaged, like there was something eating holes out of my cerebellum, making me forget how to perform rudimentary tasks and how to understand the most basic information. I searched my addled memory to try to figure out how and when the damage could have happened.

Was it the year on Zoloft? Was it too many Bloody Marys? Valium? Ambien? Was it the time, when I was two years old, that Dad threw me in the pool to see if I would swim, and I sank to the bottom? Was it lack of adequate nutrition? Not enough meat? Was it pesticide runoff in my drinking water? Lead paint? Was it the DDT in the bug spray? Too much masturbation? Aliens?

I half remembered bright flashing strobelike lights all through the house one night, as a five-year-old, when everyone else was asleep. Had aliens come to take me away as I slept and performed experiments on my brain, removing chunks of it?

When the set finally, mercifully, ended, I went straight to the dressing room and changed out of my stupid miniskirt and back into my jeans. Then I apologized to Freda and Heidi for playing so many wrong notes. Freda apologized, too, on behalf of herself. Heidi was similarly glum. None of us felt good about the show, either individually or collectively, but the fact that we were all bummed out together didn't make me feel any less terrible.

Then I announced, "I'm quitting music."

Freda smiled sympathetically and said, "It wasn't that bad. It's only the fourth show, too, remember. We'll get better."

But I still felt that I had cheated the audience, even if they didn't realize it. I didn't deserve to be getting paid for this, when I did it so poorly. Even though all the people seemed to really enjoy the show, clapping enthusiastically and beaming at me with their eager faces throughout the whole set, I wanted to give them all their money back.

Outside, Freda and Heidi and I waited by the van for Brian and Tim to wrap up the tallying of the merch and to gather their things together. When they emerged from the back door, Brian looked kind of frazzled and in need of a strong cocktail. Tim had been helping him with the accounting, showing him how to understand the details of the merch guy's job. Although Tim was sharing the burden, it was clearly more work than Brian had anticipated. Brian's a real laid-back guy, and the job was turning out to be fairly fast-paced and stressful. I had faith in my friend, though, and had no reason to doubt him. He was a smart, capable guy. He would figure it out.

And so when, once we had sat down in the van for the ride home, he said, "Jul, do you think you could raise my salary a little? Like, maybe, two hundred more a week? The job is just way more work than I thought it was going to be," I answered, sincerely, and maybe a tad overaccomodatingly, "Yes. Yes. Of course, Brian. Yes. I can do that. Yes," wanting to sound amenable so that he wouldn't have to feel like a jerk for asking for more money. "You deserve it. I really didn't realize it was going to be so much work for you, either."

I meant it. I was feeling sympathetic to Brian. A big part of me really wanted nothing more than to pay Brian more. And was happy to oblige. But there was another part of me thinking, "Wait. Wait a second. You can't do that—agree to one thing and then go trying to change it after agreeing to it. It doesn't work that way. I'm on a budget here. A very carefully planned-out budget."

I just wanted the tour to go smoothly, without any resentment or ill will floating around in the van. Brian was working harder than he had imagined he would, selling T-shirts and CDs, and he wanted a little more money for his trouble. Okay. Fine. Whatever. I could deal with that. I wasn't going to take home any money either way. The goal had originally been to break even, but as soon as I took Brian on, with his original lower salary and the extra hotel room each night that his presence on the tour would require, that goal became implausible. So it had already been established that I would lose money, even before Brian's pay raise. Now I would simply be losing a little more. Big deal. So what. In the red is in the red.

The van dropped me off at home and I slept in my bed for what would be the last time in a long time.

Now the tour could really get started.

10

Sassy

Sassy was the first national magazine to put me on their cover. *Sassy* was a hipper version of *Seventeen* but it appealed to older girls as well as teenagers. It first appeared on newsstands in 1987, when I was in college, and it was a breath of fresh air for those of us who were interested in fashion and music and movies and art and TV that was a little bit less mainstream and conservative. *Sassy* was for girls with a rebellious streak.

I liked *Sassy* because it didn't take itself too seriously. Their attitude was that fashion could be interesting and exciting but wasn't truly important. *Sassy* was hipper, cooler, smarter, nervier, more knowing and self-deprecating and irreverent than all the women's fashion magazines that came before.

When "alternative" rock, like Nirvana, and its culture started to break through and infiltrate the consciousness of Bon Jovi fans, *Sassy* was there to bridge the gap between glossy, mainstream magazines and the cheap, photocopied, black-and-white underground punk rock fanzines. There are tons of similar magazines now like *Nylon, Bust, Venus, YM,* and so on, but *Sassy* was the first of its kind. And they'd asked me to be on the cover.

It was after I released my first solo album, *Hey Babe*, in 1991. Along with the cover, there would be a multiple-page spread inside. I was honored and excited. I had the official *Sassy* seal of approval, and that meant a lot to me. Being on the cover of *Sassy* meant that I was breaking out of the pack of all the hundreds of artists out there struggling to make names for themselves, and had drawn a bit of attention to myself for doing my own thing to the beat of my own drummer. The whole world hadn't discovered me yet, but *Hey Babe* was striking a chord with a good number of contemplative, young, independent-minded people who felt that my voice was speaking their emotional language. And I was doing it, I thought, without selling out.

On the morning of the shoot I got up early and dressed for the drive to New York in clothes that I had picked out especially for *Sassy*; I wanted to arrive looking like I belonged. I wanted the *Sassy* people to feel confident that they had not made a mistake in choosing me to be on their cover. I wanted to look uniquely cool, uniquely me, but not like I was trying too hard; like a *Sassy* girl. I wore a knit black top that zipped up the middle, a black cotton miniskirt, opaque black tights and black lace-up shoes with a chunky heel. More put-together than the T-shirts and ratty old jeans I usually lived in, but not so dressy that I felt like an imposter.

I made the trip down from Boston in my old blue Volvo sedan in about three and a half hours, with my black Les Paul guitar in the backseat. The *Sassy* people had asked me to bring a guitar to use as a prop in one of the shots. I thought it was a good sign that they wanted me to use one of my own, and meant that they probably wouldn't try to remake me in some fantasy image that they had envisioned for me. They wanted my guitar; they wanted me.

I arrived at the set meeting place in Soho at the prearranged time of 10 a.m. They were going to shoot me so that it looked natural and not staged (except for the cover, which would be me playing guitar in the street), in various locations on the downtown west side: sitting on a bench outside a coffee shop, looking at flowers in a bodega, peering into a boutique window, walking down the street. The clothes choices they'd brought for me were from the fall collections of smallish, mostly independent companies like APC and agnès b. They were understatedly stylish, well cut, subtle but hip. A lot of black and gray or muted colors, none of it revealing or vulgar or tightly form-fitting or blatantly "sexy": wool trousers with a subdued flower-patterned blouse under a sweater vest, a black long-sleeved dress that came to below the knee—cool-looking, comfortable clothes; the kinds of things I would buy. Kind of like what I was wearing when I arrived for the shoot.

After the *Sassy* stylist and editor and photographer had greeted me, they looked me up and down and decided they liked what I had on, and so rather than redressing me immediately from head to toe from their own stash of garments, the stylist decided, "What you're wearing is great. Let's try doing the first setup with you wearing that."

They approved of my haircut, too. It was short in the back with the front longer, tapering down to chin length, and parted on the side. The hair person didn't need to do much to it other than run a bit of styling mousse through it with her fingers and brush it and push it into place so it looked kind of smooth and pretty.

After my face had been made up tastefully by the makeup artist, my hair subtly hand-sculpted, and an additional gray-green cardigan put on over my own black top, we began shooting. It was noon on a Sunday, and we were on a quiet cobblestone street of old brick loft buildings near the West Side Highway. The photographer directed me to stand holding my unplugged electric guitar as if I were performing, right there in the middle of the street, and to look lively as the photographer snapped shots of me. Although I was grateful to the *Sassy* crew for making me feel as comfortable as they could and for making every effort to integrate my real-life personality into the shot, and thankful the streets were fairly empty, I still felt uncomfortable.

I couldn't help it. I always stiffened as soon as I stepped in front of a camera. Posing for film was for me an unnatural act, a charades game that I had yet to master. Most big stars have a gift for image manipulation, and it has served them all well; Mariah Carey, for example, always looks poised and attractive and pleasant and relaxed and confident and uncomplicated in photos.

"If only I could send a body double," I thought, standing there in the street. "Send her to do this stuff for me, the stuff I'm no good at." The smiling and talking, the posing and answering questions. I want someone to build me a robot to do all my interviews and photographs. Program her to make love to the camera and to give fascinating, articulate, entertaining, insightful, understandable, accessible answers. Then I would no longer have to be continually pulling my foot out of my mouth or offending or confusing people. And then, and then . . . I could be free to just make my music. That's all I ever really wanted.

As we worked, and I continued my awkward guitar-playing-modeling-mime, a young man walking east on the sidewalk approached me and the *Sassy* crew on his way up the street. He was mildly scruffy, and bookish, a brainy-nerdy-arty type. Cute, about my age, with sandy-colored hair, glasses, in a button-down shirt and jeans. Probably a Sonic Youth fan. Maybe a graphic designer. He looked like a guy with whom I'd have a lot in common; I liked Sonic Youth (well, some of their stuff). I enjoyed graphic design (well, I enjoyed looking at it). He looked like the kind of guy I'd like to get to know; the kind of guy who could be my friend.

He glanced at the scene, briefly taking it all in (but trying not to appear too interested), and as he passed by I heard him mutter, "Oh, that looks real," in a sardonic, disdainful tone of voice. Evidently he had assumed I was a model who didn't really know how to play guitar, but was only pretending to know how to play guitar, and was doing it for the camera in the middle of the street in New York City, and that wasn't cool.

"Wait!" I wanted to call out to the guy as I turned and watched his back moving farther away up the street. "I'm not a model, I swear! I'm only pretending to be a model! You have it all wrong—I really *do* do this! I'm a musician! That's what I *do*. I play guitar!"

But what if I had been a model, only pretending to know how to play guitar? What would have been so wrong with that? What did that passerby have against models, or modeling as a profession, anyway, that made him so scornful of the whole thing?

Indeed, what had I? The first song on my next album was called "Supermodel," and it was a not entirely flattering portrait of one of the breed. "The highest paid piece of ass" was how I characterized my subject and her lot at the start of the song.

But in later verses, I sang, "I wish she'd trade places with me" and "I came over as soon as she called," because she's so beautiful and precious that we can't resist her. The scorn is revealed as the envy that it really is.

I would have had exactly the same reaction that that guy on the street had had, if I had come across a model in the street, holding a guitar in front of a photographer.

But I wasn't getting paid. Not with money, anyway. My wages that day were a stranger's contempt. And I was only trying to support my music. I believed in it so strongly that I was willing to go awkwardly out into the street and pretend to play a rock-and-roll song on an unplugged electric guitar for an invisible audience. I sacrificed some of my pride for the sake of my music. And to offer myself to *Sassy* readers, who I believed were the smart, appreciative, fair, freethinking, melodic pop-loving audience that I wanted.

I worked so hard on my songs and my singing, to keep it all true and pure, to make it better, to perfect it, to be an artist worthy of respect, but still I was perceived by some as "famous for nothing at all." I wanted desperately to deserve my success and all the attention I was starting to get. I wanted not simply to be showered with praise, but to be worthy of it.

Music was a lifeboat on a deep dark angry ocean, to me. Without it, I would have drowned. And I thought that without an audience to listen, it would have been like dying alone, my death unnoticed. Like a tree falling in the forest. So once in a while, to prove I was alive, I would put on some makeup and stand in front of a camera and pretend that I didn't not want to be there and that I didn't want to curl up into a tiny ball and roll away into a dark hole in the corner and disappear to work on my songs in private, with no makeup and no flashbulbs and no stylists tugging at my hem and no strangers throwing out quick, harsh judgments. Wishing my music could stand in for me and do all the heavy lifting and all the tedious, uncomfortable work—the work that wasn't musical, and that I wasn't trained to do, like standing in front of a camera trying not to look as awkward as I felt.

I knew no other way to get my music out there.

11

August 7

Cleveland

We pulled up to the Grog Shop in Cleveland Heights right on time and no one was there to let us in. The door was locked and there was no answer when we knocked. We parked out front and Tim, ever the responsible tour manager, got on his cell phone to try to find someone from the club. The girls and Brian went walking down the street, exploring the neighborhood.

I stayed in the van, ruminating on life's injustices.

My throat was throbbing with pain so relentless that I found it hard to really focus on my irritation at being locked out of the club. Every time I swallowed, it was like downing shards of glass. I tried lying down on the back bench seat and taking a nap, but the harsh late afternoon sun was pounding down through the van windows onto me. I pulled a pillow over my head to block the glare but that only made me hotter and more uncomfortable. So I moved to the front passenger seat and sat with my feet up on the dashboard, waiting.

Eventually Kathy, the club owner, showed up. She was so laid-back and personable that it was hard to stay mad at her for being late. What were we doing showing up on time, anyway? That's really not very rock and roll. The first thing Kathy did after unlocking the door and letting us in was to ask us all if we wanted anything from the juice bar down the street. She took our orders and went and fetched the drinks for us.

The Grog Shop is very small. It holds about two hundred and fifty people when it's packed to the gills. The restrooms are two closetlike spaces crammed in a narrow walkway in the back on the right side of the room. If you encounter another person on the way to pee, one of you has to step back against the wall to let the other pass. So going to the bathroom at the Grog Shop is kind of like going to the bathroom on a train. Except at the Grog Shop, there's no door to the stall protecting you from potential embarrassing interruptions by strangers. The toilet is barely shielded by a flimsy opaque red plastic shower curtain that is ripped and hanging precariously from two rings. Not a lot of privacy. When I poked my head in the bathroom, I saw that there was a fresh roll of toilet paper, and it made me smile. It's little things like that that mean more than you'd think.

The "dressing room" is behind the bar in the back on the left side of the club. It's not really a dressing room. It's really just the back room where Kathy has set up a desk and a computer next to a big ice machine and a bunch of stacked-up cases of beer. And on the other side of the room from the desk there's a shabby old couch against the wall for the band to sit on. People working at the bar walk through this room to get to the basement storage area.

On one wall of this back room I found four different renderings of graffiti phalluses, drawn by four, I assumed, different artists with four distinct drawing styles. This was exciting for me.

I had come on this tour with the intention of photographing all the penises drawn on all the dressing room walls. It was going to be a conceptual art project carried out in my free time off the stage. You see, almost every dressing room has at least one ink rendering of a twig and berries staring you in the face when you enter. I don't know why, exactly—I'm not a psychologist or an anthropologist. I'm just an observer of my surroundings and I can't help but notice that a lot of guys in bands feel the need to leave caricatures of their sexual organs behind when they go. (Caricatures that are often involved in rather violent and explicitly perverted cartoon scenes. And the schlongs—in repose, in flagrante delicto, in ejaculatory splendor—are always grossly exaggerated in scale.) So far, compared to past tours, there had been a disappointing lack of dirty graffiti this time around. It seemed many of the clubs on this circuit had been doing some cleaning up; either painting over or scrubbing off the filth. But where there was graffiti, there was always—invariably—at least one cartoon willy. Still, to see four (four!) in one place was a windfall for me. It made up for the total lack of penises in New York, Philly, and Boston. I immediately got to work snapping pictures of them all.

Later, during our first song of the night, I noticed a video camera up front pointed at me. Video cameras unnerve me, because they are so confrontational. Cameras encourage—no, they demand—exaggeration from a performer. When the person behind the camera says, "Just be yourself," he really means, "JUST BE YOUR FABULOUS FUCKING SELF, A HUNDRED TIMES LARGER THAN LIFE!!!" When he says, "Just act natural," he really means, "ACT REALLY FUCKING FANTASTICALLY NATURAL!!!" My instinctive reaction to being bullied like this is to want to disappear; to think, "Leave me alone. Go pick on someone who has a bigger ego." I am diminished, somehow, by the camera's intrusion into my reality. I can't afford to give any of myself away because I feel like there already isn't enough of it, and I want to hold on to what precious little there is, which belongs to me.

Cameras threaten my tenuous sense of self.

As the song progressed, I tried not to look at the camera but I couldn't avoid the fact that it was there—it was right in front of me and I could feel its presence even with my eyes closed. This cold mechanical eye remained fixed on me, staring me down, sucking some vital life force out of me, and I grew more and more agitated and distracted by this affront to my camera-shy sensibilities. It seemed to me that I should have some say in the matter. That someone should have asked my opinion. "Do you mind if I film you, Miss Hatfield?" before the fact would have been nice.

I was being filmed continuously for an extended period of time at close range without my permission and I was feeling increasingly violated. As the song came to an end I said, into the microphone, to the guy behind the camera, "Can you please not point that thing in my face?"

The camera stayed where it was. My heart was starting to beat faster in anger. I tried again, louder, just in case he was hard of hearing: "That's really rude, dude. I said I don't want that thing pointed at me. Can't you respect that?"

He was still filming, as if my chiding him was part of the show. People around him in the crowd murmured and grumbled, "C'mon, man," and "Turn it off." A few people booed.

Finally the video guy lowered his camera a few inches and sort of rolled his eyes at me, like I had a lot of nerve disrupting his evening like this.

Then I said, "Can't you just go stand somewhere that's not right in front of me? It's really distracting. I don't want to be singing to a camera all night long."

Still, video guy would not move. He opened his mouth, though, and said something that I couldn't hear above the crowd murmur. I sensed he was presenting some kind of counterargument.

Couldn't he see that this night was supposed to be fun and now he was ruining it? I want to sing to the people, not to a machine. This isn't TV. This is my life. And this is one place where I feel a little tiny bit empowered, and now he's trying to take that away from me, by making me really self-conscious?

A good five minutes went by, it seemed, with no music, no second song. Heidi was standing on her side of the stage silently holding her bass, looking uncomfortable. Freda sat patiently behind her drum set, her face in its usual infinitely serene almost-smile. Video guy appeared dumbfounded and too stunned to move; apparently he was unable to comprehend that I could feel the way I did about what he was doing. I think he was waiting for me to say, "Just kidding!" My negative reaction was clearly not part of his plan for the evening.

If this had been a Sheryl Crow show, the guy with the camera would have been picked up by security men and tossed out a long time ago. All I wanted, though, was a tiny crumb of respect. I know I'm not Sheryl Crow. I don't ask for much when I step onstage. Just some water, maybe, if it's not too much trouble, and no recording devices parked directly in my line of vision. I don't actually even ask for that—I just always assume it's common courtesy. Do I expect too much from people? Was I naive to figure that I, as the night's featured entertainment, could get this one face in the crowd to defer to my one request, if I kept at it?

"Look," I tried. "I'm not going to play until you move that thing away from me, okay?"

People were getting behind the cause now, saying stuff like, "Dude, come on. Just move. Turn it off."

They had come to see music, not this.

Still, the offending pimple on the evening, and his AV rig, would not go away. The standoff continued.

I tried another angle: "You know, that's not even legal. You can't record me without my permission. I own that recording, technically."

Finally video guy got the message. The pimple was popped. "Okay. All right. Jeez. I'll stop," he mumbled, and begrudgingly moved his little one-man stakeout operation to somewhere that I couldn't see it. And the show went on. For a while.

About a third of the way into the set, Heidi's amp stopped working. Sound stopped coming out of it. Tim came up onstage and unplugged it and swiftly hooked up my backup Ampeg head. The backup didn't work, either. This was when I remembered the guy from Dave Pirner's crew dropping it on the sidewalk while helping us move our stuff out of the Middle East Cafe back in Cambridge. Now our backup needed a backup.

Right about then the opening band's bass player arrived on the scene out of nowhere like a superhero and saved the day, or rather, night, by lending Heidi his amp for the rest of the show.

After the last song, I came offstage and stood by the side of it. The stage was up in the front of the club and the dressing room was all the way in the back. It was too much trouble to get back to the dressing room through the thick crowd when we were only going to have to turn around and come right back again for the encore. So the girls and I waited there, by the stage, surrounded by our audience, for the few minutes before the encore started.

A forty-ish woman immediately began talking to me. I wasn't really in the mood to get into a conversation (my head was still in the songs; in the show, and thinking about what I was going to do for the encore) but I didn't want to be rude so I stood there, trapped, hemmed in by bodies, and absorbed her chatter. I tried to be as attentive as I could through the clapping and hooting and the people talking loudly above it all around us. At one point the lady said what sounded like, "My brother, blah blah blah." Then, a couple of seconds later, it was, "Do you smoke pot? I have some really good Maui pot," which was really very hospitable and generous of her, and made me feel like a heel for thinking she was annoying.

I answered, "No, I don't smoke," but then I thought of the others in my crew who do like to get high once in a while, and I tried to backpedal, saying, "Oh, but, yeah, once in a while I do. Smoke," hoping she would reoffer it to me so I could give the drugs to my friends. But my response—both parts of it—went right over or through her head. She was still jabbering in a ceaseless stream, determinedly not shutting up, seemingly uninterested in any response I might give to any of it and, yet, directing it all toward me. I could hear only parts of it—disjointed words and phrases—above the crowd noise and the ringing in my ears.

Maybe she was nervous. Or high. Or drunk. Or crazy, manic. Or some combination of the four. Which would explain her excessively communicative behavior. At any rate, I finally interrupted the woman's torrent of chatter (well, "interrupted" would imply that I cut her off, but she didn't actually stop talking; I talked over her) and said, "I have to go back onstage now." And then I escaped onto the stage for the encore.

In a perfect world—in my perfect world—there would be certain rules of propriety, certain principles of appropriate behavior, that would be obvious to everybody. Common sense and restraint would prevail. But they don't, so I will give you my version of these rules, with regard to my situation. No—with regard to any band that just stepped off a stage. Just so you know:

When the band first exits the stage, give them a minute or two or ten to themselves, to cool off and catch their breath and reestablish their bearings and their hearing. Let the band wipe the sweat off their faces and take a drink of water and ponder what just happened. And then give them another minute to float back down into their bodies.

After the encore and after I'd cooled down for a bit in the dressing room, I went back out into the main room and signed some CDs and chatted with a few people who had stuck around to talk to me. I noticed the video guy approaching me. I couldn't imagine what there was left to say between us, and I was a tiny bit scared that he might slap me or yell at me, but he only wanted to apologize. He hadn't known that his filming would irritate me so much, or at all, and my disturbed reaction took him by surprise and that was why he had been so slow to act upon my wishes and get the thing away from me. He'd been stunned, and unsure if my annoyance was for real or a joke. Then he handed me the tape. He let me have full ownership of the recording of my show, without my even asking. It was a classy move. I'd never really wanted the tape; I had just wanted a little respect. And now he was giving it to me. I accepted the peace offering and thanked him.

Sometimes people just kill me with their coolness.

12

Big Money

I got a recording contract with Atlantic Records in 1992 and soon after that, I signed a deal with a music publishing company. Record deals and publishing deals often go hand in hand. When an artist who writes her own songs signs to a major label, publishing companies know that song usage revenue is likely coming in around the bend. I signed with Zomba/BMG, who also had both the Backstreet Boys and Sonic Youth, among others, on their roster. I went with Zomba because I figured that if Sonic Youth had signed with them, I could, too, and it would be cool; I wouldn't be selling out. Because Sonic Youth were cool and would never sell out. When contemplating the pros and cons of different publishing companies, the Sonic Youth factor, in regard to Zomba, was a major selling point. That and the money.

They gave me an initial $400,000 advance, which meant that I would receive that lump sum upon signing, all of which would be recoupable. I would potentially earn them (Zomba) back their money—through sales of albums and sheet music, and with film, TV, and commercial placements of my songs. When and if they collected that $400,000, then I would have paid back the advance and they would begin sending me royalty checks for however much came in on top of that. There was no guarantee they would ever recoup their money or that I would ever see any more. Their signing me was a risk, but that is how the business works. Giving an artist a sizable advance like that is seen as a kind of faith in the artist's money-making or hit-making or attention-generating potential. At that time I was seen as someone who could conceivably make people some decent, if not a lot of, money.

On the day the check arrived at my manager Gary's office, he called me and we arranged to meet later that day so he could present me with the check. When the time came, the two of us sat down on a park bench in Harvard Square and Gary pulled a regular business-sized envelope, with Zomba's official logo and return address in the upper left-hand corner, out of his bag. We were both smiling conspiratorially. I grabbed the envelope and opened it and pulled out the check for $400,000, made out to "Juliana Hatfield." To me. I showed it to Gary. I laughed. Gary laughed. This was absurd. It was absolutely ridiculous.

"Oh my *God*," I said. "How can this be happening?"

There was no answer. I just laughed, in giddy, disbelieving bursts.

"Is this thing real?" I asked, staring at the piece of paper. "Can someone really just write a check for this much money?"

"Yeah," Gary chuckled.

I held the check delicately between my two hands. I didn't want to smudge it or damage it. I had never seen a check for such a large amount of money—nor have I seen one since.

"What should I do with it?"

"I think you should put it in the bank," Gary said. "Maybe think about putting some of it in a retirement fund."

"Shouldn't I buy a Maserati or something? Maybe a Mercedes?"

I didn't buy a car. I didn't buy anything, really. I gave Gary his 15 percent and I gave the IRS their cut, and I put the rest in the bank. Then I moved to New York and I rented a one-bedroom third-floor walk-up apartment in the West Village for $1,350 a month. At the time, it seemed like a huge amount of rent for one person to pay, but I'd wanted to live in New York for a while. Now, suddenly, I could afford it, and so I indulged. I like to think I was living it up; living the high life in the big city, even though I knew hardly anyone there, and my apartment wasn't very big or impressive in any particular way and all I did in it was read, write, and watch TV. The new TV was my second-most-extravagant indulgence.

I bought a twelve-inch Panasonic combination television and VCR. A TVCR. I purchased it at a Sam Goody store on Sixth Avenue around Eighth Street, and I carried the heavy box (the little screen was fronting a surprising amount of junk in the tube's trunk) back to my place on West Eleventh Street near Hudson, stopping every twenty feet or so to put the TV down and rest. Not taking a cab was my penance, to assuage for the guilt I felt for having just purchased a brand-new television—an unnecessary extravagance. Hailing a taxi for the fairly short ride home would have been embarrassingly decadent, profligate, downright shameful.

I haven't ever bought another television. That original one has come with me from home to home. I eventually schlepped it from New York to a rental in Boston, then to L.A., driving across the country with all my stuff, and back to Boston again. The VCR broke down at one point and started eating tapes, so I brought it to my local Korean electronics repair man, who fixed it (for a very reasonable price), and the TV/VCR was as good as new again.

I have no wild, regretful stories to tell about blowing my big advance check on sports cars or drugs or diamond jewelry or vacations on the French Riviera. I could have spent my money on those kinds of things, but I didn't. I knew how lucky I was to have gotten recording and publishing deals. I kept the whole huge check thing in perspective, and tried to stay humble, and watchful, and relatively thrifty. Somehow I knew that that check might well be the last big money I ever saw.

When I got my deal with Atlantic Records, everyone was getting deals. I happened to be in the right place at the right time. So-called alternative rock was the great white hope of all the major labels and they were signing up everything "indie," left and right. Bands like REM had shown that it was possible for quirky, murky, uncompromising artists to successfully transition from college radio to the mainstream. Nirvana was, of course, this trend's crowning glory. They were the ultimate proof of the music industry's theory that snatching up all the unpolished "college rock" bands would pay off in a big way.

I don't know why or how I knew it wouldn't last. But I did. And it didn't.

And to some degree I'm still living off that publishing advance.

13

August 8
Columbus

The three-hour trip from Cleveland to Columbus is always boring. It feels like I've done it a million times. The land is completely flat and there's nothing to look at. We rolled into the outskirts of Columbus in the late afternoon and checked into a thirty-nine-dollar-a-night Knights Inn. When I entered my room a potent antiseptic odor hit me like a punch in the face.

I poked my head back out the door and asked Tim, who was just then opening the door to his room, next to mine, "Is your room filled with nauseating fumes?"

Tim went into his room, came out a few seconds later, and said, "No. Mine seems okay."

I went back in my room, dropped my bag, and pulled my vanilla candle out of my backpack and lit it, gasping. Then I pried open the window, which seemed to have never been opened before. I left the door ajar to try to air the place out.

The fact that I could smell the cleaning fluid residue so strongly through my very stuffed-up nasal passages was a testament to its likely high levels of toxicity and also to the probable disgustingness of some original stench that the extremely thorough cover-up job was, most likely, masking, which made me think of bad cologne slapped on a big sweaty man with terrible body odor. Which was worse? The cheap cologne or the body odor?

On the ride to the club and all during soundcheck, I was preoccupied because there was someone I needed to see. RJ, a fellow musician, whom I had known for about eight years, was in town. (I say "fellow musician" but he was in a slightly different league than I was; he was more of an icon, and more firmly established). He was on tour and by chance he had the night off in Columbus, where he would be playing the following night. He had given me a copy of his tour itinerary (which listed cities, hotels, venues) before the start of his tour, and I had given him mine, so we'd be aware if our paths crossed, and then be able to get in touch with each other.

I had a little time before the show when I could see him, if briefly. And I wanted to see him. And he wanted to see me. So after my soundcheck I took a cab to his hotel.

I spent an hour and a half with RJ in his room. This was par for the course for us: brief, intense, unsatisfying, sporadic visits, never in the same place twice.

RJ and I were a secret. Hardly anyone knew that we knew each other, or that we saw each other sometimes—mostly in hotel rooms, where it was safe and private and no one would see us—or that we had ever had any sort of relationship. I never told anyone because I believe in honoring a person's right to keep his private life private, especially if he's kind of famous, like RJ was.

RJ and I were both uncomfortable in the world, each always alternately hiding behind walls and baring our souls to total strangers through our music. We were very much alike. When we first met, we felt connected right off the bat, almost as if our bond had been established, by fate, in advance, and we didn't have to bother going through the whole tedious getting-to-know-each-other rigmarole. RJ told me he loved me right away, and he never wavered, never changed his tune, even when we weren't together (and we rarely were together), and when we didn't speak for long periods, and when time could have faded everything into hazy memories.

I could never believe it when RJ told me he loved me. It was too crazy, too unreal, too fantasylike to be loved by someone whose music I had known so well, and adored, for so many years, long before I met him. (I, as much as anyone else, was a music fan, and a red-blooded woman. The fact that I was a music personality myself, and had lots of opportunities to meet rock stars, didn't mean that I was immune to crushing on some of those rock stars.) Besides, I didn't think RJ and I had spent enough extended time together for him to know me well enough to ascertain that he loved me for real, for sure, and would stick by me through thick and thin, in hard times and good times, and be faithful and supportive and all those other things people are meant to be when they love someone.

I thought RJ mainly loved the idea of me, just as I loved the idea of him, and we both loved feeling connected to another person. To be able to think, "Finally, someone like me!" was a great comfort to both of us. We understood each other, and we never had to explain ourselves, but that didn't necessarily mean that we could ever function as boyfriend and girlfriend. So we let it be, and only saw each other every year or two, when one or the other passed through town or when we were both on tour and in some city at the same time. We let our circumstances and our schedules dictate our distance from each other.

RJ would tell me he loved me in a lull in a random conversation, without any fanfare; like it was a fact that had always been true—like the sun in the sky was a fact. Like it just was, and would never change.

It wasn't that simple for me. I would often respond, "Why? Why do you love me?" I couldn't fathom it, couldn't accept it as truth, and I wanted to understand it intellectually so that I could enjoy it and embrace it; so that it didn't feel so alien a sensation, being loved by someone who really seemed to mean it and to not be delusional.

It seemed to me that RJ and I, when we got together, or talked on the phone, were willfully indulging in a romantic storybook fantasy. On paper, it was perfect: two temperamental rockers; two lonely dreamers, social fugitives whom no one but the other understood, brought together by an inborn pain no one else felt as acutely, and forced—because of their quirks and insecurities and delicate constitutions and ridiculously sensitive natures—to live half the time in self-imposed exile and the other half onstage (another kind of exile).

But this was an only partially constructed narrative that would never hold up in the real world if we became a real couple.

How would I look after him—the sickly, tortured, depressive, substance-abusing genius—when I had to put so much energy into keeping my own head above water? Who would do the laundry? The taxes? Who would do the dishes? Who would cook? (I was used to munching on a handful of nuts or eating some ice cream out of the container for dinner.) Was RJ used to someone taking care of these things for him? Would he still be sweet on me when he learned how fiercely independent I was, and how fundamentally averse to performing any traditional wifely duties? Would RJ understand that my mind was preoccupied with music and reading and writing and that these things had always taken precedence over maintaining a presentable home, over cultivating a relationship?

Our bond was formed in a spiritual world—in music. We recognized our own souls in the other's songs. We were two resolutely idiosyncratic artists, each with our own unique voice and approach. We were so used to refusing to compromise in our art that refusing to compromise had become a way of life. We guarded our music-making process against any outside influence and I, for one, was just as protective of myself and my heart.

I wanted to love RJ, and some days I felt I did, or could, but couldn't say it. I couldn't trust myself. Did I love him, or was it his music that had attracted me to him for so long—since before I met him?

I cherished him too much to take the chance of finding out. It was easier to love him from afar.

It's easier, and safer, to love anyone—everyone—from afar, where love lives forever, like a song; lives on and on, remembered in its beauty and perfection. The truth is, if a person makes great music, that doesn't necessarily make him a great person. It just makes him an artist. It definitely doesn't make him a saint. And wouldn't he have to be a saint to be able to live with my mood swings and my slovenliness and my frequent, pressing need for solitude and quiet and space and freedom?

"If RJ really knew me well," I thought, "he wouldn't love me." He'd end up annoyed, frustrated, and angered by all my personal, human failings and weaknesses. I felt lovable only as a musical entity.

I would listen to my recordings and think, "Who is this person singing these songs? She's a total stranger. There is so much life in these songs—such spirit! Why can't I be that strong, compassionate person in my day-to-day life?"

It seemed part of me, possibly the best part, was given over to the songs and lost forever. And I was conscious of this, which made it seem almost cruel, and irresponsible, to let anyone—any man— become intimately involved with me when I knew he would ultimately be disappointed by what he would discover to be lacking in me, Juliana, the woman (as opposed to the musician).

RJ said to me, that night, in Columbus, "You know, you're really kind of autistic." He meant the way I fidgeted when we sat together on the couch, and pulled my hand away when he tried to hold mine, and couldn't look him in the eyes for more than a second, and the way I didn't return his "I love you"'s because it made me uncomfortable. But RJ didn't mind that I was weird and confused—that I went to see him and then acted like I didn't want to be there—and restless and so focused on folding my foil chewing gum wrapper in and in on itself into smaller and smaller squares so it was as small as I could possibly make it as he tried to whisper sweet nothings in my ear. It didn't faze him that I didn't say "I love you" back. It was all the same to him. He loved me no matter what, period, or so he claimed, and I couldn't argue. Or I could, but it was useless to do so. He believed what he wanted to believe. And so did I, I guess.

I think about RJ and I know he thinks about me. We have enduring warm, fond feelings for each other. That's enough. We are both, on one hand, damaged and doomed and resigned and a little insane and tragic, and we dramatize and glorify these personality traits in our songs. We are pop artists and we are suitably self-absorbed and prone to depression and various anxieties and nervous afflictions and possibly unable to really let go of ourselves enough to ever sacrifice anything for another person. Writing and playing our songs—our self-expression— comes first. Nothing else rewards us as consistently. Not money, not fame, not love, not acclaim. Can two artists be a couple when each possesses, already, what the other embodies? We don't need each other on a day-to-day basis. We don't need anyone, most of the time. And that is both the solution and the problem. How can you be with anyone if you don't need anyone? If you need only a guitar and a voice and a pen and a piece of paper to be perfectly content?

Many people admire RJ as a result of what he has accomplished in his career. Some people look up to me, too. We appear "cool" to some portion of the outside world. If those people only knew how little RJ and I knew about living in the world, and about being happy and having a satisfying, peaceful existence, they probably wouldn't look up to us.

Many people, when asked what they'd do if they could choose any dream job, answer, "Play in a rock band." But I'd bet that if the people who make these claims really knew what it was like to be us, they wouldn't want to trade.

Because the only thing we have figured out is how to make music.

Back at the club, I parked myself in the dressing room and began practicing my solos. I knew I had to start putting some time into maintaining my skills, or my playing was going to continue its slide into total incoherence.

I was starting to realize, though, that it was more than just laziness or brain damage that was causing my current guitar soloing problems. It was something else. It was a kind of pathological modesty.

But I didn't want anyone else to play the solos because no one ever got it right—no lead guitar player that I hired ever played them the way I heard them in my head. So I was forced to do it myself.

A guitar solo is like sex. It requires, first, a desire to do it, and then a certain concentration, and focus, of energy, and I don't necessarily feel like doing it every day. I have to be in the mood. This becomes problematic when I am on tour, because I am expected to do it every twenty-four hours. More than once. And it really wears me out. It takes so much intensity, and moxie, to follow through and passionately, successfully, and satisfyingly, complete the act. And it absolutely cannot be faked. The audience can sense when I am not fully committed to the act of soloing. Often, I just want to blend into the background. Lately, it had been happening a lot. Maybe I'm just fundamentally temperamentally unsuited to this role of "front person."

The club was half-full when we went on. The last couple of times I'd played here, it had been pretty packed with bodies. I didn't know what had happened this time, or why, to keep the people away. Maybe the promoter, a rumored coke dealer, had been putting too much time into the drug side of his business and not enough into the gig-promotions side. I tried to be philosophical about it:

"Yeah," I thought, as I approached the microphone. "There are some big holes in the crowd but there are people here. Anyone is better than no one. An audience of ten is better than an audience of zero. And there's way more than ten people here. It could be worse."

But if I am going to be honest, I have to admit that the disappointing showing was, in fact, disappointing, and that it did bother me, a lot, deep down.

My voice was ragged and scratchy all night long because of my cold. In my sickness, I was achieving the exact effect that I'd been aiming for when I took up chain-smoking back in my twenties. Back then, I'd wanted desperately to kill or at least maim, with tobacco, the chirpy little girl in my voice. It didn't work and I gave up the cigarette experiment after about five years, resigned to try to appreciate my God-given squeak, hopeful that the aging process would do its own natural Marianne Faithfull–esque ravaging of my vocal cords.

As the set wore on, with me blowing my nose between songs (really sexy, really rock and roll), the raspiness of my singing turned into a froglike croaking. Finally, during the last song, my voice gave out completely. I pushed and pushed and then . . . nothing. I couldn't make any more sound come out.

My voice had never, in all my years of singing and touring, stopped working before, and now that it had, I was strangely proud of having pushed myself and my throat to the point of, in a sense, collapse. It seemed like a noble goal, collapse; what the end result of any serious undertaking ought to be. Because only when you have nothing left in you to give do you know you have done a thorough job.

After toweling off, guzzling some water, popping a cough drop, and gathering my strength by sitting down for about fifteen minutes, I went back out onstage and began unplugging my pedals and coiling up my cables. There was no sense sitting around backstage—my equipment wasn't going to pack itself up. And the sooner we got out of there, the sooner I could get my worn-out, ailing bag of bones into a hot bath.

Most of the club had emptied out, but a handful of people were standing around the stage waiting for me to acknowledge them so they could have the CDs they had brought with them (or bought from Brian) autographed. I tried not to look directly at them. I wanted to finish putting my stuff away first. In my peripheral vision I saw one guy follow my path around the side of the stage as I went to unplug my amp. I felt his eyes on me and I heard him say, "Juliana. Juliana. Juliana," like a little boy trying to get his mother's attention while she's on the phone. ("Mom. Mom. Mom.") I pretended not to hear him because I knew that if I interrupted the flow of my packing and directed my attention to the guy, others would follow and I would never be able to break free. And my equipment would remain only partially broken-down and eventually someone else, probably Tim, would come up and finish the job for me, and then I would feel guilty because breaking down and packing up my equipment isn't Tim's job.

When all my guitars and roadcases were shut securely and shoved to the side of the stage near the load-out door, I looked up and headed toward the line of people waiting patiently for autographs. Freda and Heidi were already there, being charming. Both of them always seemed completely at ease with fans. Not tense, like I was.

The first guy in line handed me, wordlessly, a stack of CD sleeves consisting of, I think, every single recording I had ever released in the fifteen-year span of my career. Albums, singles, EPs, limited editions, foreign pressings, et cetera. Stuff that I don't even own. Lots of it.

"You want me to sign all of these?" I asked, my voice cracking. My throat had recovered enough since the end of the set for me to get a few words out.

"Yeah, could you?" the man answered, looking down.

"Do you have a pen?"

"No."

The guy behind him in line, eager to help, handed me his Sharpie amicably.

I envisioned the time it would take for me to sign all twenty or so of this guy's CD covers, and how the other people in line would have to wait, and how sort of greedy and unreasonable this guy's request seemed, to me, and I said, as pleasantly as I could, "I'll sign two of them. Pick two. I don't really want to sign the whole stack, okay?"

I could tell by the concerned look on his face that he didn't think this was as reasonable a compromise as I did. I tried to lighten the mood and, sounding chummy, said, "Why do you want my dumb signature over and over again? They'll all be exactly the same. One's as good as the next, isn't it?"

He muttered, "But it'll make each one special to have your signature on it."

"Special how?" I thought. "He acts like he doesn't even like me. He didn't even say hello to me—and not a word about the show—and now he wants fifteen or twenty autographs? But why? So he can sell them on eBay? Why can't he just be happy to see me, like all those smiling people over there talking to Heidi and Freda? He'd probably be just as disappointed with me if I chopped off one of my fingers right now and gave it to him. It wouldn't be enough. He'd want the whole hand."

I didn't want to argue with the guy but he wouldn't go away. He kept standing there motionless in front of me with his pile of Juliana Hatfield booklets, silently urging me to consider his point of view and sign every last one of them. But I held firm and signed just two of his things. He grumbled and went away.

Sometimes I feel that I should explain to these people that it's not part of my job description to be cheerful and accommodating all the time. I'm not Liza Minnelli. I'm not full of razzle-dazzle. And I respect my audience enough to always present myself as a real, flawed person, telling her version of the truth, and not some windup doll that can be positioned in front of the camera any way the photographer wants. I want a sensitive, thoughtful audience who can see their own imperfect lives in my songs, so that they don't have to feel as alone as they think they are, and so I don't have to feel as alone as I think I am.

I just wish the music was enough. I think that should be enough. When I'm asked to give something more, that's when I get into trouble. Sometimes I hurt or disappoint people when I'm not what they want me to be or when I say the wrong thing. I'm very shy and I don't know how to talk to people—that's why I write songs. So they can speak for me. But then people want to talk to me and so I try and I stumble and I run out of words. "Thank you a million times, from the bottom of my heart. Without you I am nothing," comes out sounding like "Go away. Leave me alone."

As we drove away from the club, Tim said, addressing us all, "We didn't get the dinner buyout. The promoter really took a loss and he asked if we could let the dinner buyout slide."

It's in the contract that each night the promoter must either provide the five of us with dinner or give us each ten or fifteen dollars (decided before the contracts are drawn up), on top of the show guarantee, to go to a restaurant. Some nights we don't get the buyout until the end of the night, when we get paid for the gig. We were expecting it tonight.

"What?" I yelled. "He has to give us our dinner money! He can't just break the contract!"

"Well, he lost money on the show and so I thought it would be okay to let the extra few dollars slide and . . ."

"That's not my problem, Tim! *I'm* losing money on this tour. It's not our fault that the club was half-empty. He's the promoter."

Then Tim said, "I'm sorry. You're right." His voice was quiet, contrite. "I'll get you guys the money."

"What do you mean, you're going to get the money?" I asked. "You're going to turn around and go back there and ask for it after you told the guy he didn't have to give it to us?"

"No, I'll give you each ten dollars of my own money. I should pay you. I shouldn't have agreed to that."

"I don't want *your* money. I want the promoter's money."

But we couldn't get it, now. The moment had passed. While I understood that being diplomatic and sympathetic with the promoter was good for Tim's career in terms of future run-ins with the guy, from my point of view Tim had allowed this disreputable character—who was untrustworthy to begin with—to screw us out of something that we were legitimately entitled to. Guys like that are the ones that you should always try to squeeze the money out of, because they will always try to rip you off. And though it was clear from the half-empty club that the promoter had legitimately lost money on tonight's gig, he still should have given us our dinner buyout because it's the right thing to do. Maybe I was being petty but so was the promoter—fifty bucks more on top of whatever else he had lost was not going to make much of a difference.

He'd reneged on something he had agreed to in writing, months beforehand, in the signed contract, and that wasn't cool.

14

The Story of "My Sister"

Sometimes I am awakened from sleep by music in my head. A melody and a chord progression that I have never heard before has carried over, still vivid and vibrating with life, from the depths of unconsciousness into this other, "real" life with a brand-new message from the other side. When this happens, I know from past experience that I need to jump out of bed right then and run to grab my little handheld cassette recorder so I can at least hum the melody into it before the music—elusive, evanescent—flits away and out of my head. If I don't capture it immediately, the sound and all the feeling it evokes will slip away, like vapor, in a matter of seconds, and it will be gone forever, never to return. Like a dream whose details have gone blurry and then dissipated, only a vague shadowy sensation remains; a delicious refreshing breeze rustles my hair and caresses my skin for a lovely second or two and then, it is gone.

I believe there is an underground stream of inspiration that is always there, always flowing, and always filled with truth and beauty and meaning and importance, but it's out of sight, hidden. I can't always find a way to tap into it, so sometimes I have to just hope for leaves and twigs (new, unwritten song fragments) to flow downstream to me as I wait, crouched on the bank (on my couch with my guitar, at my desk with pen and paper), my fingers dipped into the cool, clear water, ready to grab whatever comes to me.

When I get something I jump, pick up a guitar or keyboard—whatever is closest—and struggle, quickly, to figure out the chords of what I hear in my head, then press RECORD, and get it on tape before it's too late and the whole thing has evaporated and doesn't seem real anymore and I can't believe the music—the powerful, heartswelling music—I swore I heard in my head was ever even real. It's like trying to capture a ghost.

Some songs are more consciously, diligently crafted, with hours and hours of dutiful, disciplined effort and will and sustained concentration and toil, like the metal a blacksmith pounds into the shapes he has envisioned and then mapped out.

But other songs—the dream songs, the phantoms of the netherworlds—are like woodland sprites that jump out from behind a tree and dare you to try to catch them as they giggle and run away, disappearing among the thick camouflage of the forest. They tease, but don't want to be caught.

There's a reason that the word "capture" is used when describing what a writer is doing when he tries to get down on paper what he experiences. We writers are all hunters on a never-ending hunt. Hunting for the right words and chords and melodies.

When I wrote "My Sister," my most commercially successful song, I was hunting for music—words and melody and harmony—that would express something about longing and loneliness and bereavement. I didn't know *exactly* what I wanted to say with the song—it was one of those woodland sprites rather than a concrete conceptual idea; a vague yet powerful state of emotional being that lived in my mind.

When composing the song, I drew from a combination of references: first there were my own ever present feelings of inadequacy, the feeling that I was never the best at anything, never good or talented or smart enough for me to feel worthy of anyone's love. "I hate my sister/She's such a bitch" was pure hurt. I was hurt because the object of my respect and admiration had looked down her nose at me, not taken me seriously, and had then left, never to return. My beloved wouldn't love me back. The "she" in "She acts as if she doesn't even know that I exist" was someone I perceived as better than me, smarter than me, more important than me, living the full and exciting and meaningful life that I wished I could have. She had overlooked me or never really even noticed me, and rejected me, when all I'd wanted to do was to love her.

I thought it was interesting and kind of funny to think that some people who were listening might put me in the position of the "she" in the song—exalted and admired—when I felt I was on the other side. I knew that there were people out there—fans—who held me in high esteem, regarding me with longing and awe, because I was a musician making music, and people often exalt the people who make the music they love. Since *Hey Babe* had come out and gotten a lot of attention, I had won many new devoted fans. Some of them even idolized me. I knew this, and it was surreal, because I felt so worthless, and like I had *so* many failings, and this song was actually *talking* about it.

When I sang, "She's got a wall around her nobody can climb/She lets her ladder down for those who really shine/I try to scale it but to me, she's blind/So I lit a firecracker. It went off in my eye," *I* was the fan, musing on the aloof, impenetrable bearing of the ice-cold sister, wondering what it would take to reach her, to have an effect on her— someone so reserved, so distant, so removed, so seemingly above it all that she's like a statue on a pedestal.

One of my brothers once accused me, only in half-jest, of having a heart like a "cold, hard nugget." But my apparent unresponsiveness and imperturbability was a front for an almost unbearable, pathological sensitivity and anxiety; I was frozen in fear knowing that if I moved or opened my mouth, I would say and do the wrong thing. Or if I let anyone push me, or touch me, in a certain way, all my sealed-in emotion might explode out of me like the air from a popped balloon.

And then there was Maggie.

Maggie was the onetime girlfriend of my older brother. She was a few years his senior—he was in his last year of high school and she had already graduated. She had a difficult home situation and for a while, when I was in high school, she came to live with my family: my mom, my two brothers, and me. (Dad had moved out when my parents split up when I was eleven.) Maggie was like an older sister to me while she was with us. She drove me to school most mornings in her old Volvo, so I didn't have to make the nearly two-mile walk. Maggie and I went to the beach together, and shopping, and to movies, and she introduced me to the joys of frozen Junior Mints, which the two of us would scarf down together, united in our giggling, secret, gluttonous guilt. More importantly, Maggie recognized and had compassion for my teenage angst. She was the one genuinely sympathetic presence in the house during a very volatile family time. She encouraged me, and at times even tried to *force* me, to cry on her shoulder, to let it out so I could have some relief from its burden, something I never did in front of anyone.

Maggie liked cool music. She was very knowledgeable on that subject and she had brought her record collection—two milk crates full of the most important and influential punk and postpunk; vital, crucial stuff—with her to my house when she moved in. And that was how I learned all about punk rock and Boston rock history. Maggie's two milk crates were my education. Black Flag, the Misfits, Minor Threat, the Clash, the Stooges, the Germs, the Gun Club, the Minutemen, Hüsker Dü, the Dead Kennedys, X, the Replacements, the first REM EP. I had never heard any of it before.

There was no record store in my town, forty miles south of Boston, and no noticeable alternative subculture at all, and the Internet and cable television had not yet arrived to spread the news about everything to every suburb and backwoods. Before Maggie, I was listening to the Fixx and the Police and Billy Joel and Duran Duran and Pat Benatar. That was what was being played on the mainstream rock radio station that I listened to, and that was what I watched on Friday Night Videos, the one late-night network TV show that featured the most popular bands' newest videos. Maggie opened my eyes and ears to all the college radio stations in the Boston area that were playing underground, non-mainstream rock, like WMBR, WZBC, WERS, and WHRB.

As I made my way through her pile of old issues of *Boston Rock* (which featured articles and interviews and photos of current local and also national and international underground music), printed on big, cheap, black-and-white newsprint pages, I discovered all kinds of fascinating, compelling creatures of the night who were making strange and wonderful new sounds and looking like charismatic aliens from other, cooler planets, like Siouxsie Sioux, and the young, Young Snakes–era

Aimee Mann and Exene Cervenka from X, who would almost immediately, upon my hearing the first X song Maggie put on the turntable for me ("Motel Room in My Bed"), become my first female rock-and-roll role model.

Maggie took me to an underground rock show in the city. It was the first rock club I had ever been in, a place called Storyville, in Kenmore Square, and it was a dark, dungeony basement space made up of a few interconnected rooms underneath a Japanese restaurant. It was an all-ages show so I was able to get in without an ID (I was seventeen). The Del Fuegos, who didn't look much older than me, were opening for the Violent Femmes. The Violent Femmes had just released their first album, the one with "Blister in the Sun" and all those other future classics on it.

That night I saw a whole new thrilling world, a world that I wanted to be a part of: the underground rock world. These bands were just kids, like me! Scruffy kids from right here in Boston were doing what I wanted to do—what I *knew*, all of sudden, right then, I *could* do. Before this night I had always thought it was only a fantasy that someone like me, someone shy and unspectacular and unpolished and untrained, could make records, and be heard, playing her music in front of crowds. Before this night, and before Maggie's record collection, I hadn't even known that this world and all its amazing opportunities and manifestations existed. I thought that people in bands either played at the Worcester Centrum (the local enormodome) or they didn't play at all. Before all this I hadn't known that there was a place for me. And now I knew there was. It was right here in front of me. Maggie had brought me there. Maggie played a big part in pointing me toward my destiny, and I wanted to pay tribute to her, in song.

In "My Sister" I sang, "She's the one who would have taken me to my first all-ages show." I was thinking about the sister I never had, the sister I wished I had, and putting Maggie in her place: if I *had* had a sister, she would have done all the things that Maggie, my adopted, temporary sister, had done for me.

But Maggie had actually treated me better than the sister I imagined. And that was part of what made the song a sad song. I was longing for something that, like most kinds of love, in my experience, was complicated and painful.

When I went from Mammoth Records to Atlantic and recorded *Become What You Are*, my first album for them, the label chose "My Sister" as the first single. Many people had strong personal, emotional reactions to the song. It reminded some of a sibling who had died. I was amazed that I was able to connect with people so deeply using a fictional, symbolic construct. The success of this song showed me that my feelings weren't so unusual or special—they were the same as everyone else's. I could write about my sad, lonely, tormented inner life, and people would understand and identify. It gave me hope. I wasn't so alone after all.

15

August 9

Indianapolis

We were booked to play at a place called the Patio in Indianapolis, as part of a local annual music festival featuring an eclectic lineup of bands. Freda knew the young promoter, Johnny, and he had initially contacted her to try to woo us onto the bill. He lobbied hard to get us, telling Freda, "Name your price." So naturally, we were thinking, "Five or ten thousand dollars! Cool!" But then we got serious and went back to Johnny with a proposal that was more modest and, we thought, feasible. Something along the lines of "How about three thousand? We'll do it for three thousand." We didn't want to appear greedy or unreasonable because we knew we were not in a position to demand a whole lot; we didn't have a song on the radio or anything. In Indiana, we did have a bit of a hometown draw, because both Freda and Heidi lived there, but it wasn't like the festival would have stiffed if we hadn't been there.

I'd transferred the discussion over to my manager to deal with the boring stuff—the contracts and details. But in the end, in the final negotiations with my booking agent, Johnny agreed to pay us just fifteen hundred dollars, flat. Which was nothing really special. Nothing like "Name your price."

This is so typical of what goes on in the music industry. People—ambitious people—are always bending the facts, sweetening reality, hyping things up to make them seem better than they are.

Fifteen hundred dollars was pretty good money, though. I couldn't complain, really. But I also couldn't help thinking, "Johnny will go far in this business. He has all the right moves, already—he knows how to flatter with the lure of an enticing offer and then not exactly follow through. He will probably be a very successful recording industry executive some day."

The Patio was packed by 10 p.m. It was a typical festival crowd, determined to party down. I wasn't the main draw, I don't think. No one really is at a festival. People come as much for the supercharged carnival-like atmosphere as for the music.

One of the bands on the bill was a strongly hyped new quartet of young guys from Chicago. All the buzz in and around the club was that this band had "just gotten signed" by a major label and that they were "going to be huge."

I watched them play for a few minutes. They were one of those loud, modern rock-rap bands that were making a lot of harsh, computer-enhanced noise but weren't really "rocking" at all, in terms of generating actual organic, sexy power, or a groove. All of the guys in the band had a lot of tattoos and piercings, and the singer was thrashing around and moaning about his miserable, tortured life, while his complicatedly spiky hairdo managed to keep sticking, kind of magically, up and out.

I felt nothing. I could see that the band was trying to convey an edgy nonconformity, but I had a hard time believing that the angst was genuine. Because edge is conformity, these days. "Edgy modern rocker" is a proven formula and a uniform that bands wear, because they know it sells. It's popular with the youth. It's the easiest route to rock stardom, because it is recognized and accepted by the masses.

The dark and enraged stuff is shtick. And for that reason, it's impossible to take any of it seriously. One edgy rocker is the same as the next. They are practically interchangeable. They must know that their piercings and spikes and overdriven guitars and dark eye makeup

106

and self-pitying wails are so tame and commonplace and played-out that they are completely worthless as signifiers of rebellion anymore. They are hollow and banal cartoonlike gestures. Whenever any one of these guys raises his middle finger to a camera, it is like a well-known sitcom character uttering his familiar wacky catchphrase that never fails to get a laugh from the laugh track. Like "Whatchoo talkin' 'bout, Willis?" from *Diff'rent Strokes's* little Arnold Drummond, or "Ayy" from the mouth of the Fonz, it's just what we expect and want from the character.

These days, what used to be symbols of defiance, like tattoos and toothpaste-crusted mohawks and leather motorcycle jackets, are almost quaint. It's kind of adorable, really, that guys in bands still believe that these kinds of things still have any power to convey cool or danger or anything at all. But all the meaning has been drained out of the flipped bird by a voracious, bulimic media and a jaded populace that has seen everything and questions nothing and accepts it all.

These guys in these bands are really nothing more than the twenty-first century version of Pat Boone, if you think about it. They are playing a role that has been market-tested and preapproved and pronounced harmless and inoffensive to all. They are popular. Don't they know that being popular is not cool? Pat Boone wasn't cool, and neither are they. If gum-chewing middle-school girls in ponytails are buying your T-shirts, you are definitely not radical or menacing or challenging. Why isn't this new wave of punk-styled hip-hop emo-aggro/metal/hardcore tough guys embarrassed by this state of affairs? Because underneath it all, they are just a bunch of dorks who want to be loved. They're only pretending to be tough. I should know.

We are all essentially pimping our own versions of Weltschmerz. If I feel absolutely nothing when confronted with boys in eye makeup scream-singing their brains out, then why should anyone give a rat's ass about what I'm doing? What's the difference? The problem with making music in this new millennium is that everything has been said—and done—before. Unadorned authenticity and more manufactured sorts of rock theater—they're just categories. None of it seems to mean anything, anymore. I ask myself, is it my own malaise, or my age, making me feel this way or is it the world today? Has music been co-opted and exploited and overanalyzed—by TV, by the Internet, by the media—until all the life and longevity has been sucked out of the whole enterprise, fan and bands alike?

I sat in the van, which was parked in front of the entrance to the club, and waited as my time to play slowly approached. The party was inside but I didn't want to stand around in that loud, crowded smoke-filled hell. There was no dressing room to sit in so I lounged in the passenger seat. I watched people walk by, entering and exiting the Patio, unaware of my presence. I was blissfully invisible.

In a while Tim came from the direction of the Starbucks down the street, toward the van. He spotted me and approached. I rolled the window down and Tim said, "Here. Put these in the glove compartment."

He was holding out his two hands cupped together and they were full with little individually wrapped honey packets that he had pilfered from Starbucks. It was the most exciting thing to have happen to me all day. Since I'd been sick, I'd been craving tea with honey.

I said, "Wow! Cool! Thanks! I need these!"

The time to play finally came, and I performed sloppily, again. I botched a couple of solos and was ashamed of myself. We had a pretty good set in terms of mood, though. The crowd gave us a lot of positive energy, and we fed off it and gave it back to them. Their consistent enthusiasm and encouragement helped me get back up on my feet, so to speak, after each self-inflicted embarrassment.

After the gig, a bunch of us—people from bands, crews, friends—hung out on the sidewalk next to our van, since there was no backstage area. I was introduced to Johnny, the promoter. He seemed thoughtful, funny, and smart. Not at all the crass industry wheeler-dealer I had imagined. We shot the breeze for a while, talking about nothing, and when the subject of the show came up, he said, "You know, I thought your solo playing was messy tonight."

This candor, coming from a stranger, shocked me, momentarily. It was the first time on the tour that I had been confronted with outside confirmation of the awful truth. Usually people say something innocuous and neutral and basically meaningless when they don't want to admit they didn't like the show. Something like "Right on!" or "Heyyy!" (accompanied by a light, friendly punch on the shoulder) or "All right!" or the old standby, "You guys rocked!" Or worst of all, "You looked like you were having fun up there," which is code among musicians for "God, I hated it."

Johnny's critique was absolutely correct, and after the initial sting subsided, I realized that it was actually quite refreshing and even a little exciting to have someone give me an honest opinion about a less-than-great performance.

I think many performers have a sort of masochistic desire for painful negative feedback. They hope someone—some friend—will cut through all the complimentary bullshit and disparage them a little, so they can feel authentic, and alive, and not like they are dreaming. Bad press is something they can really understand and relate to, because they are used to hearing it from the little voice inside of them that says, "You are pathetic. You are worthless. You are stupid and untalented and you will never amount to anything. You will be forgotten. Oh, and you're ugly, too." We are so used to this voice that everything else seems like lies. And so we are always fishing not for compliments but for scathing negative criticism. Begging for it. "Come on," we say, "tell me what you really think. Just give it to me straight. I can take it. I was bad, wasn't I? I know I was. Come on. Just say it!"

This is the only critical stance, in regard to ourselves and our work, that we can take seriously. But no one—no one who cares about us—ever has the guts or the heart to give it to us. And we need it. We need to hear verification of what we suspect at least some people out there are, inevitably, thinking, so that we are prepared for the worst, when it hits. And it will hit, we are sure. Some heartless critic or some mean-spirited heckler or some huge misunderstanding about a new piece of work of ours—which we believed was an artistic triumph but which is, soon after its release, universally acknowledged as nothing but a commercial flop and, therefore, subject to ridicule and pity—is always lurking around the corner, to put us in our place. We want to be familiar with that feeling—of hitting the bottom with a thud—so we can withstand it with some sort of dignity; so we don't die of heartbreak or go home and kill ourselves when it happens.

Also, we really want to know what was wrong. Because we can't believe that there is nothing that needs fixing. On some level we feel like failures, like eternal fuckups, no matter what we do or how many accolades we acquire. And we want someone to acknowledge this, to acknowledge who we really are, because if they don't see the flaws, they are not seeing the real person. And then we—then I—feel like a fraud, like an imposter, and I am convinced that they couldn't possibly keep loving me if they really knew me and understood me.

I don't perform because it makes me feel good. (Well, I can't count on it to make me feel good, anyway—sometimes it does, sometimes it doesn't.) I do it because I am deeply troubled and insecure. I want attention, and acceptance, and love, but then when I get it, it's not what I wanted. Praise and only praise muddies my sense of self. Adoration frightens me. It makes it seem as if the world has spun off its axis and that people have lost their minds. If my pathetic loser ass is being kissed, something is definitely not right with the world. Now, for once, I'd been given some unfavorable and, incidentally, spot-on criticism that I could mull over. It hurt so good.

I told Johnny, "I'm on it," and that I would try to do better. Then he invited me to a party. (I liked this guy. He put me down and then asked me out.) And I kind of wanted to go because he was kind of cute, but I was tired and still pretty sick and I hate parties so I said, "No thanks, but I'll see you in Chicago," because he was planning on driving the two or so hours up from Indy to see our show at the Double Door the following night. I told him I'd put him on the guest list and then I said, "I'll try not to fuck up any solos tomorrow. I promise."

I said good-bye and got in the van with Tim and Brian and Freda and Heidi and went to the hotel and tried to forget all the mistakes I'd made. Why can't I ever remember what I did right?

16

Cool Rock Boys

I once asked a male friend of mine why guys rarely seemed to hit on me. He answered, "It's because you give off a 'Don't touch me' vibe."

Well, I never knew. I wasn't sending out that signal on purpose. Anyway, the truth was, I was sort of relieved few guys ever approached me. Because usually, when they did, I never knew what to do or how to react; I'm not what you would call a smooth operator. I trip all over myself; I blush, I sweat, I forget how to put words together, I slink away.

It was hard enough for me, as such a shy person, to meet men. And after meeting them, *then* what? Then began the impossible courting process—a complicated set of projections and misread nonverbal cues and roadblocks into which I found myself always stumbling and, sometimes, plowing over, when I should have been heeding their warnings.

I found that the easiest way to meet guys was to play in a band, and to go on tour. Sharing a bill (and a stage, and a backstage area, and meals, and sometimes a hotel) or doing an extensive multidate tour with an eligible rocker or singer/songwriter was a good way for us to get to know each other in a natural (for us) work environment, as opposed to planning, and then dreading, and then suffering through a series of awkward, nerve-wracking, artificial situations, like dates.

With guys in bands there was a built-in ice-breaker: our common love of music, and our drive to write and perform our own. We didn't have to try to think of things to talk about—we were comfortable, doing our jobs; doing what we loved; doing what we felt comfortable and proud doing, together.

A few of these road situations developed into affairs, but nothing lasting. Of course, I hoped it could happen, but no long-term love connections were ever made. The guys and I may have had the music and the lifestyle in common, but at the end of every tour we would realize that it was a tenuous connection. We'd say good-bye, over and over again, to people we'd felt close to.

Saying good-bye was always difficult, after having spent time together in the bubble, but after a few days the departed would fade into history. We'd move on because we had to—the touring musician can't afford to get attached to everyone he gets to know on the road. We always know we will be leaving soon, on to the next town, the next gig, the next collaboration, and so we don't allow ourselves to get too close to anyone. But we can't help it if we are drawn to those like us—those who understand what drives us.

For most of my adult life I'd been exclusively attracted to rock musicians as romantic objects but, like I said, I was wary of getting too close to any of them *and* I was incredibly shy. That is why I have had very few bona fide boyfriends. I can count them on one hand. Once in a while an acquaintance or a friend or a colleague would ask me if I was "seeing anyone." My stock answer was, "Nope."

"You don't have a boyfriend? What?" my interlocuter would say, surprised.

"No, it's good," I would say, a little defensively. "I don't want a boyfriend. Guys don't really like me, anyway, I don't think. But it's cool, though, 'cause I'm not good at being a girlfriend."

"Jule," this person would say, as if a little encouragement was all I needed. "You could have *anyone*. Any guy you wanted. You're beautiful. Talented. You're a rock star! You're every man's fantasy!"

"Every man's nightmare, you mean."

Even if it were true that I could have any man I wanted, that I could point to some random studmuffin and snap my fingers and he would come to me, that didn't mean that I could *keep* him. Maybe I could *get* a guy, even a highly desirable guy (and I had surprised myself by proving it to be true on a few occasions), but I couldn't necessarily hold on to him.

Nor would I necessarily *want* to hold on to him, once I got to know him.

For example, I had gone to New Orleans in 1999 to work on some music, and I met James there through mutual friends. I was excited to meet him. He was the front man of a great but largely unknown band. There was a small group of fans-in-bands (people like me who had achieved varying degrees of success in the music business) scattered around the country who were in awe of James's band's first album, when most laypeople had not even heard of them.

I wondered why James and his band weren't hugely popular, and worshiped by millions. I'd had a similar feeling about Nirvana when their first album, *Bleach*, came out. I went mad for it and thought, "What the hell is *wrong* with people? Why isn't *everyone* loving this?" I even wrote a song about my love for *Bleach*—specifically for a favorite song of mine on it called "Negative Creep." I called my song "Nirvana" (clever, right?) and it ended up on my first album. My instincts were right about Nirvana—they eventually blew the world's mind, with their second album. And I thought James's band would probably explode into the public's consciousness, too, in the near future. They, like Nirvana, had made a brilliant debut album for an indie, and had recently signed to a major label.

James was tall and skinny with big black eyes and a quasi-consumptive pallor, which emphasized the bigness and blackness of his eyes. Even though he wasn't a rock star yet, he looked and carried himself like a rock star, with a dramatic, exaggerated slouch, which made him look as if the mundane tasks of everyday life were a burden to him; like he was too important, too precious to be bothered with things like walking and eating and paying rent and stuff like that; like he ought to be ministered to—served, fed, carried, chauffered. James's obvious general physical discomfort and apparent anorexia were, I thought, symptoms of his genius, of the great artist's inner torment.

James's band was a cross between the Rolling Stones, the Sex Pistols, Nirvana, Neil Young, and Lynyrd Skynyrd—full of devils and angels and an irresistible swagger. His singing voice, a southern drawl, was alternately plaintive and menacing, going from snarling and sneering to sweet as syrup. That voice drove me crazy.

It was sexy music. And so it followed that James, as the composer and guitarist and singer and mastermind behind the sexy sound, was sexy himself. So I let myself respond to his advances. He seemed as determined to be with me, mere minutes after meeting me, as I was to be with him. But as I jumped in, some instinct—some all-knowing, protective, sensible recessed part of my psyche—told me that it would end badly with James. It was happening too fast; I didn't even really know him. It was dangerous and stupid. James could be so caustic, so negative toward the people around him. I had the sense that he was on his best behavior around me. But I went ahead with it because I was so crazy about his music. And I loved the way he called me "baby." I was entranced.

I think I wanted some of James's rock-and-roll mystique to rub off on me—that's the real reason I wanted to be with him. Part of me wanted to *be* him—to be a tough, snotty, street-smart, tubercular, glamorously skinny, stylish, beautiful, cool, rock-and-roll boy—and so my desire for him was wrapped up in all that. He represented all the qualities that I thought I lacked as an artist and frontwoman: swagger, gravitas, a dark, low, powerful voice that people would take seriously and not slag off as cute or coy or girly or a novelty. I wanted to bask in some of James's rock-and-roll glow, in the energy that lit fires in his music.

I objectified him. I would walk into a restaurant or a club with him beside me, hoping people would notice us, and thinking, proudly, "Look! Look what I got." I thought that being with James—this ultra-cool rock-star-on-the-rise—would make *me* cool by association. That's how confused I was. Looking back, the depth of my shallowness shocks and appalls me.

I thought at first that I was falling in love with the guy, but really I was just in love with his sound—with some ineffable spirit in his songs, his voice, his music, his words, his distinctive guitar playing style. All of it was so powerfully evocative of something I couldn't place—something that I felt already existed in the world's collective unconsciousness, and in me, before we met, before I was born; something elemental that he, James, and his music were tapped into. His music pulled me to him like mosquitoes to a primordial swamp.

When I left Louisiana after we got together that first time, James asked me to leave him my little half-empty bottle of vanilla oil fragrance when I flew home, to keep some part of me (my smell) close to him. We kissed at the airport and James said, with urgency and gravity, "I wanna come see you soon," and then I flew back to Los Angeles, where I was living.

He did come, a week or two later, and from that moment on it was official: James was my boyfriend and I was his girlfriend. On that first visit I noticed, one day, when we were sitting on my couch, a grayish scar, a thin mark about an inch long and a centimeter wide in the crook of his left arm. I pointed to it and asked James, "What's that?"

He hesitated a second and then said, "It's a burn."

"Oh," I said, and resumed making out with him.

Months later, after the two of us had gotten to know each other better and realized that maybe we weren't so compatible after all—maybe he was a little *too* rock and roll for me, and I was a little too cautious for him—James confessed that his "burn" was actually needle track marks. James was a heroin addict. And I hadn't known because he hid it well. And I'd had no reason to suspect that his "burn" wasn't a burn. It *looked*, I thought, like it could conceivably have been some kind of a burn scar, like maybe from a flaming twig that landed on his arm as he stoked some fire, somewhere, or possibly some kind of a soldering accident?

Also, James was temporarily clean when he met me, and had been abstaining for a few weeks, trying to make a new start, away from the drugs. But at some point, when he went back to Louisiana after one of his visits to L.A., after the cracks were starting to show in our hastily conceived relationship and he realized the two of us together wasn't going to be as perfect a rock-and-roll fantasy as he thought it would—as I knew from the start it wouldn't be—he escaped back into getting high.

James broke up with me by pretending that I didn't exist anymore. Back in Louisiana, back on heroin full time, he simply stopped calling and stopped returning my calls. I grew quite frantic and distraught, not to mention confused, before I finally figured out what was happening: James's disappearance and his determined attempt to will *me* into non-being were his way of ending it.

His behavior seemed so cowardly, so immature, so irresponsible, so needlessly cruel, so pathetically weak, so pathologically passive, so fundamentally *wrong,* and so absolutely inconceivable that it took a couple of weeks—two horrible, agonizing weeks (of not eating or sleeping much)—for me to fully believe that James was really breaking up with me by not calling. It was very hard for my mind to get around the fact that a person could *do* such a creepy, ugly thing.

I was disgusted with James and with myself. How had I, who considered myself reasonably intelligent, been so stupid? How did I get myself entangled with someone who so lacked the character and decency and bare minimum of guts that he was unable to extend the *tiniest* bit of common courtesy—like a break-up phone call or at least a letter—especially to someone with whom he'd been intimately involved for half a year? This was a person I had *chosen* to be with, and so that made *me* an idiot for making such a bad choice; made *me* pathetic, immature, irresponsible, wrong, et cetera. It left me shell-shocked, and afraid of what other terrible, harmful decisions I might make in the future.

Jackson was another southerner, another musician, another addict. Another dead-end street. Vulnerable, sensitive, friendly, charming, handsome. He sang like Neil Young and looked like Montgomery Clift (but skinnier, and blond), and he called me "darlin'." It seemed to me that Jackson was probably a kindred spirit, since we both had the same urge to lay bare our wounded hearts in song.

But as I got to know him, I saw that there was more to Jackson than his pretty face and his southern gentlemanliness, and the way he crooned. Jackson was a mess. Prone to panic attacks and ulcers and other anxiety-based afflictions, he'd grab for cocaine, pills, pot—whatever he could get his hands on to obliterate his reality and take his worried mind off the fact that he was only pretending to have his shit together.

Jackson had no job and no consistent band lineup and he never had any money (though that didn't stop him from behaving as if he did). I paid a couple of thousand dollars worth of his expenses—cell phone bills, car payments—during the nine months we were together (I wanted to help—he seemed so helpless). And on top of that, he lived with his mom, and he was twenty-seven years old.

I started to feel like his mother, paying his bills, picking up tab after tab, driving him around because he was, I thought, too high to drive safely. It's a real turnoff to feel like your boyfriend's mom, so that was the end of that.

Sam was ten years younger than I was, a talented (but penniless) guitar player, singer, and songwriter. When we started dating I said to myself, "Haven't I learned *anything* from my mistakes? I'm an idiot—a *fool*—to get involved with Sam, another cute, poor guy in a band, and so much *younger* than me on top of that."

Sam was starry-eyed when we met, as was I, though Sam's star had not yet risen. I saw potential (for musical greatness, and for disaster). And I think he saw in me some kind of idealized fantasy version of womanhood (pretty, thin, semi-famous, financially solvent). In the very beginning, Sam, in the throes of new, young love, said to me, "Let's get married." I declined to play along. I said, "Sam, wait six months and then ask me again. I guarantee you won't still want to marry me then. I'll bet you a million dollars you won't."

And then I thought, "I know exactly how this is gonna end."

I even told Sam my prediction: "Sam, you're gonna leave me for a model one day. Just wait." I would repeat this every few weeks, as a way to preemptively save face—to let Sam know in advance of when it happened that I'd seen it coming; so that when he dumped me, I could pretend it wasn't a shock, or a big deal, or a humiliation, and that I had even had a hand in my destiny.

Sam would counter with, "No way, Jule, *you're* gonna leave *me*. I'll *never* leave you." And for a while, he believed what he was saying.

But he sounded less and less convinced as time passed and the months turned into a year and the year became a year and a half.

And then he left me for a model. A model/actress, actually.

I did have a hand in my destiny. I picked the ones that I knew would ripen quickly and fall off the vine in a relatively short cycle. The fruit would go bad and I could taste the rot in my mouth and yet I kept eating. Was I a masochist? Or were bad boy decisions a way for me to avoid getting too deeply into anything very serious and potentially painful? Was it because I felt no one could ever really love the real me (because I felt essentially unlovable) that I made sure to choose the ones I knew never had a chance to begin with?

I was attracted to their music and to some extent their appearance (a unique, off-center, scruffy, interesting untraditional handsomeness), and I assumed they were attracted to me for the same reasons. I didn't believe I had much to offer anyone other than those two things. Every failed relationship reinforced this in my mind and drove me deeper into a hole of low self-opinion and isolation and fear of any kind of closeness. All my worth and my identity were tied up with my music (my job) and to some extent my looks (which provided a visual accompaniment for those listening to my songs). Take those two things away, I thought, and I was nothing, no one; I ceased to exist.

After Sam and I had been together for a few months I learned that he, who'd seemed for the most part so sweet and shy, had a dark side. A dark, mean, pugnacious, crazy, jealous side. He was Dr. Jekyll and Mr. Hyde.

Sam played guitar in my band on one cross-country tour. The brooding, sulking Mr. Hyde persona took over for most of the tour. The other guys in the band took to calling Sam "The Darkness" when he got like that. After gigs, The Darkness would corner me and accuse me of cheating on him with, say, my drummer, or of flirting with other random men.

One morning in San Francisco, I woke up with The Darkness standing at the foot of our hotel bed, glaring at me. He asked in a frighteningly flat, coldly murderous tone, "Where did you go last night?"

"What are you *talking* about, Sam?" I said as I wiped the sleep from my eyes. "I was right *here*, in *bed*. With *you*. I didn't go anywhere!"

Sam, unconvinced, said, "Where did you go? I know you left. When I was sleeping. You went to Steve's room, didn't you?"

Steve was my drummer.

"Sam, you're fucking crazy. I was *right here*."

It was pointless to try to reason with him when he was being so crazy, out of nowhere. His delusion had nothing to do with me. It was his own affliction. And so I couldn't convince him that the truth was something other than what he believed.

This became the routine: After each show, Sam and I would go back to our hotel room, and most nights, Sam would begin his demented, groundless harangue, accusing me of cheating on him/flirting with other guys. I would at first deny everything (because none of it was ever true) and try to get Sam to recognize how wrong he was, but then I would invariably come to the conclusion, within minutes, that Sam was simply insane. At that point I would stop talking—stop engaging—and Sam would storm out of the room. That's when I would close the door, chain it, and take a sleeping pill. Then I would jam my earplugs into my ears and get into bed.

In the morning I would meet the boys outside at the van. Sam, transformed back into his sweet old now-apologetic quiet and sober self, would tell me with an embarrassed smile that he'd banged on my hotel room door for a while and when I didn't hear him knocking, and didn't let him in, he'd gone and slept in one of the other guys' rooms. Then the guys would chuckle and rib Sam about it for a minute ("Ah, Sam, crazy Sam, you nutty kid!")

But I was often still really angry in the morning after a fight.

It was exasperating being with someone who vacillated hour by hour between good and evil.

The tour wasn't any fun. In fact, it was horrible. Sam ruined it for me, and made it very unpleasant for everyone else.

And then *he* broke up with *me*.

Sam was the last straw. I'd foretold it to Sam, in a jokey-but-serious tone, in the early days of our relationship, after we'd made up yet again from yet another fight: "Sam, when you leave me for Kate Moss, I'm done with guys. Guys in bands, anyway. This is it for me. You guys are too much trouble."

Sam would smile. He thought I was kidding. He didn't believe me. But I meant it.

After Sam, "No more rock guys! No more rock guys!" became my mantra. I would pray, "Please, dear God, just keep them *away* from me! *No more.*"

They were just so hard to resist, like junk food—and so bad for me.

I was drawn to to the *puer aeternus*—the archetype of the "eternal boy" (the "beautiful creature" of my album of the same name, full of songs about these boys). The *puer* is narcissistic, immature, sensitive,

119

and artistic but not so good at coping with the demands of the world, wanting to escape into fantasy rather than dealing with the reality of a situation. The *puer* doesn't have to grow up because he is playing a child's game (rock and roll); *playing*—playing guitars, making up rhymes, playing dress-up and jumping around onstage.

Was I drawn to these boys because *I* hadn't matured—because *I* was still a child and couldn't see my way to growing up? Were they a way to *avoid* the difficult task of growing up? Had rock and roll, and my doomed relationships with rock and rollers, stunted my emotional growth? When—*how*—would I ever become a woman if I kept getting mixed up with these confused, selfish, damaged, fragile, capricious boys, so careless with their own and others' feelings? How could I transform my *own* carelessness, confusion, selfishness, self-absorption, childishness, and hurt into strength, sense, sureness, patience, knowledge, confidence, maturity, and kindness?

It was never the guy's fault when it fell apart. It was my fault for falling for the guy who was born with the voice that made my knees weak. The man with the voice that helped to heal my wounded heart could also break it. The man could not help me; only his music could do that. That was what I finally learned through all that trial and error.

I loved rock and roll. And so I loved the rock and rollers. I always wanted to be one of them. I believed that only the godforsaken (or rock-forsaken) sound of my voice, and my debilitating self-consciousness, kept me from being admitted into that (mostly) boys' club. I yearned for recognition and accomplishment in the rock arena and I gravitated toward those who possessed or at least deserved what I wanted for myself. But I was misguided.

Because at heart, I am not a rock and roller. At heart I am a librarian, a bird-watcher, a transcendentalist, a gardener, a spinster, a monk. I was like a fish out of water in the modern rock world. That was why I was so often discontented and unsure of my self and my place. I was in the wrong environment—that's why it always seemed to me as if something wasn't quite right.

I don't want loud noise and fame and scandal and drugs and late nights and flashing lights; I want peace and quiet and order; solitude, privacy, and space for contemplation. I want to awake at dawn and listen to the birds, and drink a cup of tea. I need to face facts.

None of those cool rock boys—those skinny, pale-skinned beauties you see slouching down the street in their jeans and sunglasses and postcoital mussed and matted hair—are as cool as they seem to the untrained eye. Of course, they won't admit it.

But I have seen the truth. They're not cool, I'm not cool. None of us ever was. We are all secretly freaking out.

17

August 10
Chicago

I woke up in Indianapolis in a good mood. I had slept well, and today was PD day. "PD" is short for "per diem." Fifteen dollars a day for each of us, given out by the tour manager in weekly batches. It was money for the coming seven days' worth of breakfasts and lunches, ostensibly, but more often than not it was blown almost all at once on an impulsive shopping spree at a truck stop. Belt buckles, iron-ons, herbal stimulants, lottery tickets, Foreigner's greatest hits on cassette—stuff like that is hard to resist when you have a big wad of cash in your pocket.

Tim doled out the money, first thing, when we got in the van. One little pile of $105 for each of us.

We did some errands on our way out of Indianapolis.

First we stopped at a Radio Shack to get a couple of spare fuses (always good to have on hand) for our amps. Then we went to Target so Brian could buy some plastic bins to help better organize the T-shirts and CDs we were selling at the shows. The rest of us ran around the store with our cash like kids in a candy shop. I bought a little Nikon 35mm camera, a notebook, a blue camouflage CD traveling case, some film, a Plen-T-Pak of Big Red gum, and another vanilla candle. I spent all my per diem for the week, and then some.

An hour later, we were in Chicago. We checked into the Omni Hotel down near the Great Lake. Tim handed us our keys and we dragged our bags over to the elevator opposite the hotel's "world-famous" Pump Room restaurant. Framed photographs of many of the celebrities—Oprah Winfrey, Bill Clinton—who had dined there over the years attested to the world-famous-ness of the place.

At the Double Door, the rider had been all set up for us before we arrived. Grapes, oranges, apples, bananas, carrots, celery, cherry tomatoes, broccoli and cauliflower florets, three kinds of hummus, chips and salsa, all manner of soft drinks and really good Odwalla juices, Jolly Rancher lollipops, a case of bottled water, rice cakes, various kinds of Clif Bars, two bottles of wine (one red, one white), a big bottle of Absolut vodka, a box of Throat Coat tea, a plug-in tea kettle, honey. It was so above and beyond what we ever get, or expect, that I had to celebrate. I picked up two oranges and stuck them in my bra, one on each side, and jumped for joy around the room, sticking out my super-perky new breasts at Tim's camera, which he had gotten out when he saw me putting oranges in my shirt. I grabbed two apples and handed them to Heidi and made her do it, too.

After soundcheck and after Brian had finished setting up his merch stand next to the coat check, we all (Tim, Brian, Freda, Heidi, and I) walked down the street to a soul food restaurant that Tim claimed was really good. The place was crowded with festive Saturday night revelers and we were seated in what appeared to be the only unoccupied table, a banquette in the corner next to a window looking out on the street.

I'm a vegetarian so I ordered the grilled portabello mushrooms—they were the only thing on the menu that wasn't meat or fish—although I'd always thought of the mushroom as more of an accompaniment to other things; just a vegetable, to be used in a strictly auxiliary capacity. Freda, who tries to eat a healthy diet, too, has an easier time of it in restaurants because she eats fish. She got the salmon.

When my food arrived, I took a few bites and put my fork down.

The portabellos were scaring me. They weren't like any mushrooms I'd ever had before. They looked and tasted just like meat.

A couple of hours later, Freda and Heidi and I were sitting in the dressing room as the opening band played, and my stomach began to rumble. I'd had only three forkfuls of the mushrooms, but I had the disturbing sensation of having recently eaten a steak or a burger.

"Freda," I said to Freda, knowing that she, as a non-red-meat-eater herself, would sympathize with me in my red meat–related distress. "I think there was meat on my mushrooms."

"Oh, really?" she said, sounding genuinely concerned. "Why do you think that is? Do you think they used beef stock or chicken stock in the cooking sauce ?"

"Maybe. Or maybe the mushrooms were cooked on the same grill that all the meat was grilled on, all night long, and some meat remnants got on my mushrooms."

Being a vegetarian on the road can be problematic.

But the show had to go on, so I started putting on my makeup and tried not to think about the cow juice churning in my gut. Freda and Heidi did their own primping. Freda put on a pretty flowered dress and I changed into my denim X-Girl stretch miniskirt and my cowboy boots. There was a good, big crowd waiting for us.

Joe Marcus, a local alt-rock success and all-around good, cool guy, showed up backstage about a half hour before showtime. Joe and I had had a thing once, for a little while, when we were touring together, and which didn't have a clear-cut ending and so was always sort of unresolved. But we both wanted to remain friendly, because we respected each other as musicians. It meant a lot to me whenever Joe came to see me play. He and I made small talk, somewhat awkwardly, for a while and then it was just a few minutes until set time so he left to go back up into the club. Freda, Heidi, and I put the finishing touches on our hair and makeup and outfits and made our way upstairs to the stage and began setting up our equipment.

There was little reaction when we walked onto the stage. The crowd, a full house, just stood there, watching us set up. As I crouched, uncoiling my cables, I heard a male voice near the front say to his buddy, "Hey, check it out—they have all female roadies."

He thought that we, the band, were the road crew and not the band.

I wondered, "When these guys find out that I am Juliana, the singer they paid fifteen bucks each to see sing, will they feel sorry for me for having to set up my own equipment? Will they pity me, when I start singing, for having to carry my own luggage in and out of hotels? For having to drive my own van? For not having 'people' to take care of all the menial and unglamorous details; for not having handlers handling everything that isn't stepping into the spotlight and shining?"

I'm not embarrassed or ashamed to have my hands and knees dirtied in the trenches of my life's work. I feel incredibly lucky that I still even have an audience to kneel down in front of and uncoil my cables, after all this time. And they pay to see me! I'm living my own version of a rock-and-roll fantasy. Because all I ever wanted, really, was a chance to have an audience who gets it and likes it.

The energy coming from the crowd was strange. Slightly off. Not quite right. Hesitant. They seemed confused by all of the brand-new material, which none of them had ever heard before. Chicago had always been a great town for me, with especially appreciative and knowledgeable audiences, so I was bewildered and a bit shaken by the crowd's lack of comprehension and enthusiasm. I had thought that they, Chicago, of all crowds, would be happy and curious and interested to hear new songs. But they cheered only for the old stuff. Which was a totally understandable reaction. I just didn't expect it from Chicago, where I'd always felt welcome and well-liked, no matter what I chose to play for them.

And so, after a couple of songs I began to feel just like Anthony Patch in *The Beautiful and Damned*: "His confidence oozed from him in great retching emanations that seemed to be sections of his own body." Maybe my band and I were just not any good. Maybe I'd lost my touch, or gone stale. Maybe this was the end of the line. Maybe it was time to hang up my guitar for good.

And then I went and confirmed my suspicions: During the solo in "The Prettiest Girl," I hit an ugly couple of notes. Clams.

"Oh my God," I thought. "Not again. I'm such a loser."

I suddenly thought of Johnny the promoter, who had driven up from Indianapolis to see us play, and of my vow to not mess up any more solos. He was out there in the crowd somewhere.

At the end of the song I said into the mike, with sincere embarrassment, "I'm sorry I fucked up, Johnny."

Joe Marcus didn't come back to say hi after the show. He was nowhere to be found. He was gone.

"Joe has impeccable musical taste," I thought, "and if I had put on a good show he would have stayed until the end and he would have been excited and he would have come backstage and told me how much he'd liked it. The fact that he left means that the show must've stunk."

And so, at the end of the night, I had worked myself up into a state of utter dejection. Only a few hours earlier I had been dancing around the dressing room with fruit in my bra, looking forward to a great night, and now I was back to feeling pitiful and stupid.

It was the opening band's last night with us. They lived in Chicago and they would be staying at home while we moved on. I hadn't bonded with any of them. I still hadn't even learned any of their names. I went outside in back of the club and posed for a few pictures with them minus their lead singer, who wasn't around, and then I got in the van and lay down and waited for everyone to say all of their good-byes. The singer eventually showed up (I could hear her on the sidewalk) and she was a bit drunk and very emphatic about wanting a photograph with me in it, but I was one hundred percent committed to being done—with everything and everyone—for the night. I stayed where I was, supine and lifeless and out of view on the backseat, ignoring all pleas for camaraderie and fraternity, pretending I was deaf and invisible. Trying to will myself into nothingness, wishing I was somebody—anybody—else. Dying to get out of the van and into my hotel room, where I would be alone and free to cry, out loud, like I so wanted to.

There had been people—fans—hanging around outside the back door as we were loading out, wanting autographs and handshakes and saying, "Great show," to me, but I couldn't shake the feeling that something wasn't right tonight. Both the performance and the crowd were lacking something—some essential spark—and it was my fault. Who else could be blamed? I was supposed to be the ringleader. I was supposed to be able to summon the necessary magic. But it seemed the magic was increasingly just not there.

Finally everyone was ready to go and we made our escape. When we were getting out of the van in front of the hotel, Freda asked me, "Hey, Juliana? Do you think I could have one of those sleeping pills?"

I said, "Yeah, of course," unenthusiastically. But then, suddenly worried, I said, "But promise me you won't drink anything with it. I don't want to be responsible for your death. It says on the bottle, 'Do not drink alcohol with these pills,' okay? Look—it says it right here." And I showed her—I held the bottle out to her, made her read it.

Freda laughed and said, "Okay."

But I wasn't joking. Tonight I felt cursed, doomed, like darkness personified; the darkness that could snuff out even Freda, who was so full of light.

I unzipped my backpack as we got into the elevator and took out my pill container as we rode up. I handed an Ambien to Freda just as the elevator doors opened on my floor. I said good-night and the elevator doors closed behind me and the tears came instantly, even before I could get to my door.

I ran a bath, still crying, and got in the tub, my warm tears mixing with the bathwater.

As long as I've been doing this, I have felt this way half the time. It's like God wants to make sure I stay humble, so I can really appreciate the good stuff, when it happens. Like maybe all these little depressions and disappointments that come out of nowhere for practically no real reason keep me balanced, in a weird way. All of the joy and wonder need to be tempered with dejection and doubt so I am better able to recognize and be thankful for my good fortune.

When I was done with my bath, the red light on my phone was flashing, so I picked up the receiver and dialed into the room's voice-mail system. It was RJ. He had left me a sweet message and in my fragile state, I was highly susceptible to these tender utterances. If I called RJ back, I was likely to dissolve completely, pouring my tears onto him pathetically, self-pityingly, greedily, grasping for his sympathy and kindness. But I knew that in the morning, with a clearer head, I would regret being so profligate with my emotions. To call RJ back would be to lead him on, selfishly perpetuating the fantasy—the fantasy of me and RJ—for my own benefit. We were both, at that moment, far from home and sad and lonely and needing comfort. Phone calls were an escape from the drudgery of being on tour, from the occasional misery of our lives and minds.

"It's not real," I reminded myself. "We're not real. RJ can't help me. I'm on my own. RJ and I will never be together. And I don't want to be. It wouldn't work. Nothing—no one—ever does."

There's a certain pleasure in wanting what you can't ever really have. It's like believing in Santa Claus—you're incredibly excited that he's coming, even though time has proven, Christmas after Christmas, that you'll probably never actually get to see him. That was me and RJ.

But I didn't believe in Santa Claus anymore

"What am I doing with RJ?" I thought. "What do I know about loving or being loved?"

Nothing. Nothing at all.

So I didn't call RJ back.

I got into bed and closed my eyes.

18

Guns N' Roses and Me

In 1993 my first single for Atlantic Records, "My Sister," was in pretty heavy rotation on both modern rock radio and MTV. I *never* got used to the shock of turning on the radio or the TV and hearing or seeing my song come on the air. It was an unexpected thrill, every time. Like the sudden drop-off from the top of a roller coaster—but totally unanticipated—jerking me out of my normal foggy, dazed, slightly numb state of mind, like I'd been dreaming my life, and now suddenly I was awake. But at the same time it seemed unreal, like this was someone else's life, someone else's voice on the radio and face on TV. After all, I, Juliana, was here, in, say, a hotel room wherever I happened to be, doing whatever I happened to be doing. The Juliana on the radio was a disembodied voice separate from me, a whole different entity that had a life of its own, apart from me. I didn't create my voice, and I didn't control it—it simply existed, and came through me, from some strange exotic shadowy half-world dimension to this one, via my body. That enigmatic, unknowable creature on TV—the voice and face of my music—was almost as foreign to me as it was to everyone else out there.

I was on tour as radio and video airplay of my song were snow-balling. One afternoon in San Francisco, after a day full of promotional activities (interviews, a photo shoot, a radio station visit, lunch with the local label rep, et cetera) my crew and I found ourselves with a couple of hours of free time at our hotel before we had to get on the tour bus and go to soundcheck.

When I entered my room, I sat down on the edge of the bed and turned on the TV. It was tuned to the MTV channel. I watched as Guns N' Roses' epic, pain-drenched power ballad "November Rain" drew to its dramatic conclusion. It ended and then my "My Sister" video came on, identified in the corner of the screen as a "buzz clip."

Guns N' Roses and then . . . me. Me and Guns N' Roses. Back-to-back. Joined in the same block of heavily rotated music videos in some kind of surreal union. It seemed so completely unlikely. So *bizarre* for the two of us—me and GN'R—to be lumped together.

I had nothing against Guns N' Roses. It was just that me and them seemed so fundamentally, philosophically unlike one another. They were rock icons—the biggest band in the world, in fact, at the time—and they *knew* it and believed in their mythology and were *working* it. *All the time.* They *lived* rock and roll, twenty-four/seven. They seemed to *breathe* rock and roll. They *ate* rock and roll. They probably *shat* rock and roll. You knew that they knew that rock-and-roll stardom was their birthright, that they fuckin' *deserved* to be rock stars.

As for me, I seemed born not to raise hell but to doubt everything. Had I earned my place on the charts next to GN'R? Did I deserve my current success? Did I fit the role—fill the rock star shoes—like they did? It was open to debate. And I, for one, was decidedly skeptical. I certainly didn't *feel* like a superstar, or have any sort of clue as to how to act like one.

Guys in bands like GN'R, with their top hats and scarves and tight pants, and swilling Jack Daniel's out of the bottle, believed in pop stardom as a way of life from the beginning and were aiming for it as if it were a clearly marked destination on a map. For me it was always a fanciful dream, an amorphous and somewhat delusional fantasy. So when it actually *happened*, to *me*, I couldn't understand it or make sense of it or accept it or believe it or deal with it. It didn't seem real. Or rather, it seemed *too* real, and that took some of the shine off it.

Fantasies are visions of perfection and they serve as escapes from the recurring letdowns and disappointments of reality. They aren't supposed to come to life. When they do, they inevitably lose some of their sparkle in the journey from dream to the here and now. That's why people warn, "Be careful what you wish for." In a rock-and-roll fantasy you're better, more beautiful, more interesting, more talented, more desirable, more charismatic. In order to sustain this kind of vision, day-to-day, you have to actively play along and keep the fantasy afloat by deluding yourself, and others, into believing you are as wonderful and dazzling as the ongoing fantasy. There can never be any untidy or unpleasant or uncomfortable moments, moments that are always in reality sprouting up during the life span of any long-term situation.

I'm not saying that dreams can't come true—they can and they have. (*I* fantasized about hearing my music on the radio and then one day I heard my music on the radio.) But reality intrudes upon and transforms the impossible perfection of the fantasy. You dream of hearing your music on the radio but you don't think about what comes along with having your music played on the radio. Negative criticism. Record company pressure to not only *stay* on the radio, but to *top* your popularity and do better with the next release. Loss of free time. Loss of privacy. Rude, obnoxious, sexist radio station DJs who ogle you and ask you stupid questions. You adjust to this new existence, wherein your altered fantasy becomes your normal life, with its ups and downs. And so then you construct new fantasies, perfect ones. And the cycle of discontent continues.

My record company continued, for a while, working to disseminate and build upon the fantasy of Juliana Hatfield as pop star, but from my perspective becoming a "buzz clip" and sharing the airwaves with Guns N' Roses was a fluke, a tiny blip that was soon-to-be-forgotten history. I could only make sense of the hoopla surrounding me if I thought of it as some freak accident. I just continued to do my thing—the same thing I had always done and in the same way I had always done it (although I *had* upgraded from a van to a tour bus, and the crowds were bigger) and continued to be baffled by what was happening to me, and by all the little storms raging around me. My success was bound to slip away eventually, because I didn't think I really deserved it, and I didn't grab on to it very hard or try to cultivate it in earnest. It really wasn't my fault that I was swept up in the wave of popular culture, for a minute. It was just something that happened to me.

I guess I beat my commercial and pop-cultural demise to the punch, in a way, by not taking my pop star status completely seriously. I never really believed in it, never really believed it was real.

Who wants to keep pumping his fist for someone like that?

19

August 11

Iowa City

I joined Tim and Brian in the van and said good-bye to Freda and Heidi, who were going to get a ride back home to Indiana with Johnny (so Freda could have some time with her family). Tim and Brian and I were going to head off on our own to the West Coast. I was scheduled to stop and play shows on my own, without the band, in Iowa City, Minneapolis, and Denver. Freda and Heidi would then, six days later, fly out and meet us in San Francisco, and the whole crew would resume the tour.

We got to Iowa City about an hour before we needed to be at the club, so we checked into our hotel, a Red Roof Inn near the highway. Tim handed me my key card, in its little paper holder, on which the front desk clerk had written my name: "J. HATEFIELD."

"How perfect," I thought.

Up in my room, I threw my bags on the bed, switched on the TV, and turned down the air-conditioning, which was blasting out of the vent under the window and making the room feel like a refrigerator.

A Kmart commercial came on the television. The music in the

background of the ad sounded familiar. When I realized what it was, I said to myself, out loud, incredulous, "There's a fucking Nico song in this Kmart commercial."

What did it mean? Nico and Kmart were completely incongruous.

The song was "These Days" from the *Chelsea Girls* album. The ad was using just the song's instrumental intro, a sweet and pretty finger-picked guitar part; the part that happens before Nico's mournful Germanic alto comes in singing about being depressed. The ad featured a mixed-race Earth Mother type in a comfortable shirt and loose-fitting cotton drawstring pants smiling beatifically and bouncing a big beach ball to a happy child in a room with summer-colored paint on the walls. The room was clean and empty except for a stylish low-slung faux-leather couch positioned against the wall. The ad was selling everyday all-American Kmart stuff, but with a fresh new spin on design, to compete with the much hipper Target, probably. And Nico was the soundtrack! Nico, dead Nico, the embodiment of darkness and decay and decadence. And German-ness.

Was this a brilliant stroke of post-postmodern marketing mischievousness, putting the two together?

I turned off the TV and went outside. The whole sky was completely packed with dense swirly cloud cover as far as the eye could see; a vast gray ceiling, with luminous slivers peeking out here and there, glowing. It was enchantingly ominous and strange, the billowing clouds motionless, and mute, like storm clouds in a photograph.

After a while Tim and Brian came outside and the three of us got in the van and went to the venue. The venue was a sports bar with zero charm or personality, shabby with years of accumulated grime. Neon beer signs hung on the walls, and under our feet was the kind of cheap, gray, industrial wall-to-wall matting that covers the floors of so many college-town hangouts, worn thin, stinking up the room with all the spilled beers and crushed-out cigarette butts that had been absorbed into it through the years.

There was no dressing room ("You can hang out in the hallway between the bar and the back door if you want," said the bartender) and no rider. ("You want some water? I can get you a water.")

"No thanks," I said.

I didn't want water. What I wanted was just to get out of there as soon as possible, leaving immediately after soundcheck and returning just before going onstage. And then not hanging around after the show. That's the kind of place it was; the kind of night it was going to be. Do the show, get paid, and leave.

I opened a low window behind the "stage" (a slightly raised platform in the corner of the room) to let some air in. The window overlooked a parking lot. I sat on the windowsill and looked at the parking lot while Tim worked at getting the PA in working order.

I didn't know anyone in Iowa City.

Tim was muttering under his breath about the pitiful state of the house sound system. When he approached the stage and began setting up a mike near me, I tried commiserating, for lack of anything else to do. "This place sucks," I said.

"No kidding," Tim said. "How am I supposed to make you sound good in these conditions?"

"Ah, I'm not worried. You're a pro. You'll make it work, I'm sure. If anyone can do it, you can."

Then I added, "I'm bored."

And I followed that with, "I'm hungry."

Tim said, "We'll go and eat after soundcheck. I'll try to get this set up as quick as I can, but it might take me a little while. This PA isn't in very good shape."

Then he went back to the soundboard to twiddle some knobs. Soon he was testing the system's power with the same Blue Nile song he used to test it with every evening. The singer's sniveling, easy-listening moan blasted through the room: "Now that I found peace at last/Tell me, Jesus, will it last?"

The song was starting to really get on my nerves. With each successive soundcheck, I came a little closer to ripping the CD out of the stereo and throwing it on the ground and stomping on it.

"Stop it," I wanted to tell the singer. "Just shut up, okay? Just be happy you found God. Don't whine about it. And you can't rhyme 'last' with 'last.' That's totally lame."

I went to the front of the club, near the entrance, where Brian was setting up his merchandise display. This involved taping a Juliana Hatfield T-shirt to the wall. I sat behind his table for a while watching him work, silently.

135

After a couple of minutes Brian said, half to me and half to himself, "I wonder if I can get a beer."

I jumped up and said, "I'll get you a beer. What kind do you want?" excited at having something to do.

After what seemed like an eternity, Tim was ready for me and I did a quick soundcheck. It was just me and my electric guitar, so it only took about five minutes. Then the three of us went to find some dinner. I had been hungry since we arrived at the club and by the time we got out of there, two hours later, I was feeling weak and irritable.

We headed downtown, figuring there would be a decent restaurant that would appeal to the three of us. Tim parked the van at a meter and we walked a block to the nearest open place, something called Finnigan's pub. Inside, the stools in the dingy bar section were all occupied but the booths in the restaurant half of the room were all empty.

It didn't look promising. People were drinking but no one was eating. And it was dinnertime. There were no waiters or hosts around, so Tim asked the bartender for a menu. The man produced a grimy laminated sheet from behind the bar. The offerings were regular stuff like pasta and salads, but one look around the room told us that they clearly did not specialize in food here and that the locals didn't come here to eat.

My stomach growled, loudly. The inside of my mouth tasted bad, rotten.

Tim asked the guy behind the bar if they were serving dinner, and the bartender said, "Let me see. I'll ask. I don't know if the cook is here yet."

He yelled into the room behind the bar (the kitchen, presumably), "Hey, is Bart here?"

I heard a muffled reply, which I couldn't make out. Then the bartender turned back to Tim and said, yeah, he thought they could make us something to eat.

I was halfway out the door already. Brian was still outside, waiting to see what we had found out.

Tim followed me as I stormed out onto the sidewalk and he ventured, gingerly, hopefully, "Should we try this place?"

I answered, "*No.*"

My blood sugar sank down another notch with the effort it took to get the one-syllable word out. All I'd had to eat all day was a Clif Bar in the morning and a handful of peanuts for lunch, seven hours ago.

I sat down on the curb in front of the bar while Tim went back inside to inquire about other places to eat in the neighborhood. I hung my head down and put my face in my hands.

"I am a miserable wretch," I thought. "I hate this. I hate this place. I hate this town. I hate this restaurant. I hate this sidewalk. I hate everything. And I hate that club I have to play in tonight. It's so depressing being there. Do I have to keep playing these ugly, smelly places with no dressing rooms forever—for the rest of my life? Is this really my life? This is my life. My stupid pathetic washed-up no one cares anymore life. Sitting on a curb in Iowa City complaining and whining like a stupid spoiled baby. Why can't I just be happy?"

Brian, sensing intuitively that anything he said or did could set me, in my funk, off, kept his distance and stood by the street sign up at the other end of the block from me. A lack of nutriments in the brain, or something, was making me delirious with teeth-grinding frustration and gall. I wanted so badly to cry or scream but I knew I didn't have a legitimate reason.

In a minute Tim came striding out, maintaining his usual peppy demeanor. He looked as if he was about to say something encouraging, but before he could, I said, "I. Need. Food." in a bloodless monotone.

Someone had to be informed, at least indirectly, of how horrible it was to be me at that moment, and I chose Tim, because he was there.

It felt as if my skin was sliding down off me and toward the ground. I didn't have the energy to even lift my head to look at Tim when I spoke. The corners of my mouth were as if weighted, pulling my lips down so that they were stuck in a frown.

Tim, eager to swiftly and diplomatically remedy the increasingly volatile and unpleasant situation (my raging hunger/psychotically bad mood), kept on his happy face and said, "A guy in the bar told me about a cool vegetarian place not too far from here and I got directions. Okay? Wanna try it? Let's go."

I managed to let out a groan of assent. But I hated having to agree to something. I wanted reasons, more reasons, for feeling the way I did, more reasons to be angry, to be bitter and disgusted, to lash out.

I got up slowly from the sidewalk and followed Tim and Brian back to the van. The short walk was painful and seemed to take forever. I felt like a dead person. Like my bones were made of cement. Like I was walking through water, on the bottom of the ocean, with all of my clothes on.

I sat in the back, stewing silently.

"How can anyone stand to be around me?" I wondered. "Why am I like this? Why do these guys stick around? Why don't they quit?"

Tim located the recommended restaurant, in a quiet residential neighborhood, and parked out front. It was a homey (in a house, actually) little vegan place run by friendly, apple-cheeked hippies with dreadlocks and Birkenstocks.

After a few bites, I felt the life coming back into me. A few more mouthfuls and the world was a nice place again and Tim and Brian were my faithful compadres and I was the luckiest girl in the world, being blessed with delicious, lovingly prepared, cruelty-free sustenance, in a peaceful town full of kind and generous and forgiving folks, some of whom I was going to get to sing my songs to (!) later, and I was going to get paid to do it!

"Hey, you guys," I said to Tim and Brian between bites. "I'm sorry I was such a bitch back there. I was just so hungry that I couldn't see straight. It put me in a bad mood. But that's no excuse for being such a bitch. I'm really really sorry. I'm so embarrassed."

"Ah, no worries," said Tim nonchalantly. "It all worked out okay. We found this place."

Brian added, smiling, "Yeah. Isn't this place great?"

"Yeah," I said. "It's perfect. It's just what I wanted. Thanks for finding it, Tim. I wish we could eat like this every night."

When we got back to the sports bar, Tim and Brian went inside while I sat in the van and watched people file in. It was an all-ages show tonight and a large part of the crowd seemed to be teenagers; high schoolers and college kids, who probably couldn't get in to most club shows because they were underage.

They clapped and yelled and hooted enthusiastically when I took the stage. I thought, "Wow. If these people are this glad to see me, they must be starved for entertainment. They must really not get out much."

Despite the warm welcome, I felt naked and nervous up there

without Freda and Heidi and with the crowd so close, right there in front of me, staring at me, waiting, anticipating something great; greater, probably, than what I was about to give them. I so didn't want to disappoint them, but I feared I was going to.

The minimalistic stage lighting—a few colored bulbs pointed at me—was throwing shadows onto the neck of my guitar, making it hard for me to see what my left hand was doing. There was no lighting person to adjust them (they'd been set up hastily by Tim at soundcheck and left like that) so I was stuck either trying to feel my way through the blind spots or concentrating way too much on the placement of the chords. Neither strategy was successful—both limited my freedom of movement and expression, and my singing and my playing suffered. I was never able to fully let go and lose myself in the music; I felt tethered. It took most of the set just to loosen up, and then it was over.

I tried to make it up to the kids by staying on the stage for a really long time after the show, signing stuff and answering questions. Most of them seemed to think it had been a really good show. ("So easy to please!" I thought.) None of them complained at all. They seemed happy and satisfied and so innocent in their eagerness to shake my hand.

One girl handed me a folded-up piece of paper. I took it, said "Hi," and, "Do you want me to sign this?" and she said, "No. That's for you," and then she added, "Great show," smiling shyly. I said, "Thanks," and she walked away as I stuck the note in my back pocket.

Later, in my hotel room, I would remember the piece of paper as I undressed for bed, taking the note out of my jeans and unfolding it and reading:

> Juliana,
> Your music has gotten me through sadness, loneliness, breakups, being homesick, car rides, plane rides, sleeplessness, finals, and even the best times of my life. A million thank yous could not express my gratitude, but THANK YOU and please never stop making music.

And the girl had signed her name at the bottom.

I was crying by the second line. It was just about the sweetest thing I had ever read. I hadn't done my best that night, and I had in fact shown just about the worst of myself earlier in the day, but still people were giving me their love. I didn't deserve it. But I realized, as I cried, how much I really needed it and, at that moment, it was the best present I had ever been given. My reward. It made up for everything.

Brian was in the last stages of loading his merch stuff out to the van when he came back in to get the one last display T-shirt down from the wall. It was gone. Someone had taken it when Brian was outside.

"What?!" he exclaimed upon realizing he had been robbed. "I can't believe someone stole a shirt! Who would do that?"

"Teenagers," I chided, jokingly. "We are such chumps. I can't believe we fell for their sweet and innocent act."

"I know! Shit, that pisses me off. Jul, I'm really sorry I let that happen. I really didn't think any of those kids would steal from me in the two seconds that I wasn't looking."

"God, Brian, I don't care. Don't even worry about it."

I was in a good mood. The crowd's tender, unguarded attitude had softened me up. They really had seemed thoroughly unjaded, and friendly, and glad to be there, and it cheered me to know that there were still people in the world—in America—who didn't appear to have seen and heard everything. I even had warm feelings toward the thief. In my mind he was probably not a hardened criminal but, more likely, a serious young guy—a true music fan—who wanted a T-shirt and knew this was his only chance to get one but didn't have the money. I was flattered that someone wanted to steal a shirt that had my name on it. I really didn't mind losing the one shirt. Some of the merchandise always gets written off as giveaways or promotions, anyway. We could put the stolen T-shirt in that category.

But Brian continued to fume about the evil teenage thief who had taken advantage of him, and of us. I continued to try to console him.

"These things happen," I said. "Don't let one bad apple spoil the whole bunch. I think most of them really were genuinely excited to be there tonight. They had a good time."

As we pulled away from the club and started back toward the hotel, I asked Brian, "Hey, how many T-shirts did we sell, anyway?"

"Not that many. We only did about seven."

"That's it? Shit. The kids must really not have any money. How many CDs did we sell?"

"Four."

"God, that's bad."

Anyway, I'd put in my time, and gotten paid, and gotten out, just like I'd planned. And I'd gotten some love.

20

My Idol

The Replacements played on *Saturday Night Live* in 1986. I was home from college at my mom's house for the weekend. I sat alone in the dark on the shag carpet in front of the glowing TV, my face about two feet from the screen, and screamed and wept like the band was the Beatles on the *Ed Sullivan Show* in 1964. No one that I knew of in my small town forty miles south of Boston shared my love for the Replacements, and the rest of the house was asleep, or away, so I celebrated the band's exhilarating *SNL* performance by myself.

They did an impassioned, loud, on-the-edge-of-the-precipice-and-about-to-fall-off version of "Bastards of Young" and then later in the show they came back, having mischievously traded outfits with each other, and played a raw, sweet, hard "Kiss Me on the Bus," with front man Paul Westerberg dropping to his knees at the end and falling forward—guitar banging on the soundstage floor—in mock prostration to the TV cameras and the audience.

The whole brief spectacle was triumphant and life-affirming: everyone's favorite fuckups, the band that was always sabotaging themselves and their chances at success and seeming to deliberately shoot themselves in the foot by getting really drunk and flouting the rules of propriety in high-profile gig situations, had just delivered a wonderful, winning rock-and-roll performance on national TV in support of their new album—their major label debut, *Tim*. The pressure was on, the stakes were high, and they had *done* it; they had proven that they *were* one of the greatest living American rock bands and that maybe people should stop doubting them now, once and for all. All of us loyal supporters who rooted for the Replacements even though they were incorrigible rebels, always making a mess of things, pissing off the people they most needed to impress and offending those to whom they most needed to ingratiate themselves—we were so proud that night, watching our favorite band on *Saturday Night Live*. They had come through.

The Replacements had greatness in them, a gorgeous, scraggy majesty that sometimes refused to come out and show itself, leaving the band flailing and stumbling, wasted. But even then, on the not-so-great nights, the mess they made was a kind of beautiful, endearing, funny mess, not an ugly or angry one. That night on national television they knocked *us* over with a great, shining rock-and-roll blast of feeling and humanity, and they did it without compromising any of their ragged spirit. I just about died of happiness, seeing it happen. Westerberg became, with this performance, *The* Man of My Dreams.

I bought my first electric guitar later that year, soon after meeting John and Freda. The three of us were in a music store around the corner from my dorm building at the Berklee College of Music, and I spotted a guitar that looked just like the one Paul Westerberg had played on *SNL*. His was a scratched-up, all-black, Les Paul–shaped thing with no pickguard. The one hanging on the wall in the guitar shop was a Gibson "Challenger" and it was the spitting image of Westerberg's. It cost me two hundred dollars. I didn't even plug it in and try it out to see how it sounded before I bought it. I simply grabbed it and made it mine, just like I wished I could do with Westerberg himself.

Eight years later, in 1994, I was invited to open for Westerberg on a series of tour dates supporting his debut solo album, *14 Songs* (the Replacements had split up by then). That album and my Atlantic Records debut, *Become What You Are,* had both come out the year before (1993).

Mammoth Records, who in 1991 had put out my first solo album, *Hey Babe,* had then sold my contract to Atlantic, which meant that I had transitioned, through no real effort of my own, from an indie (Mammoth) rocker into a major label (Atlantic) recording artist. It was an upgrade, like getting a promotion, and it felt like a natural evolution on what had so far been a nice, steady, manageable career track. Now that I had access to Atlantic's radio, video, design, and publicity departments, which were better-staffed than Mammoth's and had more money to spend on promoting and marketing their artists, I was getting more airplay than ever before with *Become What You Are,* and more press, and I was playing to bigger crowds. I was selling more records and reaching more and more people with my music. Evidently, even Paul Westerberg had heard of me.

Receiving his invitation was one of the high points, if not the very highest, of my career—of my life—up to that point. I responded immediately, hyperventilating and yelling at my manager (who'd brought the news over the phone), "Yes Yes Oh My God Holy Shit Are You Kidding Me? *Yes!*"

Paul Westerberg was my hero, my idol; he was the first modern-era (postpunk) rock icon whose music and persona affected me in a profoundly, uniquely deep and personal way. When I discovered, as a teenager, the band's *Let It Be* album in Maggie's milk crate full of records, it was like finding the long-lost soul mate that I hadn't realized was missing until that moment of discovery.

Westerberg's voice, and words, and melodies, and even his face, and the aura surrounding him grabbed onto some primal, elemental part of my psyche and wouldn't let go. It stayed with me for years, through serious bouts of isolation when it felt like Westerberg was my only friend, my best friend, lonely like me, sad like me, damaged like me, confiding in me. I *needed* his music; it helped keep me sane; it was something to focus on outside of my confused, aching head, reassuring me that I wasn't alone in my confusion. It was as if Westerberg *was* me. Talking to myself. Through his songs. Experiencing all the mood swings I did and saying all the things I thought and felt and wanted to say, myself, and one day would, with my own songs.

Westerberg had a big influence on the way I presented myself and my music to the world, in that he made me feel that it was okay for me to just be myself—with all my doubts and faults and insecurities and idiosyncracies—in a way that didn't really fit into any preestablished patterns or molds or pop/rock singer/musician archetypes. *He* didn't fit any mold. He wasn't really comparable to anyone I had ever seen or known—not in my town, not in the music world. He seemed more real, more human—and as such, more complicated, and interesting—than other music-makers.

His music was tangled in varying points of view. It was funny, and fun, and romantic, *and* it was coarse and kind of mean. It was sweet, vulnerable, and sensitive without being sentimental or drippy, *and* it rocked, hard. As a result, Westerberg was sometimes misunderstood. People questioned how he could be both sweet-vulnerable and punkrock tough. Was his soft side for real? Was he joking with the folky ballads? Was he punk or was he pop or was he rock and roll, or what?

I understood the complexity, and the need to explore all sides of one's personality—to look into the dark corners of any given situation and try to express feelings that were normally hidden or obscured, or embarrassing.

It seemed as if a girl singer like me had to be either Joan Jett or Joan Baez—and nothing in between—or people would get confused.

Westerberg was everything. He was alternately cocksure and doubt-ful, down on himself. Listening to his albums was to experience a fascinating back-and-forth conversation between cynicism and hopeful-ness. Westerberg was a world-weary dreamer. So was I. Everything about him screamed, "Juliana, we are kindred spirits." Everything about him made sense to me. Everything: the way he moved when he was onstage—on the edge of danger and collapse, raw emotion struggling to bust out like a heart attack, but always just restrained and self-conscious enough, with enough solid good sense to keep it all together and not drop over the line into falling apart embarrassingly in a regrettable pub-lic breakdown; his perpetual grace, even when shitfaced; the sweet melodies of his softer songs (sung in that craggy, raspy ache of a voice), which somehow managed to coexist alongside his dirtiest, scabbiest, punkrockest rave-ups; his gentle-looking fingers which betrayed, I was sure, a gentle soul, and which pried—delicately, somehow—grungy, loud, ringing, defensive fuck-you chords from his nicked and scratched guitars; his utterly unpretentious, self-deprecating stance; the way he sometimes really listened, respectfully, to the questions during inter-views, and gave thoughtful, honest answers, even when his bandmates were falling and laughing and yelling and taking the piss out of every-thing around him and generally behaving badly and not taking any of that interview business the least bit seriously.

His hair, that he let run a little wild, seemed to say, "My *heart,* too, is untamed, windburned, homeless, in need of care" and at the same time to thumb its nose at respectable society and all its shallow, mean-ingless conventions, like grooming and hairbrushing. ("*I* don't brush *my* hair, either!" I would think, as a teenager. "We're soul mates!")

His clothes were scruffy, secondhand, but he wore them with panache. Westerberg's bearing was simultaneously regal and slightly dis-solute, like a descendant of an aristocracy that had lost all its money and social standing, but not the blood and pride. (He'd even named his publishing company "Elegant Mule.") His dad sold cars for a living, but I was convinced their people must have once been kings. German Catholic royalty—the "*Ves*tuhbahgs" (pronounced with a German accent).

There was an inherent dignity in what Westerberg was doing, in his devotion to the pursuit of music. There has to be, I think, an ingrained self-love—independent of anything or anyone else—already present in one's genetic makeup if he is going to have the guts and the will to devote a major part of his life and time and energy to art or music. I myself have always been a cup half-full of equal parts self-loathing and self-glorification. In my head and heart I was often falling apart (sim-ply as a matter of course) but my songs and my voice had conviction and strength and vibrancy, and they were often the only things that made sense. That was why I fell so hard for Westerberg, whose music and persona seemed to embody all my shifting, dramatic moods which, up until I'd found him, had made me feel that there was something wrong with me—something that no one else could understand. West-erberg seemed to be clinging to his music as I was to mine—like any artist compelled to produce clings to his work—like the music was a life raft, saving us from drowning in the meaninglessness of everything else.

He was tough and street-smart and smart-alecky and rock and roll, but he was also sincere, compassionate, fragile, fractured, and tuneful. His sad eyes betrayed an empathy for the suffering of others, and his fans knew that when he sang, he was singing for and about them as well as himself. He sympathized with all the so-called losers and outcasts and social misfits—the downtrodden—of the world, but he hung out with movie stars, too, because he was so fuckin' cool that movie stars wanted to hang out with him. He was beautifully, perfectly imperfect, and he was our hero.

And now, eight years later, I'd been chosen, by my musical hero, to be his personal opening act every night for an extended run of concerts. I used to daydream as a teenager and think, "I *know* that if we could just meet, Paul would fall in love with me. I just *know* it. I *have* to meet him." I think that's why I started a band in the first place. So that I could meet Paul Westerberg, and on a level playing field, where I'd be seen as a peer and not just a lowly fan. And be taken seriously. And now that was *happening*, and it blew my mind. One of my most prominent long-running fantasies started out *exactly* like this. Paul and I would spend time together, get to know each other. And then what would happen next was that Paul would fall in love with me. He would fall in love with me because we were soul mates, destined to meet and fall in love. It was a foreordained spiritual connection, and up until this point we'd been separated only by physical distance (he lived in Minnesota, I lived in Massachusetts) and the fact that we had never met.

I wrote Paul Westerberg a fan letter when I was about sixteen years old, a couple of years before that *Saturday Night Live* performance. He was far away out of my range but he was, I thought, in my adolescent agony, the only one who understood me. I yearned to know him personally, but I couldn't, and it was torture. I had to try to reach out, make some kind of contact, so I did it in the only way that seemed possible: a brief "thank you for your music—it has gotten me through some hard times" note. I suppose there were other ways I could have made contact; I could have, for example, found his address in Minneapolis and then bought a plane ticket and shown up on his doorstep with, like, flowers or something. But that would have been a big turnoff for him, I'm sure (and incredibly awkward for me). No, that was definitely not the scenario I envisioned for our first meeting. I was a fan with a big crush, but I sure as hell didn't want the object of my affection to think I was insane, or desperate, or annoying. So I went with the letter, addressed to Paul care of his local (Minneapolis) record company at the time (Twin/Tone). I was nobody then—just some lonely teenage girl—and anyway Westerberg probably received piles of fan letters every day, so I tried as hard as I could to banish from my mind any hopes I might have harbored for a response.

He wrote me back on a smallish piece of notepaper torn off a notepad, with black and white piano keys running along the top of the page. It was a short, self-deprecating handwritten note whose whole purpose, it seemed, was to make me deliriously happy for a moment. It began, "Dear Juliana," and crescendoed with "I forgot to take my ass-hole pill this morning" and ended with "I have to go tune the drums now." He'd given me a small, guarded glimpse into his head and his life, and the kindness of this little act of generosity was—and is, still—incredibly touching.

When I got his invitation to tour, I could have quit, right then, in 1994; quit everything—singing, writing, touring, breathing—and just expired, completely content, with no regrets, knowing my life had been a complete success.

The dream was about to come true. Everything had been arranged by our respective camps—booking agents, managers, promoters, publicists. Paul and I were going to meet for the first time in Denver, at our first double-billed show, which was scheduled for a theater downtown.

On the way to that first gig my tour manager got a phone call from Westerberg's tour manager informing us that Westerberg had thrown his back out at the end of his concert the night before, and that since then Paul had been in extreme pain and was barely able to stand upright (let alone hold a guitar and play another concert) and so was at present on his way home to Minneapolis. He was canceling the remainder of the tour.

My heart was broken, but only for a moment. I didn't even cry. I had been working in the music business for long enough at that point that I had almost come to expect this kind of huge letdown. Disappointments were so commonplace in the world of rock that they didn't shock me anymore. When music is your life, and when your colleagues and collaborators are artists with temperamental, mercurial dispositions, great and wonderful things are bound to happen; but the law of averages dictates that some of the great and wonderful things that *almost* happen or *could* happen or *might* happen never come to pass.

And anyway, I had always been so grateful and awed by just the *possibilities;* by the everlasting promise of brilliant moments, musical and otherwise—surreal in their "pinch me" unbelievability—that it was almost impossible to stay sad for long about any one particular letdown, no matter how major a letdown.

By being born into a dream of music—by simply being one of the lucky ones able to live an artistic life, I'd been given the best gift that the world had to offer anyone: A purpose. An identity. A reason for existing. Sure, fantastic opportunities were constantly falling through, but amazing things were often happening, too, and could always happen, and might, and would. So much had already happened to me—meeting John and Freda, getting a record deal and being able to quit my day job, hearing my songs on the radio, gaining the respect of some of my heroes—that it was hard to be truly, lastingly disheartened or really beaten down by the events that failed to by materialize. Disappointments balance out all the wondrous things that do happen from time to time, and disappointments keep me grounded, and humble.

Getting to the point at which I was seen by Paul Westerberg as a suitable touring companion, and musically and temperamentally compatible, was a major achievement. A dream had come true. Well, almost. The beginning of a dream. I had been awakened too soon. Still, what *had* happened was pretty unbelievable and wonderful: I had worked my way into Paul Westerberg's—my idol's—consciousness. I had existed as an image, a thought, an idea—a good idea—in his mind. This was incredible to me. And it was, strangely, quite satisfying—it was *enough*—to have been merely a word on his lips. (He had most likely spoken my name to his manager, band, or booking agent). To be seen as a real person, and as a legitimate artist, and taken seriously, by him, was all I'd ever *really* wanted from him. Westerberg's response to my wispy young fan letter had been a thrill that I still savored, and being invited on his tour was a thrill, too; a proud, exciting moment; a memory that I could take, grinning as I thought about it, to my grave.

It was a humongous downer when Paul Westerberg canceled our tour, but I took comfort in knowing that I'd been the one chosen to do the tour. I'd been invited. I would always have that, and that's more than most people—I mean, more than most Replacements fans—have.

And we did eventually meet.

21

August 12

Minneapolis

I walked into my room at the downtown Best Western and was nearly knocked over by the smell of men's aftershave. I envisioned a polyester leisure suit–clad swinger with greased-back hair, a thick gold chain around his neck, and a smoker's cough clumsily knocking over his bottle of Drakkar Noir as he went to make a muscle man pose in the mirror.

I immediately pulled my L'Occitane eau de vanille out of my backpack and sprayed it into the air, waving it back and forth, but the vanilla was almost instantly overpowered by the heavy-duty cologne stench.

I tried plan B: I went to the window, praying it wasn't bolted shut. Nine times out of ten they are. But I lucked out; it opened and I stuck my head out and breathed deeply.

Fresh air is a rare luxury in these chain hotels. The builders who build them and most of the people who come to occupy them seem to agree that the weather's whims are nothing but a nuisance. "Nature is temperamental," the unopenable windows seem to say, "and uncomfortable, sometimes, so if we can at least control the indoor climate, from command central, that's one less worrisome thing to have to think about while we watch TV or sit at our desks looking at our computers." Which I guess kind of makes sense.

But if something happens to disturb the pleasant synthetic consistency of this indoor air, like, say, someone accidentally spills a bottle of cologne, we have a problem. Because there is no way to air the place out. So then, sometimes, like in my room at the Knights Inn in Columbus, a cleansing agent—something ostensibly "fresh"-smelling—is introduced. But the artificial "lemon" or "gardenia" or "pine, tinged with ammonia" scent is often no less noxious than the original odor and is often, in fact, a whole lot more so.

Besides, fresh air just feels nice sometimes. And when the windows are sealed shut it makes me feel like I'm in jail. Or like the hotel authorities think that I am incompetent and can't be trusted to take care of myself. But I can. If the windows open.

An hour later Tim, Brian, and I left the hotel to go to the 400 Bar. I left the window in my room open to let the fumes dissipate. When I got in the van Brian asked, "What's that smell?" Apparently the stink of aftershave had thoroughly saturated my physical being and was emanating from my clothes and body. I grabbed a fistful of my hair and sniffed it and, yes, there it was. Disgusting cheap cologne vapors had seeped into and between and under and on top of every strand and follicle on my head.

I sprayed more vanilla on me and tried not to think bad thoughts.

A local guy, with his guitar, was the opening act. I forget his name. Tom something. He was kind of Dylan-esque. He had good songs and his manner was unpretentious. I liked it.

Later, in my set, during my performance of "My Sister"—my one ancient, quasi-modern rock hit—people sang along really loudly. I could hear the crowd above my own voice in the monitors. Three pretty young women (late teens? early twenties?) in the front had their arms draped across one anothers' shoulders as they sang together, along with me, looking right at me and smiling broadly, openly, sharing their good feelings. It took me by surprise because that kind of outward intra-song contribution from the crowd—the hearty group singalong—doesn't happen to me much these days. My audiences are genuinely pretty reserved. But tonight it was as if the audience was stuck in a time warp and "My Sister" was still on the radio and its video still a "buzz clip" on MTV, and they reacted accordingly, with the resultant excitement at seeing the real thing in front of them in the flesh. But it was . . . today. Not then. It was strange, but it was nice to see people having a really good time.

I had a good time, too. Unlike the night before, in Iowa City, I was comfortable. There were no badly placed stage lights throwing shadows and obscuring the neck of my guitar. And the audience's very vocal enthusiasm toward not only the familiar oldies but just about every song I played had the effect, after my initial shock subsided, of defrosting my heart. Warming it. Relaxing it. Opening it up a bit. And I let go and sang hard.

Following the show, I met some fans, signed some things, answered some questions, and posed for a few photos, like I usually do. After I thought I'd talked to everyone, and was turning to go down the stairs to the dressing room to gather my things, I saw one more girl. Not until I looked at her did she approach me. It was as if my seeing her was an invitation, the invitation she'd been hoping for, to talk to me. I'd noticed her before, when I was chatting with other people. She was the pale, slightly overweight, concerned-looking dark-haired girl, about eighteen, waiting patiently by herself off to the side. As soon as I said hi, she kind of burst out—quietly, though, and controlled, like she'd practiced it—with what she'd apparently been holding in, and needing to say, for a long time: "When I first heard your song 'Choose Drugs,' my younger sister was downstairs being beaten up by my mother. My mother's a pill-head. And when I heard the song, it was, like, 'Whoa. That's my life.'"

The girl's desperation and pain were so palpable—emanating out from her like some terrible, tragic perfume—that I took it like a punch. Her whole being was so sad and serious and heavy, so resigned to the fact of the complete and utter shittiness of her situation, that I didn't know what to say. I felt hopelessly and criminally ill-equipped; this girl needed so much, too much, and what could I possibly do? What could I possibly say, right now, at this moment, to help make her life any less horrible? What this girl needed was a professional. Someone trained in these situations.

I kind of froze, and then felt myself backing away involuntarily while blabbering something about how "we all feel things, and so I know how you feel 'cause we all feel these things and I guess the music expresses it and I just write about the stuff we all feel and I know you're in pain and I hope you'll be all right."

What I'd said wasn't what I'd wanted or meant to say and then I was saying good-bye and the poor girl had the remnants of a faded black eye, herself, that I'd just noticed then in the poorly lit room, and I almost couldn't bear the thought of what horrible things were waiting for her when she got home. And I just didn't know how to deal with this.

I walked out of the 400 Bar feeling shaken and scared for the girl. The fact that one of my songs had helped her, in some way, to see that she was not alone, wasn't really making me feel any better about the whole thing.

"I should've hugged her," I thought. "Why didn't I hug her? Was I afraid her pain was contagious? Was I worried she would follow me home, like a stray puppy? I should have just hugged her to me and whispered, 'I know. I know how much it hurts.' I totally failed. I let that girl down."

Then we drove away. I abandoned the stray. I just left her there, standing on the street corner outside the club, looking lost and just as sad and desperate and serious—like she'd never smiled a day in her life; like she'd never had a reason to—as before I'd talked to her. I should've taken her with me. But then, what would become of her little sister? This is what I told myself.

When I returned to my hotel room, all traces of the malodorous man perfume from earlier in the day were gone. The night air had, over the course of a few hours, dispelled the funk of humankind. Or rather, one of them. This particular problem had been solved. Thank God for windows that open.

22

The Harpsichord

I wanted to be loved by audiences and critics. I thought it would make up for the absence of close, meaningful, supportive personal relationships in my life. I put myself out there, over and over again, in front of people, when it sometimes felt so masochistic, as a way to counteract the isolation and aloneness I felt. I should have known that this audience-performer bond would prove to be much more complicated and fragile and unfulfilling and insufficient than the love I had envisioned. Of course it wasn't simple or comfortable or unbreakable or easy to sustain. Love never is.

I never dreamed of finding Prince Charming and living happily ever after. I never dreamed of getting married, never believed a man would save me from anything or make my life any better. I never had any faith in romantic love. I put it all into my music—all my fairy-tale dreams and wishes. I believed it was more conceivable that I would grow up to become a rock star than to ever have a stable, healthy, enduring relationship with a man. I had no reason to believe otherwise.

My parents' marriage was not a happy or successful one. It was doomed from the beginning. If I used my parents as a template, I had no reason to believe a marriage, or a man and a woman, or two people, could work. I had seen with my own eyes from a young age that love is painful and sad and lonely and messy. Love brings out the worst in people.

When my mother gave up her dream of being a concert pianist, she also gave up the man she loved. My mother was in love with a man who wasn't my father, all through my parents' marriage. And my father knew it. Mom met Felix when they were both music students at the University of Michigan. They were engaged to be married but at the last minute my mother got scared and decided that marrying a musician with no prospects, no security, no guarantee of future employment—a man of whom her parents did not approve—wasn't the smart thing to do and she broke off the engagement, right around the time she switched her major from music to journalism.

Soon after that she met my father, a medical student, and agreed to marry him. They ended up in New England and had three kids. Felix went on to play bass in the rock group Mountain, who were known for their early 1970s hit "Mississippi Queen" and for their rather large, Meatloaf-like frontman, Leslie West. Felix also produced other people's records, including Cream's *Disraeli Gears*. My parents managed to forge a quasi-united front until I was eleven, and then they finally split up for good.

Felix drifted in and out of my mother's life. I knew, as a child knows everything, that he was often on her mind. He came to visit the house once when I was about nine years old. Dad must have been out of town at the time. I remember Felix falling asleep on our couch, sitting up, in the middle of the day. "This is the guy Mom is so hung up on?" I thought.

After the birth of her third and last child (my younger brother), my mother experienced a terrible spell of postpartum depression. In this agonized, weakened state of mind, all she could think was that she had to get away from her life, and my Dad, and go to Felix. She left the baby and me and my older brother, who was five, with a neighbor and took off from Boston on the first plane out to Chicago, where she knew Mountain was scheduled to play on a tour stop.

Felix was married to someone else by then, plus he was on tour and preoccupied with that, so my mother's impulsive, desperate visit was a short one.

In the music room of our house there was a harpsichord that my father had built, as a gift for my mother, with his bare hands, from a harpsichord construction kit. (He was always building things—skiffs, tables, desks. His last big project before he died was a small airplane which he was putting together in his garage and which he hoped one day to fly.) When my mother returned from Chicago, my father knew where she'd been. She hadn't told him but he knew. He'd managed to find us kids and gather us up and bring us back home where he'd waited, fearful that she might not return.

When she walked up the brick path and into the house, past my father standing in the doorway, my mother said nothing. My father didn't speak, either. He went to the garage, grabbed the ax he used for chopping wood, and started back toward the house. My mother, watching him from the kitchen window, wasn't scared, and didn't move or run away, even as she thought, "He's going to kill me." She was so depressed that she didn't care. Her next thought, after "He's going to kill me" was, "I don't care if he kills me."

Dad walked in through the kitchen door and past my mother, holding the ax. He went through the dining room and into the music room and he brought the ax down hard on the harpsichord—the beautiful harpsichord that he had built for my mother. He destroyed it, methodically, as my mother watched, numb, and when he was finished he looked at her, with sweat streaming down his face, and said, "Stay with me." She did, for eight more years.

I, naturally, concluded that love, and men, and marriage must always lead inevitably to smashed harpsichords. But music, my loyal and constant companion, would never break my heart or love me too little or destroy anything. Music would be an alternative to secular, romantic love and to marriage and misery. The audience and I would love each other from a safe, platonic remove and no one would get hurt.

Felix's wife murdered him in 1983. She shot him with a gun and killed him, in their bedroom. I was fifteen years old and had no idea how to handle my mother's grief for a man I never knew, and who wasn't my father. My mother still says, "I should have married Felix. He'd still be alive today if I had."

But I, in all my infinite wisdom, still try to convince her otherwise whenever she brings it up. I tell her, "Mom, you'd have probably ended up wanting to kill him, too. You're lucky you didn't marry him. Mom, come on, he was a musician. He was in a rock band. Musicians are selfish, immature, and narcissistic and they love their music more than they will ever love you. Most of them have serious emotional problems—and substance abuse issues, too. Felix was young and innocent and clean-cut when you guys fell in love in college. But you have no idea what he might have gotten messed up in. Remember when Felix came to the house and passed out on our couch? Was that the kind of life you wanted? Do you realize what it's like to deal with a drug addict boyfriend, Mom? Trust me, it's a fucking nightmare. And what about groupies? How would you have dealt with his sleeping with girls on the road? They all do it, Mom. I'm sure you would've wanted to kill him, too. You can romanticize him because you never had to live with him."

My mother never listens, though. She continues to believe in a silly romantic fantasy of true love.

23

August 13

Minneapolis to Kearney

We had 559 miles to go on our day off. The scheduled stopping point for the night was in Kearney, Nebraska, about two-thirds of the way to Denver.

First thing in the morning, as we pulled out of the Minneapolis hotel parking lot, Tim, who was driving, put on a live Richard Thompson recording.

The unofficial policy in the van was that whoever was driving got to choose the music. It was a reasonable rule, but unfortunately Tim and I had pretty opposing tastes and I dreaded his playing DJ.

Usually I didn't give voice to my displeasure if Tim put on something I didn't like. I felt I shouldn't complain. He was on driving duty, so he got to pick the tunes and I had to respect that. So I would suffer silently, cringing mutely to myself while some irritating contemporary jazz-funk played. Or some 1980s adult lite-rock—Talk Talk, World Party, latter-day (read: not good anymore) XTC—or something from his large collection of overearnest lesbian folksinger-songwriters.

Conversely, Tim was liable to scoff, indirectly, at my more ragged rock choices like the Stooges or the Runaways, or the Scandinavian bubblegum pop (Annie, Ace of Base, ABBA) that I like so much. He would never say anything, but I could always sense Tim's disapproval by his sour facial expressions and lack of head-bobbing or foot-tapping.

We were all generally pretty tolerant and forgiving of each driver's choices (at least outwardly), unless a passenger was in a bad mood, or hungover, and really couldn't take it. In that case he or she might issue a plea for mercy which was, usually, granted graciously by the hands at the helm, and the music was changed or just simply stopped. There *were* a few artists who appealed to the sensibilities of the lot of us, though, and whose music made the whole van happy, in a pinch. Everyone liked Neil Young and Bob Dylan and AC/DC and the Rolling Stones.

Anyway, Tim had Richard Thompson going at a fairly loud volume. Tim was a serious Richard Thompson fan, and played his music a lot in the van. Every time he did, I would at first listen for a while, with an open mind, but then, invariably, not be able to get into it, except maybe on an intellectual or conceptual level appreciating Thompson's "skill" as a guitar player. I *wanted* to like Richard Thompson because almost every musician friend I had held Thompson in high esteem— particularly his guitar playing—but I just didn't dig it. It was just one of those things. Jimmy Page and Jimi Hendrix and J Mascis floated my boat as lead guitarists, but Richard Thompson didn't. My head told me that I *should* like Richard Thompson, but my heart wasn't feeling it. And Tim knew it.

The last time Tim had played Richard Thompson in the van, I had tried to explain my position. I had said something like, "I keep hoping this'll grow on me or I'll have an epiphany and suddenly it will become clear to me why everybody loves him so much. I mean, I'm just not get- ting it. I keep trying to find something about it that I can like. But I don't really like his voice or his songwriting and I don't really care for his guitar playing style, either. I really don't even like the *sound* of his guitar. Hey, what is that, anyway, that he's playing? A Strat?"

"Yeah," Tim had answered.

"I thought so. I never liked the sound of Strats played clean like that."

So Tim knew how I felt about Richard Thompson. I knew he knew. And he knew I knew he knew. And at this early hour, at the very beginning of what was going to be a very long drive, Thompson's cutting vocal tone and trebly, epic-length fret gymnastics were particularly grating.

I looked over at Tim. He was enjoying himself, moving his head up and down in time to the music.

After about the third eighteen-minute guitar solo, I couldn't take it anymore. It was too early in the morning for eighteen-minute guitar solos. And I hadn't slept well. And I was still suffering the unrelenting effects of a bad bad cold.

I said to Tim, "Tim? I'm just curious. If you know how I feel about Richard Thompson's music, why do you always play it?"

Tim stiffened and immediately ejected the CD and put it back in its case with the hand that wasn't on the wheel. He didn't say anything, didn't answer my question. Just kept his eyes on the road, straight ahead. I had obviously hurt his feelings.

"Oh, fuck," I thought. "What did I just do? Why did I do that? What is my problem?"

I felt like a schoolyard bully who had picked a fight, only to be knocked flat on his face. I was mortified by Tim's shaming silence but determined not to show it. I tried to hold my ground, to save face, and said, "Tim, I'm serious. It's a legitimate question. Why are you so mad?"

There was no response from Tim. He continued to look straight ahead at the road in front of him.

"I was confused and I thought you could explain to me and, you know, help me understand why you would play Richard Thompson's music, the music that you *know* I really don't like, first thing in the morning when you know I don't want to hear it and I'm tired and not feeling that good, and it just seemed kind of insensitive of you to do that."

Still there was nothing.

I was digging myself deeper and deeper into a hole that I never should have jumped into in the first place.

"Why are you ignoring me?" I continued. "I wasn't trying to upset you. I just wanted to know the answer to a simple question. I really was seriously curious. I mean, I have a right to say what I want to say. I was just being honest. What? You can't take it? Would you rather I played games with you and got all passive and not said anything about it but then just be pissed off at you for playing the *one thing* that you *know* I don't want to hear? Come on! What's your problem?"

Still there was no response from Tim.

"Why won't you answer me? Say something."

I looked at his stone-cold profile as he drove.

"Oh. I get it. You're giving me the silent treatment."

Still no sound or movement came from Tim.

Then I said, "God, you're such a baby," and gave up.

Now that I had finally shut up, Tim opened his mouth and in a quiet, measured tone of voice that seemed to be almost imperceptibly straining to carefully contain a seething disdain just below the surface, said, "I just thought that you might want to listen to him because you're always saying that if you heard more you might learn to like it."

That was the final, silencing slap in my already red face. Still, I scrambled to defend myself, to myself.

"Oh my *God*. What a load of crap," I thought. "He put on Richard Thompson for *my* benefit? That is such a crock. He *knows* I was only trying to be nice all those times I tolerated Richard Thompson politely. He needs to just accept the fact that not everyone worships his precious Richard Thompson. I'm *sorry*, Tim. *I just don't like Richard Thompson.* Deal with it."

After that, Tim continued to give me the silent treatment, and no music at all, for two more hours. I spent the greater part of that time curled up in a fetal position in the seat behind Tim with my jacket over my head, pretending to be pissed off but actually crying muffled tears of shame and frustration, cursing my errant tongue, wondering how I had messed everything up so early in the day, thinking, "Why couldn't I have kept my mouth shut? Why couldn't I have respected the driver-gets-to-choose rule? Why couldn't I have just said it nicely like, 'Tim, would you mind maybe playing something else, please, if you wouldn't mind too much?' Why can't I just be a nice, normal person?"

This incident reminded me of something that happened with me and my father a few years before he died: I, along with my brothers, was visiting Dad at a house he had rented for Christmas vacation in Florida, and he had cooked a vegetarian stew for dinner. He was concentrating, with a dish towel over one arm and beads of sweat on his brow, on preparing bowls of this stew, one at a time, for each of us. He would ladle out a bowl of stew and then, as a finishing touch, he would grab a handful of feta cheese (Dad *loved* feta) from a package on the counter and dump it on top. I happened to be going through a militant vegan phase at the time. After he had served my two brothers, Dad filled another bowl with stew and I knew it had to be for me. I saw Dad turn toward the feta and as he grabbed a handful I said, "Dad, can I have mine without the feta?" and just as I was finishing the question, his hand was opening over the bowl—it all happened so fast—and Dad snapped, "No, you fucking can't," and the feta dropped onto my stew. Needless to say, the cheese was no longer an issue, since I wasn't hungry anymore.

My father's reaction—suddenly quite angry, and hurt, because of my rejection of something he had offered to me—was similar to Tim's. In each case, something that the man had wanted to share was in a sense thrown back at him and so he had snapped back, or in Tim's case, recoiled, like a wounded animal. In both cases I felt terrible, but confused: I hadn't meant to hurt them, had I? I simply didn't want the extra cheese on top of my stew, and I didn't feel like listening to Richard Thompson. In neither case did I mean to attack either man's personal . . . personhood, or being; his Dadness or Timness. So why were their reactions so extreme, like I'd sucker-punched them? *Had* I really meant to hurt them? How could this be? Were there deeper resentments at work that I didn't understand? Am I a horrible person? Are all men, deep down, little boys?

On tour, tensions build up quickly and sometimes they seep out or boil over and feelings are hurt and sensitive artistic egos bruised. You see the best and the worst of people when a small group is forced to be together day and night for weeks on end. When you want to get away you can't, really, not for any substantial length of time. You are all collectively stuck in the van, in the clubs, in the dressing rooms and backstage areas, sometimes in the same hotel room. It's like a marriage or a family. Band and crew are bound to one another for better or for worse.

You learn how to push one another's buttons. And unconsciously or not, that is just what I had done to Tim—by vocalizing, snarkily, my dislike of his beloved Richard Thompson—and of what Tim had done to me by playing Richard Thompson.

Sometimes, being passive-aggressive is, or seems, easier than being direct. You don't want to hurt anyone's feelings so you try to skirt around the issue at hand and in so doing, you make a mess of things. (Freda, however, has an amazing ability to always be both direct and sweet, at the same time. It's awe-inspiring.)

Eight hours later, the Richard Thompson business was a distant memory. Tim and I had both cooled off and we were friends again, just shooting the shit. Over the course of the day, Brian had driven for a couple of hours and then I had taken over for a couple of hours and now Tim was back behind the wheel. We were coming up on the exit to our Ramada Inn in Kearney, Nebraska. And Tim wasn't slowing down.

"This is our exit," I told him as we approached the big green and white sign for Kearney.

"No it's not," Tim said, matter-of-factly.

"Yes it is."

"No it's not."

"Yes. IT IS."

"No it's not!"

"Okay, it's not. But it is."

Just then we passed the exit and in that same second Tim's brain came to life and he realized his mistake and said, "Oh shit! You're right. I missed it. Sorry. I'll get off at the next one and turn around."

It's frightening how utterly convinced you can be that something is right when it's not. And it's equally humbling how, in one shocking instant of clarity, everything can change. And you realize how completely wrong you were.

24

Hair and Makeup

Sometime in the early 1990s, I was scheduled for a photo shoot with a glossy music and pop culture magazine. I had arrived at the downtown Manhattan hotel where the shoot was to take place. I was sitting in the makeup chair while the photographer and his assistant set up their equipment and a stylist unpacked all of the trendy fashions that she was going to want me to try on. My eyebrows were being plucked by the makeup artist. It was part of her concept for the shot. My eyebrows were to be strategically yanked, with tweezers, until they were about half as thick as their normal, naturally occurring state. I'd never had a dramatic eyebrow reshaping done to me before and I was game.

"Why not?" I thought. "I'll give it a go. Maybe it'll look cool. A new, improved, fabulous Juliana!"

But after about fifteen minutes of the plucking, I was starting to feel very uncomfortable. It was a much more time-consuming, painstaking process than I had expected, this redesign of my brow. Hair after hair after hair after hair after hair was pulled, one by one, and it was painful. Each tug hurt more than the last and my eyes began watering. The situation, from my perspective, was becoming masochistic.

After half an hour I thought, "Why am I letting this woman *do* this to me? It *hurts*! My eyebrows were *fine*; there was absolutely *nothing* wrong with them the way they were when I walked in here today. Ow! (That one *really* hurt.) This woman is a sadist! She *must* be aware of the pain I am in. Look how my body winces and tenses, involuntarily, with each yank!"

I let her continue manhandling me, like I was a hunk of clay, until she had finished her brow masterpiece. Then it was time for makeup. And an hour and a half later we got down to the business of making some photographs.

As I said, we were set up in a hotel room. (Hotel rooms are very popular sites for photo shoots.) My hair and makeup done, and my eyebrows plucked to near nothingness, the photographer's eyes quickly scanned around for ideas and then suggested to me that I "jump up and down on the bed" while he captured me in motion.

I can't tell you how many times the photographer on the job, when shooting in a hotel room, has made this particular suggestion. My immediate reaction, as a fairly dour, unperky person, was usually something like, "You're kidding, right?" accompanied by a nervous laugh, or "Please, no. Please don't make me do that" or "Uhh, couldn't we do something else, like could I maybe just sit here in this chair or on the edge of the bed, maybe, and look out the window while you work your magic?"

What I really wanted to say was, "Maybe if you give me a *reason* to jump up and down on the bed, then I'll jump up and down on the bed. I'm not an actor and I'm not a model and I'm not a twelve-year-old girl at a slumber party so why would I want to jump up and down on the bed?"

Why did they always want me to jump up and down on the bed? Were photographers constantly nudging Kurt Cobain to jump up and down on beds?

It was as if the press had some preconceived idea of me as a bubbly, happy, accommodating girly-girl. I guess I can't blame them for assuming this about me. My young-sounding, chirpy singing voice probably put the idea into their heads; it may have led people to believe that I was a fun-loving adolescent who could frequently be found jumping up and down on her bed out of sheer delight and innocence.

But didn't they ever listen to the lyrics? Their message, if there is one, is pretty much the opposite of fun-loving.

As for all the grooming and styling and fussing and detailing that was pushed on me when I was in the public eye, it took up unbeliev-able amounts of time and energy. I assumed it was something that came with being a girl musician in the pop world, so I tried to go along with it, within limits, and to not protest too much. How does one say to a hairstylist, "Don't do anything. Don't touch it," when the hairstylist, whose job is hairstyling, has been hired to style my hair? How does one say it without coming across as "whiny" or "difficult"?

Usually, before I had even said anything—before I had figured out a nice way to say "thanks but no thanks"—I would already have started to feel bad for the hairstylist, envisioning her standing off to the side, sad and unwanted (shot down before she had even had a chance to show off any of her skills), holding her brush and blow dryer forlornly, and I would give up on finding a diplomatic solution, and just let her do whatever she wanted to do to my hair.

Most magazines would send not only a makeup artist and a hair person along with the photographer, but also a clothing and accessories stylist. A stylist is someone who is paid, essentially, to go shopping. As if we didn't know how to dress ourselves. A stylist sometimes comes in with a particular concept that has little or nothing to do with the aes-thetic or the personality of the subject who is being "styled." Once in a while I, for example, would have to put my foot down and say, "No, I am not going to wear the push-up corset and the leather hot pants and hold the whip. Sorry. It's just not *me*." Other times I just didn't have the will or the energy for a face-off with a particularly strong-willed stylist, and I would end up in a photo wearing some dumb, totally inappropri-ate outfit, sometimes with way too much makeup slathered on my small face, overwhelming my delicate features, and with a blank, defeated look in my eyes.

At one photo shoot for a major young women's magazine at the height of my fame, somehow I ended up in pigtails wearing the (male) hairstylist's clingy boxer shorts, and my bass player's star-patterned T-shirt. Overall, a ridiculous ensemble. I had on my own shoes—my trusty, well-worn combat boots, the one lone concession to my original, authentic self.

When the issue with the pigtails-and-men's-underwear photograph in it came out and I opened it and saw myself, I thought then, as I think now, "How the hell did this *happen*? I look like an *idiot*. Who in her right mind could have possibly thought this was a good idea? "

Maybe they were right to want to enhance my appearance. Maybe they were really only trying to help. Besides, in my line of work, *shouldn't* I have been making more of an effort to be more fabulous? Wasn't looking fabulous and sparkly and fierce part of doing my job well?

I was playing on bigger stages, with brighter lights, bigger crowds, and that called for bigger gestures, bigger colors, bigger everything, right? Bigger hair? Heels? Lips? Breasts? At any rate, I needed to, I thought, make some adjustments in order to adapt to my new higher-profile situation. What could I do in order to not be obliterated under the bright lights? Should I go blond? Isn't that part of being a good pop star?

But did I want to be a pop star? Or did I just want to be a working artist, generating a decent, livable income? Hadn't my record label taken me on because they liked what I was doing and believed an audience would, too? Couldn't I continue to be my unglamorous, mousy-haired, low-maintenance self and still keep everybody—the label, the audience, the magazines, MTV, radio—happy?

I decided to have my hair bleached platinum in 1995, around the time of the release of my second album for Atlantic Records. I was surprised at how much the process hurt.

I left the salon after that first bleaching with tender, raw scabs all over my head, under my shining, newly whitish hair. It was horrifying. I felt like a zombie in a sci-fi movie who had been doused with some deadly slow-killing alien scalp-burning disease-virus. Needless to say, I didn't stay blond for long.

What does this have to do with music? That's what I was always asking myself.

25

August 14

Denver

I had been subsisting on peanuts and V8 juice from gas station convenience stores for a couple of days. So when the front desk lady at the Colfax Avenue Ramada told us there was a Whole Foods market just a few blocks away, I smiled and clapped my hands together and said, "Yay."

Immediately after checking in and before even getting our bags out of the van or looking at our rooms, we took off for the Whole Foods. Brian, Tim, and I knew that good, fresh, healthy food was going to be hard to come by from here to the West Coast. The route we were about to take tomorrow, after tonight's gig here in Denver, was a vast, thousand-mile stretch of land and sky (and beef and pork) where few, if any, have ever heard of a "vegan alternative." So I needed to stock up. Otherwise, I feared I might die of starvation before we got to San Francisco.

The Lion's Lair, the night's venue, has a kind of skid row vibe by day. It's not a rock club. It's just a neighborhood bar—in a bad neighborhood—with a jukebox and a small PA set up in a dark corner. Some enterprising young promoter had come up with the idea of booking national acts, which brought in younger people who came in on show nights and mixed with the regulars.

The regulars, a handful of grizzled drunks and dentally challenged drug addicts, were sitting around the bar on bar stools chatting wearily, hunched over their afternoon spirits, when I showed up at about four in the afternoon. I set up and prepared to do my soundcheck in front of them.

When I first approached the microphone to test it, I instinctively touched my electric guitar, which was plugged in to my turned-on amp, to the microphone like I always do. It's a simple way to check if there is any potential shock hazard. When my guitar strings touched the mike, a very strong and evil-sounding *crackle zzzt* accompanied by sparks made me jump back.

With a surliness that comes from having almost been fried to a black char, I said loudly to Tim, and to God, and to whoever else among the winos and bums wanted to listen, "I don't want to die HERE."

And then I thought, "Why am I even here? Don't I ever get to graduate from playing dives in the bad part of town? I didn't know Denver even had a skid row. But here I am. Is this electrical interference God telling me to quit, already? Or is this yet another test of my faith? Do I have to actually *die*—of an electric shock—to prove I'm serious about my work? Do I really want to waste my last precious breath standing on this dirty beer-stained cigarette-burnt floor in front of a handful of smack-addled strangers who couldn't care less about me or my music?"

I flipped my amp's polarity switch and put a gray plastic cushioning adapter on the amp's plug while the bar's hired soundman fetched a windscreen to put over the microphone. He and Tim messed with cords and knobs and things that I don't understand, trying to get rid of the scary crackling sound that was still coming through the PA system.

Finally, after about ten more minutes, it was safe for me to put my mouth on the mike (I like to get right up on it when I sing). I was sufficiently buffered and there were no more jolts of electricity. I would go on, as scheduled, and I would do my show, and I would probably not die.

Later that night, during my set, in a brief pause between my songs, a man sitting in one of the ratty, torn-vinyl booths against the

169

wall a few feet to my left asked me in a slurred voice, "Can I have your autograph?"

He was about fifty, scrawny and unkempt, with long greasy hair, an apparent holdover from the afternoon bar crowd.

I turned and faced him and answered, into the mike, "You want my autograph? Right now?"

"Yeeahh."

"Do you have a pen?"

"Nnno."

"You want my autograph, right now, and you don't have a pen?"

"Yyeh."

"Well, I don't have a pen, either. How about I do it a little later, like when I'm done playing, maybe? Would that be alright?"

"Awright," my new fan answered, seeming to have lost interest in the subject, and he turned away from me, to his beer.

In the middle of "Ride with Me" I became bored and found myself wishing I hadn't started the song. I really wanted to abandon it right then but I didn't think that would be the right thing to do; it might make the audience uncomfortable. So I pushed through it.

As I played and sang, my mind split off from the playing and singing, on a parallel tangent: "This is the last time I'm ever going to play this song. I'm totally sick of it. I am definitely going to retire it after tonight. Can the audience tell that I am bored? Do they care or are they just happy to have me here playing my songs? Well, they should care that I'm bored. They should be angry. They should boo me. They deserve more than this stale, colorless, uninspired version of this song. It really doesn't seem fair to make them suffer through this with me. Even if they don't realize I am sucking right now, that doesn't change the fact that I am sucking. Maybe I should stop the song. Since I'm really not feeling it, quitting might be the most respectable thing to do.

"My other option is to forge ahead and try to find something; some vestige of an energy or a feeling that is authentic and that I can work with, even if that feeling is frustration (I am frustrated because I am not feeling any passion for the song) or desperation (I'm desperate to get to the end of this song so I can stop feeling so bad about not enjoying it) or despondence (I'm despondent because I've lost the love I used to have for this song). Frustration and desperation and despondence are real and the expression of such truths can be a unifying experience for me and my fellow humans—for me and the audience—because we all feel these things. I will use these emotions, which the performance of this song is generating, to give resonance to the remainder of the song. Yeah."

And thus, I rode out "Ride with Me." It actually got better toward the end, as I willed it into something resembling real emotional fervor. Do you remember John Lydon, in that old PiL song, singing, "Anger is an energy"? Well, so is frustration. And I felt some satisfaction at having used it to my advantage.

Sometimes I wish that I, as a perfomer, were a better actor, but I always assume my audience is perceptive enough to know when I am bullshitting them so why should I even try? (If they want to be "entertained," in the traditional sense of the word, they can go to a Madonna concert, or Lenny Kravitz, or David Lee Roth.) It would be so nice to be able to sustain a high level of crazy boundless vibrating rock and roll magic all through every set, but it's very difficult to do every night, after years and years of doing it, week after week, town after town. That's why musicians sometimes use cocaine, and all those other drugs that make them forget that they just don't care anymore. Don't let Lenny Kravitz fool you into believing that he is that excited, that transmogrified into the archetypal rock-and-roll animal, with each and every performance. It's not possible. He must have bad days. He's got to be faking it, onstage, at least some of the time.

My audience at the Lion's Lair seemed to enjoy themselves and to appreciate whatever I had to give to them, even when I was struggling. They didn't demand that I pretend to love every minute of it. They let me be myself and they even applauded me, generously, for it and I was so grateful to them. Because I am incapable of being anything but myself, all the time. I can't bullshit anyone. I wish I could. But I can't.

26

August 15

Denver to Wendover

I took my complimentary copy of *USA Today* from the floor outside my door and made my way down to the lobby of the Ramada to meet the others and to check out. It was 10 a.m. and we wanted to get going in the direction of San Francisco. Our destination: Wendover, Utah, one hundred miles west of Salt Lake City, right on the Nevada border. The next show wasn't until the seventeenth but we wanted to get to the Coast by the next night (the sixteenth) so we could have a whole day free in San Francisco. We would cover about six hundred miles that day, and the same tomorrow.

Our route took us into southern Wyoming. Wyoming was just what one would expect: very stereotypical Western cowboy land. Lots of pickup trucks and horse trailers. And cows, grazing on open land. Lots of cows. My heart swelled as we passed yet another group of these gentle creatures, and I wondered, "How could anyone kill a cow? Cows are beautiful!"

Have you ever gotten up close to one and looked it in the eye? A cow will stare right back at you, without turning or running away, forcing you, somehow, to question the depth and the quality of your own character. In a cow's eyes is some most profound universal intelligence, and calm, and solidity. And truth. It's like staring into the eyes of a Buddha.

Somewhere near the Utah border, traffic came to a full stop for a good half hour. I got out and took pictures of the seemingly infinite line of cars in front of and behind us. There was a reluctant camaraderie in the air, the kind that materializes when a bunch of strangers are starting to resign themselves to being stuck together for an indeterminate amount of time in a common bummer that none of them has any power to rectify or fight against so they may as well make the most of it and be neighborly.

People mingled outside of their vehicles, stretching their legs, chatting. Tim got out of the van to investigate what was causing the delay in movement. He started walking in the direction the traffic would be going if it were moving. Brian and I lost sight of him, among all the cars and people, within seconds.

When cars began to start up and slowly move, Brian got behind the wheel. We picked up Tim about a half mile down the road, near the site of the cause of the problem. It was an old VW bus, completely charred, through and through. The blaze had been extinguished and neither victims nor fire trucks nor ambulances nor policemen nor police cars remained. The scene had been wiped clean but for the burnt black metal shell of the old bus.

I took a picture as we drove past the accident site. It's always worthwhile to have reminders of your mortality on hand; makes you appreciate being alive.

Four kids from my high school class died in our senior year, in car accidents. One of the victims was a girl with whom I'd gone to my first U2 concert a few months earlier. Her name was Dawn. The two of us drank peppermint schnapps in the backseat together on the way to the concert, giggling at how nasty it tasted. Another was a romantic rebel named Lance, who once, in summertime, grabbed a bumblebee from the air and ate it, in a gesture meant to illustrate, I think, his punk rock–ness.

And then there was my mother's younger brother, struck dead by lightning, on a golf course, at the age of sixteen. He would have been my uncle.

Sometimes I think that just to simply be alive, still, at my age is a triumph. If I have nothing else, I have that. I'm still here.

A half an hour later, we saw a tire blow off an old truck on the other side of the highway and fly over the guardrail into the dusty scrub as the truck whizzed by in the other direction.

Brian drove most of the afternoon while Tim did some business on his laptop and I read the *New Yorker* at a leisurely pace. I took over the driving for a couple of hours in the early evening and in those two hours, Brian managed to bore through a big chunk of *The Corrections*. At one point, I looked back and noticed the swift progress he was making in his book and asked, "How many pages have you read today, Brian?"

He looked at the page number and answered, "About a hundred and fifty."

Flabbergasted, I inquired, "Do you speed read? Are you a Speed Reader?"

And he said, "No, I just read fast."

"What? A hundred fifty pages in two hours? It's not possible. You must be shortcutting. You can't possibly have read so many words in so little time while retaining all the information."

"No, I'm reading it. Really. I just read really fast."

"Are you serious? God, I feel stupid. It takes me like a whole week to read a *New Yorker*."

Months later, I caught Brian cheating: He announced one day that he had just finished reading *Infinite Jest*. Reading this book is an almost superhuman feat of endurance, which I myself was proud to have accomplished a few years before. At the time of his announcement, I said to Brian, "Weren't the footnotes hell to get through?"

"Yeah," Brian answered, hesitantly. "Well, actually, I didn't read all of them. I kind of skimmed through them."

"What!" I exclaimed. "You cannot say you've read *Infinite Jest* if you haven't read the footnotes! The footnotes are, like, half the book! No wonder you read so fast! You're not actually reading all the words!"

"Yeah, you're right. I guess I kind of cheated."

I succeeded in guilting Brian into going back and reading all the footnotes—every single one—at which point he was able to proudly and truthfully boast that he had, indeed, read *Infinite Jest*.

As we crossed into Utah, the landscape became greener and more mountainous and quite beautiful. It was like a movie set from a 1950s Technicolor Western. Small groups of elegant brown and black cows lounged around glistening natural pools under canopies of trees' leaves, and brown-purple mountains stood stoically in the background. Sun-bleached wooden fences and gentle late-afternoon sun added to the scene's charm.

The two-lane road began to wind and twist up and down hills as we got closer to Salt Lake City. I was gaining on a white compact car with two women in it. I got in the left lane to pass but as I sped up, the other car sped up, too, on my right, as if challenging me to a race. The road was curvy and potentially dangerous at high speeds so I slowed down and got back behind the white car.

We approached an eighteen-wheeler. The white car moved into the passing lane to pass the slow-moving truck and then I was behind the big rig, but then I got impatient and wanted to pass it, too, so I got in the left lane again, behind the white car. But the white car didn't make any movement to pass the truck; it was just sort of cruising alongside it.

"This is so annoying!" I yelled at Tim, who was next to me in the front. "What does this woman think she is doing?"

I looked over at Tim. He had a slightly amused half-smile on his face.

After a few more minutes, the woman gave it some gas, as if she had just then, finally, noticed that there was someone restless on her tail, and passed the truck and got back in the right lane in front of it, clearing the way for me to pass first the truck and then the white car. As I made this maneuver, Tim got a good look at the driver-perpetrator and her car as we glided by.

He reported, "She's got handicapped plates."

"What kind of handicap keeps you from cruising in the cruising lane and passing in the passing lane?" I shouted. "Why doesn't she just stay in the slow lane?"

And then, like a sinner confessing her sins, I said, earnestly, to whatever god or gods were listening, as if saying so out loud might absolve me of my irascibility and impatience, "I. Am. Such. A bitch."

I have a theory that every time I make a disparaging comment about anyone, someone in the world says or writes something bad about me. It's basically the karma principle. So every bad review I get is my fault. I brought them all on myself. But it's hard, sometimes, to keep my mouth shut, and once in a while I just let it rip—all kinds of criticisms heaped on people I don't even know and on whom I'm in no position to pass judgment, or even have an opinion.

We had planned on eating dinner at some place—perhaps a Cracker Barrel—just off the highway by Salt Lake City, but there really wasn't anything there. We had expected to see a bunch of restaurant signs all bunched together on each of the few SLC exit signs, but we didn't. There were only signs for streets. And then there was kind of instantly nothing, like civilization just stopped, right past the city limits.

"I need food now," I whined. "My blood sugar is plummeting. Help me."

"I know," said Tim, like a parent comforting a child. "There's probably going to be something in ten miles, at exit ninety-nine, the next exit."

West of Salt Lake City the land became completely flat. The lake loomed on the right, vast and creepy-looking in the fading light. Gloomy mountains rose menacingly up out of the water. They appeared black because of the angle of the setting sun's shadows. Crusty salt flats, interspersed with stinky low-tide mud, ran along both sides of the straight, level highway.

People had spelled out various messages with stones on the salty flats, like 3-D rock graffiti, laid out on the ground. The only one I could make out as we zipped by was "God Bless ———." I couldn't see the last part. We were going too fast.

"God bless what?" I asked Brian. "Did you see what that said?"

"I don't know," Brian said. "I couldn't see it. But that one there says 'U2.' And another one back there said, 'Bite Me.'"

"Oh, that's nice. Very nice."

I turned on the radio to try to find National Public Radio.

"Is there NPR in Utah," I asked Tim, "or is NPR a blue state thing so they don't have it?"

Tim answered, "Yeah, you should be able to find it."

I found the end of "Marketplace," which is standard NPR fare, but next, some guy started yammering about faith, and Jesus, and how absolutely impossible it is to beat an addiction without them and how pointless it is to argue otherwise. The Mormons had infiltrated even sensible, secular, unbiased National Public Radio with their Christian self-righteousness.

I switched to AM and on the only audible channel there was a show in progress called "Point of View." A man was talking about AIDS. He was saying that the disease, contrary to popular belief, was lately becoming as prevalent as it was in the initial boom of the 1980s, and that this was an outrage and someone should be held responsible. The radio guy's claim was, basically, that modern-day heathens (homosexuals, bisexuals, drug addicts, whores) were to blame for this recent spike in the infection rate, and that everyone out there should be alarmed and enraged—not that AIDS rates were going up but that there were so many queers and druggies getting away with, literally, murder, and that these immoral barbarians ought to be called out for their plague-spreading and evil-propagating behaviors, and stopped.

"Wait," I thought. "This guy calls himself a Christian, right? What about 'Love thy neighbor'? What about 'Have mercy on the downtrodden' or whatever?"

The radio host went on: "My show last month in which Dr. (so-and-so) enlightened us as to what unsavory practices these homosexuals are indulging in behind closed doors received thousands of letters in response including many threats from gay rights groups."

"Why doesn't he just say it?" I wondered. Really nail his point, which he was chomping at the bit to blurt out: AIDS kills bad people because they are bad people who deserve to get AIDS and die.

I said to Brian, "What a sanctimonious twit! Is this guy for real? Do people like this really exist in the twenty-first century? I mean, come on—'heathens'? Who talks like that? Is he kidding?"

Right before I turned the radio off the host said, self-congratulatorily, "I recently received a letter from a nice woman who wrote, 'That show was the most disgusting thing I've ever heard. Thank you so much for running it,'" at which point Brian and I burst out laughing.

But in the back of my mind, I knew that my criticisms of the radio host were just as biased and self-righteous as his criticisms of homosexuals and drug addicts, and as I ridiculed him I knew that someone out there was, right this very moment, putting me down or composing a negative review about me and when it was published, and I read the names they were calling me, I would remember writing that fundamentalist radio host off as a "sanctimonious twit" and a "Jesus freak."

"God," I thought." I gotta get out of this van. There's nothing to do but think, in here. I'm thinking too much."

At exit 99, the only exit for miles in either direction, there was a truck stop with a restaurant. It seemed like it was our last chance for food, so we stopped.

After dinner I took the wheel for the hundred-mile home stretch to Wendover. We were heading west into the sunset and the glare off the flat lake was blinding if you looked straight at it. The mountains were turning purpler as darkness fell and pink tufts of clouds wafted around the mountains' peaks. I turned the van lights on.

The road was still unwaveringly flat and straight, with a line of yellow headlights coming at us on the left for miles. A cluster of billboards and neon loomed just ahead.

"That must be Wendover, already," said Brian.

It looked as if the town was right there just up the road a half mile or so but the next sign said, "Wendover, 9 miles."

That's what the straight flat road does; it makes faraway things seem close. And seventy-five miles per hour feels like nothing. Feels like you're barely moving.

We exited at Wendover and drove about half a mile, to our Days Inn, and stopped. Tim went to check us in. I stepped down and out of the van and the night air was hot and dry.

"Bendover! We made it!" I said to Brian, who smiled.

My room was clammy so I turned on the air conditioner. The blowing air was loud, puffing out the curtain above it, but not loud enough to drown out the sound of a lone dog barking forlornly somewhere out there in the night. I pushed back the curtain and looked out the window facing behind the hotel. A lonely mountain rose up, dry and rocky, about a hundred yards away.

I wrote twenty pages in my journal and turned out the lights at about three. The dog was still barking intermittently. It sounded sad and lonely. I put in my earplugs, swallowed half a sleeping pill, and dreamed of dogs and wind and a dark gloomy sea.

27

Jeff Buckley

I met Jeff Buckley when I was living in New York City in the mid-1990s. I bumped into him at a crowded Chris Whitley show at a small club called Brownie's in the East Village. A man whom I was talking to at the time, and who worked at Whitley and Buckley's record label (Columbia), introduced me and Jeff. I was excited, to say the least, to meet him; I had just recently discovered his newly released *Grace* album, and was in the process of falling madly in love with it.

After the show, Jeff and I were ushered backstage to say hi to Chris, and a photographer lined the three of us up shoulder to shoulder and snapped a few shots. A month or so later, I opened up *Rolling Stone* magazine and saw one of these photographs in the "Random Notes" section, but minus me. I had been cropped out of the photo, whose caption read something like "Chris Whitley and Jeff Buckley after Whitley's recent concert at Brownie's." The two were labelmates at Columbia and they were both perceived to be on their way up, so maybe, I figured, it made sense for me to be cropped out; maybe I didn't fit in conceptually, since I had already experienced my moment in the spotlight with my last album, *Become What You Are*.

Could it be that people already sensed that I was on my way out? Atlantic would soon release my second album for them, *Only Everything*, but there were no guarantees it would do as well or even half as well as the last one, which had been my best-selling piece of work so far. The fact that I was, perhaps, old news already, if only in other people's eyes, rattled me when I thought about it.

Just before *Only Everything* came out a few months later, Jeff's manager contacted mine, presenting him with the idea of Jeff and me teaming up: "Would Juliana be into having Jeff support her—be her opening act—on a couple of weeks on her upcoming North American tour?"

I didn't have to think about it for even half a second. Yes! I responded. Ohmygod Yes! Jeff, whom I had gotten to know a little bit during the past few months in New York since we had met, was not only frighteningly, supernaturally talented but beautiful, smart, compassionate, and hilarious (his impersonations of other well-known singers were spot-on and always had observers in stitches). And his album was starting to catch on with people, and with MTV (his "Last Goodbye" video had just been chosen as a buzz clip) and with radio, so it was clear that his presence on my tour would bring in a whole bunch of people—the swelling ranks of ravenous Jeff Buckley fans—to my shows. I could try to win them over and get them to be my fans, to buy my records.

But the thing that excited me most about the upcoming tour was the fact that I was going to get to spend every day for two weeks hanging out with Jeff, and every night watching him play.

I couldn't fathom how I had fallen into such good fortune. Jeff's *Grace* was currently my absolute favorite album. I was a little obsessed with it, in fact, as one tends to be obsessed with any new love. Why had I been chosen, when I'm sure he would have been welcomed on almost anyone's tour? I didn't want to jinx it by questioning it too much. I just wanted to enjoy it.

I did ask Jeff many months later, when the tour was just a memory, "Why me, Jeff? Why did you want to tour with me, of all people?"

Jeff answered, "You seemed nice."

That wasn't a satisfying answer, nor did it seem entirely truthful—there just had to be more to it than that. (Jeff and his handlers must have had business or strategic reasons.) But again, I didn't want to question it too much. Maybe I had simply gotten lucky. Again. Really lucky, like with my record and publishing deals and being invited to tour with Paul Westerberg. It didn't make sense, maybe, but it happened and I savored every minute of the tour and every minute of every one of Jeff's wonderful, transcendent, life-affirming performances. It was like being in heaven, watching him play, like he was an angel sent by God to comfort us—the audience—and to give us strength, and hope. Jeff had a way of drawing everyone in the crowd in to his world, and raising them up with the spirit in his music, each night—not just playing to them, or performing for them—but involving them so that it felt, for everyone, like a kind of holy communion, like a collective two-hour rapture, shared by all, but intimate, too.

Jeff and I played the Roseland Ballroom in New York City. Headlining Roseland was a big deal (literally big—it holds more than three thousand). But I knew that this gig was only partly about me. Technically, I was "headlining"—my name was at the top of the bill, and I would close the show—but the night was as much, if not more, about Jeff, whose album sales and renown were starting to explode.

Besides, all the buzz that had surrounded me during my last, biggest-selling album, hadn't even really been about "me" in terms of my music or my talent or my personality, as the buzz around Jeff was about his amazing talent and winning personality. It was mostly hype. People took notice of me because girls with guitars who wrote their own music—and alternative rock in general—were being lavished with an inordinate amount of media attention. I was by chance part of a legitimate cultural trend: Liz Phair, PJ Harvey, Veruca Salt, L7, Babes in Toyland, Belly, Hole, Luscious Jackson, me, et cetera.

But Jeff Buckley was a star. It was exciting to be near him. He had undeniable charisma and charm and he was authentically, indisputably gifted with a talent that was so big and so universally recognizable that it must have been a sort of a burden to carry around. It was a blessing and a curse. Girls would scream when he walked onstage. Almost everyone who came into contact with him fell in love with him.

When we played Roseland together, just before Jeff was scheduled to go on I peeked my head out from the top of the stairway that led down to the dressing rooms to gauge the scene out front. The house was full and vibrating with palpable anticipation of Jeff's arrival on the big, now dark stage. I noticed some commotion up in the mezzanine balcony. Voices around me were buzzing and chattering with excitement and stretching their necks to try to get a good look up at the spot. My tour manager, on his way from the house back to the dressing room, said to me as he passed, "Paul McCartney is here." And he had just been ushered to a seat in the front of the balcony, with a good view of the stage.

Jeff took the stage in his sparkly gold-threaded rock star jacket, the one he was wearing on the cover of his album. Most shows, he wore a T-shirt or a button-down flannel. But like I said, Roseland was a big deal. And a Beatle in the audience was a really big deal, and Jeff had put on his special jacket.

After Jeff's set, the backstage's main, open area was electrified by energy. Someone had sent word that "McCartney's coming backstage" to meet Jeff, and people were getting ready to welcome his royal rock highness.

I never saw the man. I was in my own dressing room with the door closed. I didn't want to get in the way. It was Jeff's moment. I knew there would already be a rush of people vying for McCartney's attention, and if I stayed in my private room I would be one less person gawking at the Beatle.

After McCartney had gone, my bass player, who had observed the whole thing from up close, gave me the play-by-play: Sir Paul had come down directly following Jeff's set, with a small entourage, and been introduced to Jeff, shaken his hand. He'd congratulated Jeff on a great show and a great album and complimented him on his prodigious talent. And then, the story goes, McCartney said good-bye and left the building.

I went on half an hour later.

28

August 16

Wendover to San Francisco

I woke up early. Too early. I tried to fall back asleep but couldn't, so I lay there for a while, ruminating on the fact that I had gone to sleep at three and woken up at six. And that I would probably feel like hell all day because of it.

At about 7:30 I got out of bed and fixed myself my usual breakfast of a Clif Bar (I always have a stash) and a cup of tea, which I make by putting a tea bag in the plastic filter of the Mr. Coffee coffeemaker (every hotel room has one) and running bottled water through it to heat it.

After breakfast I watched some CNN and read my complimentary copy of *USA Today*, which was waiting for me on the floor outside my door, and then I got myself together and packed up my stuff and waited for my ten o'clock interview to call. We were scheduled to hit the road to San Francisco directly after my conversation with Jon, a journalist in Kansas who was putting together a preview of my upcoming show there for his local paper.

At 10:10 the phone had not rung so I called my publicist in

Boston, Melinda, who had arranged the interview with Jon, to see if she knew what was causing the delay. She said she would find out.

At 10:20 I hadn't heard back from Melinda or Jon and I was getting restless and bored waiting around with nothing happening, so I called Melinda again. She told me that she had spoken to Jon and that he had been ready and prepared to interview me right on time at ten and had tried to call me repeatedly, but the calls apparently weren't getting through, and neither were Melinda's subsequent calls to me.

"I don't know why the calls aren't getting through," she said. "but if you'll hold on and wait another minute, I'll call Jon back and get him to try you again right now, when I hang up."

"Okay," I said.

I hung up and waited. At 10:30 I gathered up my bags and guitars and brought them out to the van. The interview was supposed to have been completed by now. Ten-thirty was the scheduled departure time and so in my mind we had to leave, now.

Leaving at a certain time in the morning and driving for a certain number of hours and arriving at a certain time at our destination, and then getting up and doing it all again the next day and the next day, is the routine. The routine keeps me relatively calm and helps reassure me that the world will not disintegrate around me or fall on top of me, out here. Now chaos was threatening to bust in, and I could not allow that to happen.

Tim and Brian were sitting casually in the van with the doors open. They were all packed up and ready to go, and probably, I thought, thinking that my interview would be done by now. Tim was finishing up a conversation on his cell phone. I heard him say, "Okay. Bye." I threw my stuff in the back of the van and said to Tim, "I couldn't do my interview."

"I know," Tim said. "That was Melinda I was just talking to. She says the guy keeps trying to call you but his calls aren't getting through. But he still wants to do it and you can do the interview now, on my cell phone. Melinda gave me his number. Here, I'll get him on the line for you."

"No. Forget it. I don't want you guys to have to wait while I do a boring interview. Look—you're all ready to leave. And there's probably no cell service out here anyway. We're in the middle of nowhere. And now I'm in a bad mood and I won't be nice to the guy and I'll probably come across as a bitch and then he'll write that I'm a bitch. I don't want to do it. Fuck it."

That about sums up my MO: Take a mildly annoying situation, set up camp right in the middle of it, and stew in it for as long as possible, and make it worse, rather than even entertain contemplating a way out.

My tour bus was once stopped and searched on the way into Canada in the early 1990s. My tour manager at the time, a guy named Brad, had decided, right before the border crossing, to try lying to the Customs officials and saying that we had no tour merchandise that we would be selling at the shows in Canada so that we could avoid paying the high tariff on them. Canadian Customs guys are no suckers ("An American band coming, in a big tour bus, to play a bunch of concerts in Canada, without merchandise to hawk at the gigs? I don't think so. They are hiding something," they must have thought, rightly) and so they of course pulled our bus over and began an extremely thorough search. They looked through all of our luggage, under the bunk mattresses, and down in the cargo hold. They even opened a loaf of bread and looked between the slices.

Needless to say, they found the contraband (in the cargo hold)—a few big cardboard boxes full of Juliana Hatfield tour T-shirts. We sat at the border station for three hours as this black mark was entered into my records and the duty was added up, in addition to the punitive fine, all of which involved pages and pages of paperwork and official bureaucratic stamps and markings and enterings into databases.

Bored almost to unconsciousness of sitting around in the sterile, harshly lit holding room, me and my crew had been instructed not to leave, pissed off at Brad for making me suffer the punishment of his stupid lie, and annoyed at the length of time it was taking to wrap it all up ("Just give us a ticket or something, already!" I thought. "Arrest me! Bring me to the torture chamber. Something!"), I took my disposable camera out of my backpack. There was one frame left. I snapped it randomly, without looking through the eyehole—it was a shot of nothing—and then threw the camera into the trash can next to me.

Even now, years later, the Dada aspect of the whole thing does have

At the piano

Voted "Most Individual" in the Class of 1985, Duxbury High School

MOST INDIVIDUAL
J. Hatfield, Jim Maguire

Berklee College of Music student ID

Soundchecking with my high school cover band

Blake Babies with Evan Dando in the late eighties.

Blake Babies

Lounging poolside with friends at the Phoenix Hotel, San Francisco, in the early nineties

*On stage at Tipitina's in New Orleans with Bob Weston (bass) and
Paul Trudeau (drums) during the* Hey Babe *tour*

*On stage with Dean
Fisher during the* Become
What You Are *tour*

Recording Only Everything *at Fort Apache. Left to right: me, Paul Kolderie, Gary Smith, Sean Slade. (This photo is kind of dirty from being on my mom's fridge.)*

Heidi and I with fruit in our bras backstage in Chicago

With Heidi and Freda backstage in Seattle

"Some Girls featuring Juliana Hatfield" in Tucson

Some Girls

An acoustic show at the Wyndham (a recording studio, concert hall, and former hotel) in Bellows Falls, Vermont

On stage with Ed Valauskas in 2005

On stage with Exene Cervenka and John Doe of X
during the Made in China *tour*

a certain logic: Buy a disposable camera, shoot all the pictures, and then throw it away. It is a disposable camera, after all.

Besides, the gesture seemed to make a kind of sense at that moment. Not only had Brad made a serious error of judgment, in my name, but now the border guards had me in their custody and didn't have to let me go until they felt like it. The rage brought on by my impotence and inability to remedy the situation found expression in the obliteration of my undeveloped photos.

That same kind of crazed frustration was now making me want to throw in the towel on this interview, even though it could still quite easily be salvaged. When I did get him on the phone, Jon was very understanding and easy to talk to and when it was over Tim and Brian and I hightailed it out of Wendover and Utah and into Nevada.

Later in the day we passed through Reno, a dirty gray nowhere seemingly devoid of any charm whatsoever. It looked like a city that had been built, and existed, solely for the purpose of commerce. Not for living. Casinos and quickie-divorce places and faux-Western, olde-timey saloons were just about all Reno had to offer to the visitor passing through. Nature—like the dry gray-brown mountains that rose up forlornly through the smog in the distance—seemed all but forgotten.

"Why would anyone live here on purpose?" I asked the boys as we pulled out of a gas station on the outskirts of town.

"I don't know," said Brian. "Gambling?"

"I think we have all been spoiled growing up in New England, you guys. God, it's so much nicer there than here." (Brian was originally from Vermont, Tim from Maine.)

I looked out the window at the rows of identical tract houses built into the barren, razed hills along the route out of Reno, and thought, "So much of who we are has to do with where we come from and what we are born into. To the people that have lived all their lives here, this is normal."

Coming into California, suddenly everything was greener. The dry brown of Nevada had been replaced by dense pine growth. The road became more mountainous and snaky, winding more steeply and frighteningly the closer we got to the town of Truckee.

I leaned left from my passenger seat perch and had a look at the speedometer.

"Hey, Tim," I said, nervously clutching the sides of my seat. "The speed limit is fifty-five here. Are you sure you want to be going seventy? You don't want to get a ticket, do you?"

Tim eased up on the gas and remarked, as a Greyhound bus sped by in the other direction, "That must be hell being a bus driver doing the route from Truckee to Reno. They must see all manner of carnage."

I said, "Yeah," and chuckled, thinking he meant, like, the carnage of newly love-struck couples who barely know each other going to get quickie marriages at three in the morning.

Then Tim said, "This road is pretty hairy. There's probably a lot of accidents. It must be pretty tricky to maneuver all these turns if you get going too fast."

"Oh. Yeah. It's scary. I was scared. Thanks for slowing down."

When I was a child in the seventies, no one wore seat belts. No one that I knew, anyway. And there were no child car seat requirements, at least according to my mother. She claims that when I was a baby, she would lay me on the front seat next to her when she went out driving. If I fell to the floor at a sudden stop, well, babies were soft and hard to break, and Mom would let me roll around on the passenger side floor awhile, until she could reach down and place me back on the seat.

And only professional bicycle racers wore bike helmets. And drinking and driving didn't seem to even be an issue. Parents' approach to child-rearing was so laissez-faire, especially compared to today, that it's a miracle any of us survived.

Here's one of my memories, from when I was about nine years old: One night after dinner out with my family, Dad, who always ordered at least one martini before dinner and then wine with the meal, decided it would be fun on the drive home to make the car swerve back and forth by cutting the steering wheel fast from side to side. I was in the way back of the little Datsun station wagon. Mom was up front next to Dad, and my two brothers were in the middle seat. I was getting the most centrifugal action, since I was in the back, in the snake tail, being whipped back and forth. Dad was whooping and having a grand old time. I was scared and kept yelling, "Dad! Stop! Come on! Stop it! It's not funny! Mom! Make him stop!" My brothers were laughing. I couldn't really gauge how Mom, up front, felt about the whole car-swerving thing—I was too busy trying to find something to hold on to while sliding around in the back. Finally the driver's side of the back end of the Datsun banged into a tree on the left side of the road—which meant that we were way over on the wrong side of the road—and Mom yelped, "Phil!" The little bang-up wasn't enough to disable the car or to hurt anyone, but enough to put an end to Dad's fun. He drove normally the rest of the way home, with a dent in the back left side of the car. And I grew up to be a nervous passenger.

On the first cross-country Blake Babies tour I even refused to let anyone else drive the van for the whole month we were on the road. There were a few twelve- and thirteen-hour hauls (and one stretching to sixteen hours) during which I almost succumbed to the constant fatigue, hallucinating animals of all kinds darting out in front of the van, slapping myself hard in the face to stay awake. John and Freda couldn't understand why I wouldn't ever take a break and let one of them drive once in a while. I kind of lost my mind; I became convinced that the van was possessed by the devil and that if I let anyone else get behind the wheel, the van would overpower the driver and turn itself toward the guardrail and off the road or over a cliff and kill us all. The van lurched on its own sometimes when I was driving, as if someone—someone invisible—was pressing on the gas pedal, causing the gas to surge. Touching the brakes usually stopped it but, still, this strange phenomenon only reinforced my belief that the old Chevy was possessed by a malevolent spirit. I was strong, and I was the only one who could protect us. I needed to get John and Freda home alive. It was a battle between good (me) and evil (the van). It was like a horror movie.

When we were almost home, after having traveled all around the whole country, the nightmare ended. Following our gig in New York City, I drove us to the Kiev restaurant in the East Village, where John and Freda and I and a couple of our friends were going to have a late-night snack before we drove back to Boston. I parked, and when I took the key out, the van sputtered and shuddered repeatedly, the whole thing convulsing, as if in the throes of death, and then, in fact, it expired. We'd made it all around the country and then the van finally conked out for good in front of the Kiev.

We went inside and ate while our friend Metcalf, who had accompanied us to the restaurant, called one of his friends who was in a band in Hoboken, and had a van, and arranged for us to borrow it to get back to Boston for our show there the following night. John and Freda and Metcalf and I ended up sleeping for a few hours in our dead van while Metcalf's friend with the working van rounded up his band, who then met at their rehearsal space to load all of their gear out of the back so that there would be room for our Blake Babies gear. By the time Metcalf's friend's van came around to get us, it was morning. We transferred all of our equipment and luggage and tapes from our van to the other, and then we took off for Boston. I abandoned my Chevy outside of the Kiev and never looked back. I was glad to be free of it. It wasn't worth anything, anyway. I'd bought it for about a thousand dollars, back before I'd run it hard around the country.

The gas-surge thing was probably just a hose or something in the engine that needed to be fixed a long time ago. But none of us in the band knew anything about cars or engines or hoses—we all thought that getting an oil change meant telling the gas station attendant to put in a quart of oil. As a result, we never got an oil change the whole time we had the van. And it was an old van, and probably could've used an oil change, and a new hose or two once in a while. In the end, I killed that van; it didn't kill us, as I feared the whole time that it would.

I worry too much. Maybe my mother had it right: her babies could fall off the front seat and roll around a bit on the floor of her moving vehicle, and they'd be fine.

We stopped for dinner at a roadside Mexican restaurant in the town of Truckee. When we sat down, Brian said, "I like Truckee. I spent a few months here once."

"You did?" I said.

"Yeah. Every single person I met here grew pot."

"It is kind of a hippie Mecca, isn't it?"

"Yeah. I think I might move here."

"Really?"

"Yeah. I've thought about it a lot."

"That would be cool. Yeah, I can see you here. It would suit you."

Tim ordered the chimichanga, whatever that is. I got the chile relleno/cheese enchilada combo (scraped off the breading, squeezed out the cheese, ate just the chile and the tortilla). Brian had a small salad and a small cup of tortilla soup. And a margarita.

"That's all you're having?" I asked him.

"Everything I eat lately makes my stomach swell up. I think I might have become allergic to some food, like maybe dairy? So I'm trying to just not eat much at all."

I said, "That sounds like a sensible plan."

"Are you making fun of me?"

"No! I'm completely serious. It makes sense. If food is making you feel bad, by all means stop eating it. Why wouldn't you?"

Brian took a sip of his margarita.

"I don't know if your plan will work if you drink a lot of booze, though," I added.

"Shut up," Brian said.

Near Sacramento, Brian started talking about his stomach again. He restated his simple strategy for healing gastrointestinal upset: "Put the fork down. That's the concept. That's all I have to do to fix my stomach. Just put the fork down. It works for losing weight, too."

I said, "Yeah, I like that. That's another way of saying, 'Close the door in your brain.' That's how I think of it. When I quit smoking I just visualized closing the door to smoking in my head and then I threw away the key and just didn't ever open the door again. It's *so* simple."

"It's not that easy for some people, though." The conversation suddenly took a turn here, and became more like an argument.

"Well, I know, but, I didn't say it was easy. I said it was simple. I mean, it's a simple concept. You just have to decide to do it and then stick to it. And when people fail—to quit smoking or lose weight or quit drugs or alcohol, or whatever—they are simply not trying hard enough to stick to the plan."

"That's cruel."

"That's cool?"

"No, that's cruel. To say that people aren't trying hard enough."

"No, it's not cruel. It's true. You said it yourself, Brian: 'Just put the fork down.' PUT THE FORK DOWN."

"But it's harder for some people."

"I know. I know it's hard. But even if you fail you have to keep trying until you get it done. You have to be really strong, and committed, sure. You just do."

"So," Brian said. "You're saying that Miles is a bad person? Because he had a drug problem?"

Miles was a mutual friend who'd had, over the years, an ongoing problem with cocaine.

"What? *No!* That's not what I'm saying at all! People aren't bad, they're just weak, sometimes, is all I'm saying. And it feels really bad to feel really weak. Or at least it should feel bad. My feeling is that it's okay to be addicted to a drug or alcohol or ice cream or whatever, as long as you feel shitty about it. You know? Denial can only last so long before the truth of what you are doing to yourself starts to become clear. And if you don't eventually develop some sense of shame about it—about your continual gluttonous, destructive behavior—then I can't sympathize with you. Because you're a nihilist. Not that there's anything wrong with being a nihilist. And if you do happen to be a nihilist then you don't want or need anyone's sympathy anyway. Wait. Didn't Miles quit cocaine, finally, recently?"

"Yes."

"Well, there. You just made my point for me. It took Miles a while, but he did it, is my point. People get addicted to stuff all the time and people quit all the time. Or lose weight or whatever. That's all I'm saying. That it is possible. There's proof of it all over the place. Why are you arguing with me, Brian? You started it with your 'Put the fork down.' What about that? Now you're saying it's not true and that people are just helplessly, hopelessly fucked up? Are you trying to justify your inevitable failure or something? Like in case you can't keep up the 'Put the fork down' thing? Don't you have any faith in yourself? In anybody? Well, I believe people can change. People can fix their problems, if they put some work and time and dedication into it."

And then, just like that, the discussion simply ended. It ran out of gas. Remnants of the conversation lingered in the air in the van and then dissipated as we drove closer to San Francisco.

We crossed the Bay Bridge into San Francisco at about eight-thirty at night. I don't like being on that bridge. It makes me nervous. It's very long, and it takes forever to cross it. I had made sure to plan, well in advance of this day, on leaving our last hotel just late enough so that we wouldn't get stuck in traffic on the bridge at rush hour, in case someone tried to blow it up or fly a plane into it. Or what if there was an earthquake?

Freda and Heidi were at the Phoenix Hotel when we arrived. They had flown in that afternoon from Indianapolis and now the family—our musical family—was back together.

I went to bed early. The bar down off the hotel courtyard was pounding out an earsplittingly irritating techno beat which a large number of partying Friday night people were shouting over, so I had no choice but to swallow a whole sleeping pill. Had I not, I would have lain in bed all night and into the dawn cursing my lot in life. And that wouldn't have been cool. Because my life is good. And besides, God gave us sleeping pills for nights like these.

But this was the third night in a row I had taken all or part of a pill. I had to start being careful.

29

August 17

San Francisco

I spent the morning making my old brown corduroy Levi's, handed down from one of my brothers in adolescence and which had never fit right, into a skirt, with a needle and thread from the complimentary sewing kit in the hotel bathroom and scissors borrowed from the front desk. At around noon, satisfied with the results of my pants-to-skirt project, I went for a walk. I headed toward the downtown shopping district and ended up at Macy's.

I was trying on a pair of pants in the dressing room when I stepped on something wet. I looked down and saw a dark spot on the carpeting. I stood on one leg, lifted my other, damp, foot, and smelled my sock. Dog piss. Unmistakably. Somebody must have brought her little lapdog into the changing room with her, whereupon it peed.

"Goddammit," I thought.

On the walk back to my hotel, I picked up an iced tea from a Starbucks. The tea was bitterly strong. Halfway through it I dumped the rest in a trash barrel.

"God, I'm tense," I thought.

Back in my hotel room, I laid my new purchases on the bed and surveyed the booty, all three hundred dollars' worth: a pink corduroy jacket, a pair of white jeans, a brown hippie-ish tunic, a blue midriff-baring Label Whore top, a necklace with a delicate silver disk charm on a chain, a tiny watch on a thin black leather band. I felt dirty, and kind of nauseous, as I always do after bingeing on trifles. But I consoled myself with the fact that at least it was all tax deductible. Since I planned on wearing it all onstage, it could be written off as "stagewear" or "costumes" for my work as a performer.

I took all the rest of my clothes out of my traveling bag and put them next to my new stuff on the bed. I began trying things on, attempting to figure out what to wear at the show later.

Tim's friend Andrew Squire, a local photographer, was going to be coming with a camera to shoot some live photos of the band and I wanted to look good.

As a female performer who wants to put on a good show, but who also has body image issues as well as a strong desire to guard her personal integrity, I am always torn between wanting to show off my body and wanting to cover it up completely. Usually the latter inclination wins out. So there is practically no visual record of all the hours I have put in, over the years, at the gym, or of my ascetic's diet. So tonight I wanted to use this opportunity (Tim's photographer friend) to capture my form on film, for posterity, just so there was some proof, later in life, that I looked pretty good once. And that meant I would need to wear something that would show off my figure.

I tried on approximately ten different outfits and finally settled on something I thought would serve my purposes: my new sporty/sexy navy blue Label Whore shirt. It was somewhat form-hugging yet not vulgarly revealing or too tight. It was long-sleeved with a crew neck, so there was absolutely no chance of there being any visible cleavage, but it fit snugly around my torso just an inch or so below the bottom of my breasts so you could see a few of my lower ribs, my waist, my belly button, and the top curve of my hips.

When it was time to go to the club for our soundcheck, my hotel room looked as if a tornado had torn through it, leaving clothes scattered everywhere. Shirts and pants and shoes and bras and skirts covered almost every surface—the floor, the bed, the desk, the chair.

After we had gotten in the van, Freda pulled *Swann's Way* out of her bag and handed it to me. "Here," she said. "You can have this back. I'm done with it."

I said, "Oh, yeah. Did you read it?"

"I tried, but you were right; it's so boring. I couldn't finish it. I gave up halfway through."

"I told you."

"You were so right."

Looking at the book in my hands, I said, "I don't want it either. I have no use for it. Are you sure you don't want to keep it? And try to finish it?"

"No!"

"I'll leave it in the hotel. Maybe the maid will want to read it."

During the course of the drive to the club, Freda and Heidi and I discovered that we were all premenstrual and expecting our periods to hit at around the same date a few days from then.

"We are gonna be so punk rock tonight, you guys," I said, addressing Freda and Heidi. "Cause we're all PMS-ing. No one better fuck with us, man."

Freda said, smiling, "When I left home today to come here and Jake dropped me off at the airport, he told me, 'It would be great if you would leave like this every month when you are premenstrual.'"

"Oh, your husband is so sweet!"

Freda laughed. "Yeah, I know."

Tim, curious, inquired of any or all of us, "What does PMS feel like?"

"Oh, it's horrible," I said, eager to explain. "It's like, nothing feels good. Nothing feels right. You're depressed and cranky and on edge but you don't know why. Your boobs hurt like crazy and they're all swollen and tender and achy. And then, when you finally get your period, there's this indescribable piercing pain spread all throughout your lower abdomen that doesn't go away all day. And you feel huge, like your skin doesn't fit right or feel right. And you're itchy. Your face itches. At least mine does. And every little thing and everyone irritates the hell out of you and you want to scream and cry and you can't get comfortable and you don't want anyone to touch you. And then, on top of all that, there's this blood and mucus streaming out of you, down there, twenty-four hours a day."

Tim didn't say anything. He appeared to be silently contemplating the wave of information with which he'd just been assaulted.

"And did I mention the mucus?" I added. "Everyone always talks about menstrual blood but you never hear about the menstrual mucus. It's not just liquid, you know, coming out—there's chunks, too. And goo. We're shedding the uterine wall. Uterine tissue."

"Aww, I don't need to know that," Tim moaned, breaking his silence.

"Hey, you asked," I said, smiling. "I'm just telling you. What we go through every month."

Poor Tim. He probably thought that going on tour with three hot rock chicks was going to be like a Mötley Crüe video, but the reality was much less fantasylike. We all got PMS. And Tim got to hear about it.

Once we had loaded into the club, Brian set up the merchandise while I changed the strings on my SG and Tim got familiar with the PA. Freda unpacked her drum kit and started putting the pieces together while Heidi went off to make a phone call. As I snipped my low E string with my wire cutters, Brian approached me and asked, "What time do you think I should be back at the club to start selling merch, after dinner?"

I answered, "I'm not sure. Use your own judgment, maybe," confused as to why this question would come up now, when the tour was half over.

Brian walked away but came back a bit later and asked me the same question, in a slightly altered form. Again, I didn't quite have an answer. I tried a different, more philosophical, approach: "Well, I have known merch guys who made sure to be there selling right when doors opened and I have known merch guys who were more casual about it."

The truth was, Brian's role was not clearly defined. Even his salary had turned out to be elastic. I'd hired him to come along and "sell T-shirts and CDs" but I had never laid out the exact, specific parameters of the job. I had assumed Brian would kind of wing it; play it by ear; learn by doing. How hard could it be, right? Tim, who had more experience dealing with merch guys and the details of their job than I did, would help Brian out if he had any questions. Tim was in charge of the boring details of the tour and he should be the one my crew turned to for boring job-related and logistical inquiries. Not me. I

197

didn't want to have to act like Brian's boss. I was his friend and I wanted it to stay that way. I didn't want to tell him what to do.

Besides, I didn't really know what to tell him. And I wanted him to stop asking me. But he kept pushing, nudging, pressing me for stricter guidelines pertaining to the exact nature of the number of minutes he should be on the clock, and I continued not having the sure answer. The only reason I could think of to explain Brian's sudden concern about his job was that Tim had said something to him about it. Brian is a pretty laid-back guy. Tim is not. Tim's a perfectionist and very detail-oriented. Maybe Tim wanted Brian to be more conscientious (maybe Brian's math was sloppy, for example, which would make Tim's job doing the overall accounting of everything more difficult) and had told him so.

"But when do you think I should start?" I couldn't believe Brian was asking again. This was about the fourth go-round. I felt my pulse speeding up with each repetition of Brian's needling, unanswerable question and I finally could not stand the subject anymore. I blurted, "You keep asking me the same question over and over, Brian! I keep telling you I don't know! Can't you just use your own judgment? How have you been doing it on the rest of the tour up until now? Do that!"

That silenced him.

After soundcheck, Brian walked sullenly out, off, away from the club. Tim called Heidi and Freda and me a cab to take us back to the hotel for a couple of hours of rest before the show. Before leaving I asked Tim, who was going to stay at the club and tweak some knobs (and maybe get to know the house soundgirl, who was kind of cute), "Tim, Brian keeps asking me when he should be here selling merch. I don't know what to tell him. And I don't know why he's asking me this now. He's been doing fine, right? I mean, I feel like as long as he's there at his table at some point after doors open, people that want stuff can buy it. They don't have to have it right when doors open, do they? But then again, if he isn't there and the doors open, all the stuff is sitting there behind the table in boxes, and someone could easily steal something. Shit, I don't know. What do you think? When, exactly, should a merch guy be at the merch table to start work?"

Tim said, without hesitation, "I think the merch guy ought to be there selling stuff as soon as there are people in the club."

I began to understand what was happening: There was some sort of power struggle going on, covertly, between Tim and Brian. I'd had inklings that Tim and Brian were starting to get on each other's nerves; they were so different. Tim must have pulled rank and told Brian to quit slacking off and be set up to work right when doors opened and Brian was now appealing to a higher authority: me.

The question of rank was an interesting one. Was Tim, by virtue of his being the tour manager, authorized to tell Brian, the merch guy, what to do; what he, Tim, thought Brian should do? Or should Tim come to me to ask for permission to lay a particular directive on Brian? Had I granted Tim, when I hired him as the tour manager, the authority to tell all the people on the crew what he thought they should do? What if what Tim thought Brian should do wasn't what I thought he should do?

If I had had an opinion on the subject at hand—when Brian should start selling—I would have cared more about all this stuff. As it was, I was relieved to finally have a solution to the problem that I had been unable to solve myself. Tim had suggested an actual definitive no-nonsense answer with clear-cut boundaries, that I could present to Brian: He should be ready to work as soon as the doors opened.

"Aah, yes," I thought. "That makes so much sense! Duh. Why didn't I think of that? Oh, Brian will be so relieved to have his question answered at last!"

I could hardly wait to give him the good news.

But Brian was off eating dinner somewhere by himself, and the girls and I were heading back to the hotel for a bit of preshow chilling out, so Tim would be the one to break the news to Brian. Unless he already had. In which case my concurring would probably seem to Brian like Tim and I were in cahoots, ganging up against him. Which was not what was happening. As far as I was concerned, Brian had asked me a simple question and now I had a simple answer. Period. Done. Problem solved. I wasn't going to be drawn into whatever, if any, passive-aggressive drama was going on between Tim and Brian.

Later, as the opening act played downstairs in the main room, Brian came up into the dressing room, which was in a little apartment above the club, to freshen his drink with more vodka from the bottle of Stoli the promoter had provided for us. Brian seemed half in the bag already, at this relatively early hour. It was only ten o'clock and we weren't scheduled to go on until eleven-thirty.

I didn't like the fact that Brian seemed to be well on his way to getting drunk while working, but I didn't say anything. I wanted to give Brian the benefit of the doubt and withhold judgment and wait to see what, if anything, happened. But when Tim came into the room and freshened his drink, I wondered, "What the hell. Is everyone getting drunk on the job tonight?"

I meant, of course, is everyone who has real work to do getting drunk. Because if the band decided to get drunk, I would have no problem with that. The band is allowed to get drunk. In fact, the band is always implicitly encouraged to do so. Being a little, if not a lot, drunk helps. Alcohol loosens us up. The music isn't complicated or fussy enough to suffer from a little unbuttoning of the collar, so to speak. A buzz is an icebreaker between the artist and the audience, as well as between the song and the artist. When I'm feeling nervous, I take my one preshow drink like medicine.

I once had a drummer who claimed, "I can't play while sober." I took him at his word and I didn't ever try to challenge him. I just kept him supplied with his Jack Daniel's and let him do his thing. He was a good drummer.

As Tim attempted to duck out of the room quietly with his cocktail, I asked him, "Are you going to be doing the drunk mix tonight?" He gave me an "I'm-going-to-ignore-that-question" kind of a smirk and said, "Yup," and made his exit.

About a half an hour later Freda and Heidi, who had been down in the club checking out the opening band, came upstairs.

I asked, "What's the scene down there?"

Freda said, "There's a really good-sized crowd. I think it might sell out."

She added, "Brian's kind of tipsy."

"That's so not cool for him to be getting drunk on the job. Is he really drunk already?"

Freda answered, smiling, "Kinda, yeah."

"How drunk is he?"

"He seems pretty drunk. Giving us hugs and stuff."

When Freda, Heidi, and I left the dressing room for the stage, the vodka bottle was three quarters gone and none of us girls had had any.

I went onstage with my jacket on over my midriff-baring top. After a few songs I was sweating, so I took the jacket off and threw it behind my amp. I tried to ignore the whistles but I found myself suddenly extremely self-conscious, and underdressed, in my little top.

"Oh my God," I thought. "What was I thinking? What am I wearing? What have I done?"

Exposing a bare belly, especially among a group of strangers, is a confrontational act. (I had neglected to take this into account when choosing my outfit for the evening.) I deserved the hooting and hollering; after all, I was basically provoking a reaction by forcing my little hunk of naked flesh on these people.

I tried to reassure myself by reminding myself that though I was revealing a bit more than I usually did, there was a serious, valid purpose: I needed to preserve my body on film for my personal photographic archives so that I could look back and remember, "This was me in my thirties. I was kind of hot," and I would know that my life hadn't been a complete waste. I mean, at least I looked good.

Still, I thought, "I am so full of shit. I came out here in front of the audience intending to shed my jacket and titillate them. I did! Why can't I just admit it? I wanted them to see my body. I work hard at staying fit and I just wanted someone to know it! I don't have a husband, or a boyfriend, and so this body—this pretty great body—is being completely underutilized. No one ever sees it! I just want someone, once, to appreciate all of my hard work."

Most of the faces I looked into—apart from the few who whistled—appeared perplexed. My partial nudity seemed to stun them, but not in a good way, as if they held me to higher standards of integrity than they held, say, all those other girl pop singers on TV strutting around with hardly any clothes on, and these standards included keeping myself completely covered up in public. And now I had shattered that illusion—ruined their idealistic fantasy of my pureness—by showing them my belly button.

Now that I had gotten their attention this way, neither I nor the audience knew what to do. I think they were embarrassed. And so was

I. They were not convinced that I really wanted my body to be looked at. (My fans are so smart.) I wasn't selling this skin thing at all. I certainly wasn't feeling the least bit sexy or empowered or believable.

In time, within a couple of songs, I'd gotten used to the feeling of air on my waist and the whistlers had stopped whistling. The show was sailing along. But something still wasn't right. I was finally losing my soloing phobia and, without the fear, I was playing better and digging in more. But there was still something missing: I wasn't fully committing to the experience of being onstage. Not to any one of the elements. Maybe baring my skin had been a way for me to try to preemptorily distract the audience's attention from the fact that my performance just wasn't all there. I was detached. From all of it.

A degree of detachment is necessary, I think. Otherwise you give too much and then there is nothing left of you. You're just an open wound and bleeding, dying, in front of an audience. And that's not healthy. It's entertaining for the audience, sure, maybe, but you'll just end up planted in the funny farm and then what good are you to anyone?

But I had loads more to give before I lost control of myself; I was much more aloof than I needed or wanted to be. It was as if a thin sheet of gauze was wrapped around me from head to toe, keeping me separated from the people. And my mind felt disconnected from the deepest, most powerful and vulnerable parts of myself. I wanted to punch through the gauze but I felt stuck, trapped and muffled, behind the veil.

I'll never be a great performer because I will never give these people enough. It's my fatal flaw as a live act: I hold back. I won't surrender fully to the audience because I want to protect myself. I don't trust anyone, I guess. It's like every relationship I've ever had; all of them were blissful and mind-blowing, at times, but ultimately painful and unfulfilling.

But I kept putting myself out there, hoping someone would enlighten me as to why I kept doing it when I felt I was not very good at it. Maybe someone would understand what it was I was trying to do, when I didn't even understand myself. Maybe someone could tell me why this performing stuff was so fraught with conflict, for me. Why it always had been. And why it was that the only time I felt really good, really confident, really unafraid, really sexy and whole, really calm and in control of my life, was when I was in the process of writing the songs. Why it was that only while in the process of pulling melody and harmony from the ether was I truly engaged and excited and alive. Why it was that I couldn't seem to convey this happiness, this vibrance, toward anyone in my life; why those feelings so often, eight times out of ten, slipped away when I stepped up in front of an audience. And why those audiences were, still, so nice to me, and why they kept coming back.

The crowd didn't seem to notice that my performance was lacking in some essential, vital spark. Or if they did, they didn't show it; they clapped and hollered throughout and smiled and shouted for more when the last song ended. And I was grateful. Because it made me feel better to know that they were having a good time; made me realize it wasn't as bad as I thought it was.

The hot room was filled with bodies and I walked down the steps at the side of the stage with my face and hair and clothes drenched in sweat. I followed Freda and Heidi toward the stairway leading up to the dressing room. Someone deftly handed me a note as I walked by. I took the note, said thanks, and put it in my pocket to read later. Halfway up the stairs a young man, teenage-looking, stopped me. "Can I give you something?" he asked.

"Okay," I replied.

He handed me a thin plastic bag, like one from a convenience store. Inside were a box of Pop-Tarts, a small bottle of Motrin pain reliever, and a bottle of orange soda. It took me a couple of seconds to register the meaning of this odd gift assortment, and then it dawned on me that these were all items I'd listed in a song of mine called "Houseboy." In the song I send my (fictitious) houseboy out to get a bunch of things from the store: Advil, Robitussin, condoms, orange soda, Pop-Tarts. I said to the boy, mock-scoldingly, "Hey, this is supposed to be Advil, not Motrin. And where are the condoms? And the Robitussin?"

The boy smiled shyly and let out a tentative "Ha ha," not sure if I was kidding or not.

Then I said, "No, I'm just kidding. Thanks for the present. It's sweet. I can definitely use this," holding up the Motrin. And then I walked away.

I followed the girls into the dressing room and set the bag on the table.

"What's in the bag?" Heidi asked.

I showed her and explained the significance of the items. Lifting out the orange soda, I remarked, "This'll be good with vodka." Then, "Does anyone want the Pop-Tarts?"

Freda and Heidi shook their heads.

I didn't want the Pop-Tarts either. I put them in a song, yeah, sure, but I wouldn't want to actually eat one of them.

Tim and Andrew Squire, his photographer friend, came into the dressing room together.

"Good one, you guys," Tim said.

"Thanks," said Freda, smiling.

"Mmmph," I mumbled, looking down.

Andrew sat me and Freda and Heidi down to show us his live photos of us. We all huddled around his little digital camera and looked at the shots he had just snapped, moments ago.

"Look at how thick my arms look!" I proclaimed, genuinely surprised and kind of shocked, upon seeing the first photo. "Are they really that big?"

"No! No, we all look weird" said Freda sympathetically, as Andrew showed us some more. "None of us look like ourselves. Whoa! Look at that one," she then said, pointing, with a kind of horrified and then disappointed look on her face, to an unflattering shot of herself.

I looked to see what she was talking about.

"Oh my God!" I said. "Ha ha! Freda, you look like a constipated ogre!" and then, quickly backpedaling, I looked into Freda's eyes and said in a serious voice, "But you know you don't look like that in real life, Freda. You're beautiful. This doesn't look like you at all."

"Look at this one," I said to Heidi, pointing to a picture of her looking weirdly puffy. Heidi frowned. I said, "You're much more attractive in real life. The camera really does add ten pounds, doesn't it?"

Freda and Heidi both nodded in downhearted agreement.

After glancing at one more photo in which I resembled nothing so much as a grimacing cow with a guitar, I winced and turned away.

It wasn't Andrew's fault; the photos were good live action shots. It was just that his film, because of bad lighting or bad positioning of the camera, had distorted our bodies. Or at least the idea that we had of our bodies. I, for one, had thought I was looking kind of foxy in the mirror back in my hotel room. But that wasn't what the photos were telling me.

"No one can see these," I said firmly to Andrew, pointing to his camera. Freda nodded her head and Heidi murmured, "Yeah."

Andrew smiled sympathetically and said, "Okay." He understood that if any of the photos ever got out, he would have to suffer the wrath of women photographed from unflattering angles.

At the end of the night, Brian was unquestionably drunk and Tim was pretty buzzed, too. The band was stone-cold sober. Everything was all ass-backwards. After all our gear had been packed up I went and sat in the van with Heidi and Brian, waiting impatiently for whatever loose ends had to be tied up by Tim. Freda opened the side door and got in and sat down in the seat behind me and said, "Tim is flirting so hard with Kim." (Kim was the cute woman in charge of running the house sound, who'd been working side by side with Tim all night long.)

At that, I marched inside and interrupted Tim and Kim's conversation. "Tim, can I have the keys? We're ready to go. I'm driving."

I went and got in the driver's seat and Tim came out about thirty seconds later and sat next to me in the front passenger side so that he could direct me back to the hotel. I pulled away from the club and within minutes we were lost. I had started out headed in the wrong direction, as per Tim's instructions. I then circled for a few minutes, as Tim tried to figure out, with a street map, how to get back on track. He was trying to put on an organized efficient front but he was obviously kind of drunk and he obviously had other things on his mind, like maybe where he was going to meet Kim later and what he was going to do with her. And I was getting more and more angry because he was the tour manager and he was supposed to know how to get us back to the hotel. I wasn't supposed to know anything. I paid him to know these things.

Brian, meanwhile, was on the bench seat behind me trying to be a really drunk guy's version of funny, which is: not funny. He asked loudly, "Hey, can I have a rice cake?" speaking to Heidi, who was sitting directly behind him. She handed him the bag of rice cakes from the stash under the backseat (rice cakes are on our rider, and we take them with us when we leave each club, so we always have some to munch on in the van). Brian tore and twisted at the bag sloppily and exaggeratedly in some pathetic attempt at vaudevillian physical humor but couldn't get it open. Maybe that was part of the act: "I can't get it open! Haw Haw Haw!" and then, like a helpless cripple, he said to Heidi, "Can you open it for me?" while still tearing at it and then eventually spilling rice cake pieces and bits and crumbs all over the seat and floor around him. Between loud bites as he munched, he said excitedly, "Hey, let's go swimming when we get back to the hotel!"

The pool was in the middle of the hotel courtyard. The guest rooms overlooked the pool.

I pounced: "The pool closes at ten o'clock. And if you go swimming now, at two-thirty in the morning, and make a bunch of noise and wake other guests up, it will reflect badly on me because our rooms are all in my name and and I will have to take the blame for waking everyone up and I will get in trouble and probably be banned from the hotel."

Brian said, "Oh. Sorry. Sorry. *Sorry. Okay?*" feigning an over-dramatic apology. And then, sarcastically, "Jeez. Okay. I won't go swimming."

He was quiet for the rest of the way.

When we got back to the Phoenix, I said good-night to the girls, ignoring Tim and Brian, and I went straight to my room. I hung the "Please do not disturb" sign outside my door and I closed it, double bolted it, and put the chain lock on. I thought I was safely cocooned for the night, at last, but about a minute after locking my door, I heard Brian in his room next door to mine yelling into his telephone and then I heard a *slam* as he banged the receiver down, hard, in its cradle. I sprung up from my bed and went and knocked on Brian's door. When he opened it I immediately said, "I can hear everything through the wall, you know, and can you please pipe down and also could you please not break the phone 'cause I'm probably gonna have to pay for it."

Brian opened his mouth and just as he was about to respond, his phone rang and he ran to get it, so I turned and stomped back to my room.

In a few minutes there was a knock at my door. I got up and opened it. It was Brian.

"What?" I said.

Brian said, "Can I talk to you for a minute?"

"Okay," I said, motioning him in. I cleared some clothes off a chair so he could sit on the only surface that as of now was not covered in clothes. Before he had a chance to say anything I blurted, "Hey, now that you're here I just want to say that I'm really not comfortable with you drinking so much when you're working."

"I only had a couple drinks," Brian said in a combative tone. He had come over to fight.

Though I was tired and I wasn't really in the mood for an argument and I was fully aware of the futility of trying to make my case against Brian's excessive drinking-while-working, while he was still drunk, I played along and said, "A couple?"

"Okay. Well, I only had three drinks."

"A couple is two."

"Well, three isn't that much."

"I saw the vodka bottle, Brian. You drank a lot."

"No I didn't."

"Brian, you were drunk! I'm not the only one who noticed it."

Brian appeared to be contemplating this idea. Either that or his mind had gone blank for a moment.

I continued, "I don't want to argue about how much you had. I'm just saying that it made me uncomfortable. I don't care what you do after the show but I just wish you wouldn't drink so much while you're working, okay?"

"What, do you think I'm gonna fuck up?" Brian said defensively.

"No! I didn't say that. I just don't think it's cool for you to be so drunk on the job. You're dealing with money. It's just not cool. Plus you're really annoying when you're drunk."

Brian would neither yield nor concede. He continued to deny that he was drunk on the job and continued to not agree to not do it again. I realized as I listened to him, and as I found myself being drawn deeper into this pointless back-and-forth to nowhere, that I'd made a stupid mistake by bringing any of this up while Brian was still drunk, and while I was still angry as well as tired.

So I said, "You know what? Get out of my room," and I stood up. Brian stood up, too, rising to meet my challenge, facing me—still belligerent, to the end—and said, "Well, you know, I could just get on a plane tomorrow and go home," and I said, "Whatever you want, Brian. Just, please, just get out of my room," and I went to the door and opened it. Brian hesitated. I wanted him out. So I said, "Leave me alone, Brian! Get the FUCK OUT OF MY ROOM!"

And with those last words, my voice rose and started to crack and I knew that in about two seconds I would be crying and shrieking and throwing things and possibly causing bodily injury and Brian saw that this was so and figured he'd best leave now. He went out the door quietly and I closed it behind him and I took a deep breath and somehow composed myself in the tiny space between breaking down and holding it together. I'd put a stopper in it and the tears didn't come.

As I ran a bath I thought about Brian's girlfriend back in Cambridge. Brian and I lived in the same building. I would often hear his girlfriend sobbing and pleading with Brian through the floor of my apartment just above Brian's, when they fought. I always used to think her crying meant she was probably weak and overly emotional or unstable but now my heart swelled with sympathy. Brian was pushing her to the breaking point, over and over again.

"Another guy who knows how to make women cry," I thought. It felt like a revelation, something I had never known about Brian. You learn a lot about people on tour. You see the best and the worst of them. Everything comes out.

When I got into the tub, I felt a sharp pang of pain in my left hand, out of nowhere. It stayed with me through my bath, burning.

The pain was worse when I got into bed so I took a sleeping pill. There's no way I would've been able to rest without it.

30

The Telecommunications
Act of 1996

A series of outside forces, along with my own ambivalence, con-
spired to help slow the upward trajectory of my career in the
mid-1990s.

I was in the studio in 1994 finishing *Only Everything* when I
learned that the president of Atlantic, Danny Goldberg, the man who
had signed me, was leaving the company to go head another one. As
soon as I heard the news from my manager, I thought, "I'm fucked." It
was as simple as that.

When the guy who signed you—who, in effect, hired you, and
stood behind you in the beginning, helping you fight your way through
the jungle of the music industry—leaves the label, you can only hope
and pray that the next guy, and the whole new cast and crew that often
arrive with him, will believe in you like the last guy did.

But it's not likely, given the nature of the modern music business
and the frequent turnover of employees and loyalties at record companies. Unless, that is, you happen to be a major star and a consistent
mega-selling money-maker, which I wasn't. I could pretty much count
on the incoming president having bigger and fresher fish to fry than me.

In the new guy's eyes I was, probably, one of Danny Goldberg's left-overs. Not what one could call a "priority" artist at the label anymore. Moreover, I was probably not even the new president's cup of musical tea, anyway.

I had already been put to the test in the marketplace with my first Atlantic album, *Become What You Are*. I thought it had done very well and gotten a surprising amount of attention (especially coming from the indie label world, where I'd sold so many fewer albums). However, *Become What You Are* had not been as smashing a success as certain people invested in me—creatively, financially, career-wise—thought it should have been. My new label head would most likely be focusing on breaking brand-new Atlantic artists, ones whose future success he could share and take credit for.

None of this made me feel very optimistic and yet I was in the middle of mixing *Only Everything* and so I had to try to focus on that. Worrying about the future wasn't going to help me finish the album. Furthermore, I loved the album and I was proud of it. It was a sonic and musical and lyrical step forward for me, away from sensitive, melodic pop and toward something a bit darker, heavier, and louder. I couldn't change my voice—it was what it was. It would never be as cool as Chrissie Hynde's or Patti Smith's—so then, well, I would just have to beat the guitars into submission and make them sound cool. With my little-girl-ish vocals on top of big rock guitars, it was kind of like Belinda Carlisle of the Go-Go's fronting Social Distortion.

My *Only Everything* producers were the team of Sean Slade and Paul Kolderie, who worked a lot at the Fort Apache Studio. Their specialty was recording loud rock guitars (they'd worked with Dinosaur Jr., Radiohead, Hole, and many others) and they encouraged me not to hold back. During these sessions, my guitar playing improved a lot. I was even starting to develop my own unique lead-playing style: structured, yet sloppy. And I was gaining confidence as my guitar playing evolved. I was discovering that I could express things—hidden emotions and energies—with a guitar solo that the lyrics and the chord progressions couldn't. I was beginning to understand this new language and it was exciting.

My first-ever recorded guitar solo was in 1991 on a B side off of *Hey Babe*, my first album. It was a cover of a Dinosaur Jr. song called, ungrammatically, "Raisans." I played the solo softly, on a clean (not distorted) guitar, tentatively feeling my way up and down the neck, seeing where my hands took me. I let them pick out rhythms and notes that felt good and sounded pretty and made some kind of sense along with the chord changes. I wanted the solo to carry my fingers to places they had never been before. A melody emerged, from where it seemed to have been waiting to be unearthed, possibly for millions of years, in the subterranean infinite of prehuman unconsciousness. The solo may not have sounded very impressive to the casual listener, but to me, when I was discovering it, playing it, it felt important and mysterious and revelatory.

My first few attempts at soloing were scary, because I knew I could derail and crash at any second; soloing for the first time was like riding a bike for the first time. I had to balance and be careful, but I had to also let go a little and trust in both the machinery and myself (too much fear and you're paralyzed). And I would fall down but then I'd get up and start where I left off—with a partial melody, remembered from the last attempt, and I'd continue to pull out new, more and more pleasing sounds; sounds that I hadn't heard before, hadn't known existed, sounds that continuously surprised me with the loveliness that an electric guitar through an amp, and my fingers on the neck, could generate.

With *Only Everything* I was now playing harder, holding the pick tighter, digging in deeper, riding that bike hard, tackling the solos rather than gently coaxing them out. I would often start by listening to the rhythm tracks a few times. I would hum along until I had a made-up melody that I liked and then I would pick up my guitar and play what I heard in my head. Or I would take the vocal melody and play part of that with my lead guitar during the solo section when the vocal wasn't there (a trick I borrowed from Kurt Cobain—he used to do this a lot). Sometimes the lead part would develop from that constructed, transcribed melody into something else, something I hadn't planned; it would go from composed and pretty and tame to bluesy and kind of wild.

I gradually found patterns, places my hands kept naturally returning to on their own—boxlike grids in each key that the fingers would zig-zag through—up and around and back down again. I later learned that these "boxes" of notes were traditional blues scale patterns, used by guitar players all over the world since the beginning of electric guitar soloing. My fingers had gravitated, on their own, to a traditional way of playing. I felt like I was entering a continuum, that I was jumping on a mystery train full of great secrets. Like I was being initiated into some Masonic guitar club, sort of by accident.

These melodic blues-scale grids were a kind of crutch that a guitar player could always fall back on when he ran out of ideas. Once you had figured out how it's done, it was easy and natural. And it looked and sounded impressive—more impressive than it really is—to people who hadn't been initiated. It was, for many guitar players, a comfortable base from which to start a lead, but which I had found my way to backward, from another starting point (the melodies I heard in my head).

Only Everything was released at the end of 1995. Soon after that, the Telecommunications Act of 1996 was signed into law by then president Bill Clinton. With the passage of this legislation, almost all previously established media ownership regulations were eliminated. A radio broadcaster, for example, could now own an unlimited amount of radio stations across the country, and a newspaper owner based in, say, New York City, could now own an unlimited number of local newspapers across the country, whereas before the Telecom Act there were limits.

Supporters of the act claimed that its passage would foster healthy American economic competition and would generate more jobs and more entertainment choices. But what in fact happened was pretty much the opposite: a few huge media companies expanded their ownership of smaller ones and then, very quickly, there was less, not more, diversity. Fewer media companies meant fewer media choices for the consumer, in terms of product offerings. And prices were raised, not lowered, because the few profit-driven behemoths could dictate pricing since they had little competition.

Clear Channel was one of these big media companies. Clear Channel controlled many radio stations, concert venues, and billboards across the country. As Clear Channel grew in size and power after the Telecom Act, it consolidated its ever more homogenized playlists. It became harder for many new artists with no proven track record, or even for people who did have a respectable history but whose music was considered maybe a bit "quirky" or "fringe" or less traditionally mainstream (i.e., me), to get airtime on commercial radio.

But if Clear Channel was invested in an artist (let's call him Mr. X), Mr. X and Clear Channel both were virtually guaranteed success on a massive scale. If a radio station in a particular region was owned by Clear Channel, the station would publicize itself on a regional billboard, which Clear Channel also owned. When people tuned in to that station, they would hear Mr. X, who was in heavy rotation on the Clear Channel radio playlist. And if people wanted to go to a Mr. X concert, they would have to buy a ticket to a Clear Channel venue, because Clear Channel owned the venue.

This affected more than just mainstream radio in cities. Many small station owners in small communities, with their own idiosyncratic, personally selected playlists full of their own local color and tastes, were bulldozed by Clear Channel and overhauled into another of Clear Channel's many eerily similar, faceless, corporate-block radio units (McRadio). Clear Channel and its ilk basically began controlling what most of the listeners in the United States were hearing on commercial radio, more than ever before, as if there was one national playlist. If an artist wasn't added to that national playlist, he could kiss his dreams of stardom good-bye.

That's part of the reason so many so-called alternative rock bands that were signed in the late 1980s/early 1990s alt-rock explosion and had hits on commercial modern rock radio (and on MTV) seemed to fall off the face of the earth, all of a sudden, all together, toward the end of the millennium: Veruca Salt ("Seether"), Local H (the "copacetic" song), the Breeders ("Cannonball"), Lemonheads, Better Than Ezra, Live, Screaming Trees, Spin Doctors, Soul Asylum, et cetera. The Telecommunications Act of 1996 helped kill alternative rock, for better or for worse.

What all this meant in terms of me and my career was that most of the commercial stations that had previously chosen to play my music were almost immediately eradicated upon the Telecom Act's passage in early 1996. Many of the stations that had made a minor hit of my last album, *Become What You Are*, were bought out by one of the few radio behemoths that had been cleared by the act to go on a feeding frenzy.

So my *Only Everything*, which was not a typically mainstream type of record to begin with (lots of loud guitars, lots of cryptic lyrics, no glamor shot of me on the album cover) didn't have much time to prove itself, or make much of an impact on the public's consciousness, before the Telecom Act went through and everything changed.

In the years before the act, record companies' radio promotions teams would work from market to market, region to region, program director to program director, trying to talk up an artist and get him added to different local stations. And if a song started to catch on, there was a shared satisfaction for the artist and the record company in knowing that they were building something from the ground up, grassroots style.

Local music programmers would for the most part play what they liked. If a song was added to a playlist at a station in, say, Louisville, other radio programmers in surrounding areas would take notice of the new artist who was being played in Louisville; and from there the airplay might spread to the next region over—maybe to Indianapolis— and suddenly there was a regional buzz about the artist. That buzz would affect album sales in the area, and concert ticket sales. So then a programmer all the way out in, say, Oakland, California, would hear about the artist's success in Louisville (and Indy) and add it to his playlist at his modern rock station, and then the song would spread in the Oakland area. And so on. A record would have a chance to keep growing and building and working its way into the country's minds and hearts. The big cheeses at the record companies would see this happening—see their company working the way it should, succeeding with artist development, and see that the artist had a chance, and a future— and wouldn't give up on the project and pull the promotional funding right away, upon not seeing immediate humongous returns on their investments.

But after the passage of the Telecom Act a song couldn't really generate a slow and steady groundswell, anymore. Success had to happen right away, out of the box, or it wasn't going to happen, except in rare, exceptionally flukey cases. It's like the "weekend box office" tallies, with movies: if a new Hollywood movie doesn't bring in gigantic numbers (tens of million of dollars in ticket sales) upon its immediate release, it is considered "over," a failure, a flop, no matter what its artistic merits.

The film company gives up on it and moves on to start working on the next project that might have a chance to hit big. A film that wasn't being promoted by the studio could still gain a devoted following by word of mouth, just as a band without major label backing could do, but still, the Telecom Act did indubitably have a powerful and lasting effect on American culture.

With music, as with film, suddenly there were fewer risks taken with artists who were not guaranteed million-sellers, and there were more cookie-cutter, copycat acts (Blink 182 begets Good Charlotte begets Girls Like Boys begets whatever new emopop/punk band with whiny-voiced guy singer) just as with film, there was a *Die Hard 1, 2, and 3*; a *Spider-Man 1, 2,* and *3,* an *Ocean's 11, 12,* and *13*, et cetera. The aim was to repeat the successful formula.

It wasn't like this when I started out with the Blake Babies, or I might not have even had the guts to even begin to try to make a name for myself. I couldn't have competed in today's harsh, bottom-line-driven atmosphere. If Bob Dylan were starting out today, no one, probably, would care. I just thank God I got in when I did, before the business changed and everyone—even the bands—got cynical.

There were other circumstances in my life that made it hard for me to sustain my worth as cultural currency. Radio conglomeration wasn't my only problem. I also took a sudden leave of absence and canceled a European tour at a time that everyone involved in my career (record label, booking agents, manager) believed would be pivotal in my upward arc, and there was Danny Goldberg's departure from my label, and the fact that fame didn't seem to agree with me. Maybe the Telecommunications Act of 1996 was a blessing in disguise.

Like all of my albums, *Only Everything* received mixed reviews. Some people really loved it and some people really didn't. One review said that with the album I wasn't "playing to my strengths," that I should stick to jangly, sensitive adolescent-girl pop. I turned up on a couple of year-end "top ten favorites of 1995" lists, which was nice. Best of all, *Only Everything* got me into the guitar magazines—the boys' club. To be taken seriously as a guitar player by *Guitar World* and *Guitar Player*—the monthly glossies that real pros and tech heads read, the magazines that hardly ever featured girl players—was incredibly gratifying.

The magazines wanted to know what sort of gear I used—what amps, what guitars (makes and models? are they customized? what kind of pickups, what gauge string), what sorts of pedals (distortion? echo? delay?) I stomped on. *Guitar World* even gave me a column for a few months, in which I explained how I got the sounds on *Only Everything* and how I came up with my ideas. And they printed my songs' tablature so people could play along.

I wanted to be taken seriously most of all. If I had had the choice between being praised by *Guitar World* and having another hit single on radio, I think I would've chosen to be featured in the guitar magazine. So that made up for the fact the first single off of *Only Everything* fizzled pretty quickly on radio, and was gone.

31

August 18

San Francisco to
Los Angeles

A housekeeping cart rumbled loudly past my door and stopped. The next thing I heard was KNOCK KNOCK KNOCK KNOCK KNOCK KNOCK KNOCK KNOCK on a door very close to mine, by the sound of it, and then, *"Housekeeping!"* There was silence for a few seconds and then the sound of a vacuum cleaner bumping repeatedly into the wall in the room next to mine.

Outside, hotel guests were chatting and laughing over the complimentary continental breakfast in the courtyard. I could hear every word loud and clear through the glass of the big window behind my drawn curtain. Were they the same drunken revelers from the night before? Had they never left the courtyard?

I was relatively well rested when we checked out, on account of the sleeping pill the night before, but my left hand was killing me and it seemed to be getting worse as the six-hour drive to L.A. commenced.

"Hey you guys," I said to Heidi and Freda and Tim (I was pretending Brian wasn't there) as we got on the freeway. "My hand is killing me. Something happened to my hand last night."

I described how the pain had seemed to come from out of nowhere all of a sudden.

"It's probably carpal tunnel," said Heidi. "From playing guitar every night."

Freda concurred.

I had my own theory: "I think it's 'cause I played 'Ugly' last night."

"Ugly" was an old song of mine from the 1991 *Hey Babe* album that I hadn't performed in years, until the encore the night before. To play it, I have to contort my left hand and fingers in an awkward and painful stretch to form some of the song's unconventional, jazzy chord voicings. Perhaps my road-weary bones and shriveled, undernourished muscles couldn't, in the end, handle the strain of attacking these unfamiliar and very challenging note formations. Under pressure, I had sprained something.

"Look what happens when I try to give the people what they want," I said. "I get injured."

There are always people in every audience who want to hear "Ugly." People who like the old songs the best. And that's the only reason I had broken out "Ugly" the night before; people had called out for it. But if it was entirely up to me, I would never play it. It's so ancient. I wrote it when I was barely out of my teens, and it feels incredibly weird, and uncomfortable, and kind of inauthentic now, singing words that came from such a long-gone era of my life. So I was glad I now had a really good reason to retire the song, once and for all: playing it caused grievous bodily harm.

Neither Brian nor I said anything to the other during the first part of the drive. He was on the second back bench seat and I was driving and I was relieved not to have to face him; I was still raw from our argument the night before, and I didn't want to think about it.

The first words we spoke to each other came after we had been driving for a couple of hours and we made a pit stop for gas and snacks. Brian waited for Freda and Heidi and Tim to get out of the van and then said quietly to me, "I'm sorry about last night."

I sighed and said, "It's okay. But I don't want to argue with you ever again. It's impossible." And then I headed into the convenience store. I wasn't angry, just worn-out. I wasn't ready yet to commit to being his friend again.

When we got back on the road, the rest of us traded war stories to kill time on the boring highway 5, which cuts straight down the dry, flat middle of California for a long time before winding steeply up into the mountains north of L.A. Freda went first.

"The Mysteries of Life opened for the Sea Monsters once, when we were on RCA."

The Mysteries of Life were one of Freda's other bands. The Sea Monsters were a mid-1990s major label guitar pop band.

"How was it?" I asked.

"It wasn't much fun," Freda said, almost apologetically, and then, with a harder, more matter-of-fact tone, "It nearly killed my desire to play music, actually."

"Why? What was so bad about it?"

"Well, first of all, the tour was really long. It was nine and a half weeks long. And the Sea Monsters just weren't very good."

"Didn't they used to wear, like, polka-dot shirts and rainbow-striped Dr. Seuss hats onstage?"

"Yeah. And they had lots of three-part vocal harmonies."

Guys in bands like the Sea Monsters are like those overachieving know-it-all brainiac nerds in high school, parading their mastery of the genre of popular music and their knowledge of vintage gear around. But I say, just 'cause you ace the SATs doesn't necessarily mean you are smarter than other kids. Maybe it just means you test well. Or study a lot. Guys like the Sea Monsters have studied the whole Beatles and Beach Boys and Badfinger and Raspberries and Big Star and Todd Rundgren catalogs and appropriated the most superficial aspects of all of them. They're almost like curators. Of rock. Smarty-pantses. But it doesn't impress me if some guy in a band can play the solo from "I Saw the Light" note for note. I want him to show me who he is. What unique himness he has to offer. If I want to hear the solo from "I Saw the Light," I'll dig up the original Rundgren.

It's Encyclopedia Rock. That's what the Sea Monsters are. They're like scientists who have figured out the perfect musical formula in a laboratory. Their whole thing has been meticulously crafted, and groomed; there is not one hair out of place. There's no mystery, or danger, or sweat dripping into the eyes and down onto the lips. It's all brain and no balls.

Disparaging the Sea Monsters didn't keep my hand from really hurting. I tried everything I could think of to make the pain go away: I tried massaging the hand with my other, noninflamed one. I tried holding the hand in different positions: pointing up, sideways, down by my side, sitting on it. Nothing helped. The biting throbbing continued, from the wrist up through the tips of the fingers. I was starting to worry that I might be too crippled with pain to do the gig the next day.

By the time we got to Los Angeles I was resigned to a life of agony. I had decided that my hand was just going to keep hurting so I may as well be stoic and shut up about it. I would embrace it, even. It would be like a hair shirt; it would make me a better, stronger person, to endure it.

We checked into the Hyatt on Sunset Boulevard. Signs posted on each of the front doors welcomed us to L.A.: "This building contains asbestos, a material known to the State of California to cause cancer."

Although this grim warning was somewhat disturbing, I didn't necessarily think it meant that this hotel we were staying in was especially poisonous or any more carcinogen-ridden than any other hotel along the way. It's just that in California, people are so lawsuit-crazy that every business establishment feels it has to warn its potential patrons about every conceivable danger, as a safeguard. Other hotels, in other, less litigious regions, just don't tell you that they are releasing toxic chemicals into the air and killing you slowly. They don't want you to know. And frankly, I don't want to know, either.

Another notice on another of the entrance doors read, "Products made or served on the premises may contain asbestos."

"Kind of puts me off eating in the cafe off the lobby," I thought.

The Hyatt had recently been remodeled and redecorated. The last time I'd stayed there, the rooms had been plain and kind of anonymous, indistinguishable from any shabby mid-priced Hyatt anywhere in America. Its new look was "early 1980s urban cocaine den of iniquity." The room evoked, for me, porn, steroids, sleaze, hair gel, dark tans, and guys with silk shirts open to the navel, exposing thick black chest hairs. There was a lot of solid shiny black plastic and silver and hard geometrical shapes. Like a cheap, hotel-room version of what I imagined Studio 54 looked like.

I didn't exactly feel at home in my room.

We had the night off. I had plans to meet with a filmmaker who was interested in documenting the making of my next album. Her name was Françoise and she was tall and blond and French-Canadian. I met her at the Rainbow Bar and Grill to talk.

After we sat down I ordered a Jack and Coke and she got a cranberry juice. I felt instantly like a slob. I was drinking. She wasn't. I was sure I must have come across as a lush. Who drinks alone? I'd ordered a drink I didn't really want, because I'd thought Françoise was going to order a drink, but then she didn't, and it only made me feel more uncomfortable.

Françoise was tall and blond, which drew out all my insecurities. Made me feel small and mousy. And Françoise was bilingual: she told me she was in the middle of editing a documentary she had shot and directed in France, in French, about a French porn star. It sounded interesting. Much more interesting than me.

Françoise asked me some questions, in order to get to know me, her potential subject. How's the tour going, when will you be recording again, how do you like being in the studio, stuff like that. She was all business. But I felt dumb and tongue-tied and self-conscious and slightly confused, as if I were auditioning to play a more interesting version of myself and this woman across from me was trying to gauge whether I was charismatic enough to play the part of me in her film about me.

Really, I kept thinking, what could this woman want with me?

"What directors do you like?" she asked me during a lull in the conversation.

It seemed like a very important question. It was a pop quiz and the answer might settle, once and for all, the question of whether or not I was worthy of a documentary. I tensed up, sure I was about to fail the test and give the wrong response, exposing myself as the pathetic philistine loser that I am.

I thought really hard. A name popped into my head. Just one.

"Peckinpah," I said meekly. "I like Peckinpah."

Right away I regretted having said it. It was a pretentious answer.

I was once characterized, in an early magazine profile, as "remarkably unremarkable" in person. This still haunts me sometimes; especially in moments of self-doubt or shyness, or when I feel I am being judged or measured. When the piece first came out, I'd been surprised, and hurt, and angry, but at times like these I worried that the journalist had sort of hit the nail right on the head.

Françoise was of course very nice throughout our whole encounter and, when we said good-bye, she vowed to call me soon to talk more about the film idea. But I was sure it would never happen.

After my meeting with Françoise, I was tired and my hand was still hurting pretty bad, so I went to bed as soon as I got back to the hotel, at around eleven. I was so tired that I didn't even need to take a pill. I fell asleep on my own and slept for ten hours, through the pain.

32

August 19
L.A.

I woke up and the first thing I did was to assess the situation in my left hand. The pain had abated ever so slightly but a strange new and disquieting sensation had taken hold. When I opened and closed my fingers, my knuckles felt like wooden slat blinds being raised up and let down, piece by piece, as if the inner machinery of my hand was rusty and needed a squirt of WD-40, or oil, or something.

My father was a radiologist, and a fatalist. The human body was to him merely a series of interconnected tubes and veins and bones and skin and muscle and tissue and cells and organs and blood and DNA. You were what you were born with. And when you died, you died, he figured. He himself was taken down by a heart attack. His aorta exploded. That's how he would have described it, if he could have, after the fact, in his no-nonsense, medical way.

He would have said, "My aorta burst." He would have motioned me over so I was standing by his side where he was sitting at the head of the kitchen table after dinner, then he would have pushed aside the uncleared plates with remnants of food still on them, taken a black felt pen out of his shirt's breast pocket, and drawn me a diagram on a paper napkin. "See this valve here? This is the ventricular valve, okay? It pumps blood to the arteries of the heart. The aorta—this tube here—is the main artery, which sends the blood from the heart to other parts of the body. The aorta is the main pathway for the blood. It needs to be clear for the body to function. But there was some blockage somewhere—either the blood couldn't get into the aorta or it couldn't get out and the blood was stuck and couldn't travel to where it needed to go. So this here—see? the aorta—broke open from the pressure of the buildup, kind of like how a chewing gum bubble will pop if you blow enough air into it. It's simple physics," he would have explained, so I could understand. So it wasn't a mystery, and I wouldn't have to be afraid.

My father enjoyed explaining biological processes to his children, when we asked. Those were the only times he had any real answers. If we had a specific medical or scientific query such as, Where do babies come from? or What is a heart attack? Or, How do X-rays work? he knew just what to tell us, but most of the rest of the time, he didn't pretend to know any more than his kids did.

Freda had suggested I try acupuncture. I'd never had it done before but I was willing to try anything to make my hand feel normal again. I looked in the Yellow Pages under "A" and I made a few telephone inquiries. All the experts I talked to said that acupuncture probably wouldn't work in just one session—I would need follow-ups to get palpable results. As I only had one day here in LA, the whole experiment would be pointless. Needles were out. Instead, I downed a couple of Advil and filled the bathroom sink with hot water and soaked my hand in it, which was soothing.

I stayed in my hotel room all morning and into the afternoon writing in my journal with my good hand. Concentrating was difficult because of a constant gnawing drill sound coming from somewhere on the outside of the building. It grew more and more annoying the longer it continued; it became a sort of sonic torture.

At noon the phone rang and it was Tim, asking, "Are you affected at all by what's happening on the roof?"

"You mean the noise?" I said. "Yeah! It's driving me fucking crazy."

"It's really bad up here on the tenth floor." (I was on the eighth.)

"What is it? What's making the noise?"

"It's some workers doing construction on the roof-deck pool. I want to try and get a discount on our rooms because this is really out of control and I can't get any work done."

"Yeah! This noise is totally impinging on my leisure time, man. It's totally stressing me out."

I hung up and went back to writing about the noise in my journal. Tim called back a few minutes later.

"They went for it. They're gonna take some money off our bill."

"Yay, Tim! Right on! What did you say to them?"

"I explained to them that 'we are a traveling musical group and we have precious few days off and we were hoping to use this day to rest and recuperate from a grueling schedule and now this construction noise is making that impossible so I think we should get a discount.'"

"Aaawwwesome. Nice work, Tim."

"Thanks. So I'll see you later?"

"Yeah. I'll meet you guys at the club at four."

"Cool."

My phone rang again. It was my friend Metcalf calling for the second time that day. We were formalizing plans to get together later.

"Hi!" he said.

"Hey."

"You know what? Both times I called, the man at the front desk told me to 'have an exceptional day' just before he put me through to you."

"Really? I hate when they make them do that. They say 'Have a nice day' so many times in a day that it sounds completely robotic and totally insincere."

"Well, yeah, but he didn't actually tell me to have a *nice* day. He said 'Have an *exceptional* day.' Exceptional doesn't necessarily mean *good*. It just means *exceptional*. 'Have an *exceptional* day' could mean 'Have an exceptionally *bad* day.'"

"You're right! That's funny."

Metcalf picked me up an hour later and we went to Amoeba Records. I bought a bunch of CDs because me and my crew were sick of most of the music we had brought from home, which we had listened to over and over again in the van, and we needed something new. I wanted Brian Eno's *Music for Airports*, because I'd been told it would "blow my mind," but they didn't have it so I bought *Music for Films* instead. Then I grabbed Hot Hot Heat's *Knock*, an EP someone had recommended, saying, "It sounds kind of like early U2 mixed with the Cure." I thought that sounded like kind of a bad combination but I bought the CD anyway, for lack of any better ideas. I also got Linda Ronstadt's *Heart Like a Wheel* and Silverchair's recent one, because I loved *Neon Ballroom*. And Metcalf bought me some modern jazz CDs that he thought I should hear, to expand my horizons: Sun Ra, Albert Ayler, Roland Kirk. I was pretty sure that I wouldn't enjoy these picks of Metcalf's, either; modern jazz is not what I usually go for.

Things were still chilly between Brian and me when we all met up at the Knitting Factory to load in late that afternoon. I avoided eye contact with him and didn't say much. Not because I was still upset, but because I just couldn't quite figure out what to say or how to say it. I was shell-shocked from our fight and I sensed that Brain felt the same.

After soundcheck Tim, Freda, Heidi, Brian, and I congregated in the dressing room, like we usually did after soundcheck, to talk about set times and where to go for dinner and stuff like that. As Freda spoke to Tim about some inconsequential matter, Brian and I happened to look at each other. We both smiled, shyly, and the tensions between us suddenly disintegrated, palpably, just like that.

Freda and Heidi gathered their things together, Tim zipped up his laptop case, and as we all made to disperse, Brian stood and walked over to me and said, "It's so nice to see you smile again."

I looked down and said, awkwardly, "Well, you know, my hand really hurt earlier and I didn't feel good." It was the only way I knew how to acknowledge, without actually saying it, that I was sorry, and that I missed him. Brian said, "I know, I know," so sincerely and sympathetically, like he was reading my mind, and he squeezed my shoulder on the way out of the room.

And, just like that, we were friends again.

After the show the pain in my hand had completely disappeared. I have since come to believe that the hand thing was a physical manifestation of emotional pain. My hand wasn't hurting because I'd played

"Ugly" in San Francisco. It was hurting because I'd fought with my friend. The sudden onset of physical agony that seemed, at the time, to have come out of nowhere, coincided perfectly with the denouement of my horrible fight with Brian. And making up with Brian made the pain go away.

Brian's girlfriend, Jackie, had flown out from Boston to be with him for a couple of days and nights. She wore a low-cut camisole to the gig. With this top and her long blond hair and heavy makeup she looked like a starlet. She fit right in in L.A. She sat by Brian at the merch table and helped him work. They ended up selling a ton of stuff; it was the best night so far for sales. I thought it was because of Jackie's cleavage that they did so well but Brian was convinced it was her exemplary selling technique. When a guy approached with a twenty dollar bill and asked for either the twelve dollar *Gold Stars* full-length CD or the eight dollar Blake Babies *Epilogue* EP Jackie would say, smiling coquettishly, "Oh, why don't you get them both?" and the guy would, more often than not, hand over the twenty.

I guess Brian and I were both right: The hard sell wouldn't have worked without the cleavage, but the cleavage on its own, without the verbal persuasion, might not have been enough to get the guys to give up the twenties.

When we all pulled up to the Hyatt at the end of the night, Tim turned to me and said, with a wounded look in his face, "Can I talk to you later?"

I said, "Yeah. Sure. Just call me after you park the van and you can come to my room and we can talk there?"

My spirits sank as I rode the elevator up to my room. I knew something bad was coming. The fact that Tim needed to deal with the issue *now*, at two in the morning, meant that it was something serious.

"Shit," I thought. "What did I do? What am I in trouble for now?"

Fifteen minutes later, Tim came to my room and sat down in the chair by the desk. I sat on the bed facing him and asked, "What's up?"

Tim answered with a question: "Do you have a problem with me?"

I had no idea where this was coming from.

"No," I said. "What do you mean?"

"Because if you have some kind of problem with me, I wish you would just tell me and I could correct it."

"What are you talking about? I don't have a problem with you. What did I do?"

Now Tim's voice sped up. There was hurt in it and he seemed on the verge of tears.

"It's just that the way you spoke to me in the dressing room this afternoon made me think that I must be doing something really wrong and that you're really disappointed with the job I'm doing. And, you know, I take this job very seriously and I do the best I can so I don't understand why you are so negative toward me."

Suddenly it all flashed back to me, like a bad dream whose memory I had, up until that moment, successfully repressed: Just before soundcheck I had laid into Tim about the absence of food and drink in the dressing room. There were a few people in the room at the time and I had said, in front of all of them, "Tim, why isn't our rider here? It's supposed to be here when we get here. Didn't you advance the show?"

Part of Tim's job as the tour manager was to call ahead in advance of each show to make sure the load-in part of the rider (snacks, water, tea) was there, upon our arrival at the club, as per the contract.

At the time in question, in my aching-handed, hungry, still-estranged-from-Brian, worried-no-one-would-show-up-at-the-gig, late-afternoon state of mind, my nagging hadn't seemed out of line at all, to me. Tim's failure to procure what I was paying him to procure had seemed to me like just another in a long list of minor annoyances contributing to my then-present unhappiness. But now, in my pain-free, well-fed, temporarily satisfied and magnanimous post-good-show condition, I could see all too clearly what an insensitive bitch I had been, embarrassing and demeaning him, when sometimes it's impossible to get the club to deliver the rider on time. Even the best, most efficient tour manager can't satisfy every single demand, on the spot. He is somewhat at the mercy of other people. Always.

"I'm really sorry, Tim," I said. "I didn't realize I was being so uncool, until now. I had no idea I upset you. There's no excuse for treating you like that. I know that you take pride in your work and I think you are really good at it. You're a great tour manager and a great soundman and I don't have any complaints, truly, and I'm *really* sorry I acted like that toward you this afternoon."

Then I looked down and shook my head and said, "I don't know what gets into me."

Finally, after all that, Tim seemed to believe me. He relaxed and breathed easier and we said good-night.

But I felt awful. Tim looked so sad when he came in, and because of me! "Why am I so intolerably sullen sometimes?" I wondered. "Why can't I be nicer? I can't believe Tim hasn't quit the tour by now. And everyone else, too. I really want to be a better person. I want to change but I *don't know how*.

"I wish Dad were here. Maybe *he* could explain it, and convince Tim that it's not my fault that I am the way I am. 'It's hypoglycemia—it's a medical condition, which, when she's in its throes, affects her brain's functioning—clouds her good sense,' he would say. Or 'It's chronic, untreated depression—a genetic, chemical disorder, handed down generation to generation, and which can manifest in irritability or as an inability to get along well with others or as an inclination to sabotage friendships or relationships with coworkers or loved ones.' Or 'It's hormones—out of control, unpredictable flushes of estrogen, generated in her ovaries, circulating wildly . . . making her feel crazy, murderous, persecuted, helpless. She can't help it. She's female. Women have no control over their emotions. They are born doomed to suffer mood fluctuations, and to be bad-tempered and intolerable once in a while.'"

I didn't ask to be born! Can I use that as an excuse? Can I blame Dad, for impregnating Mom? Is it simply my genes that I have to keep apologizing for? Maybe Dad could vouch for me and say, "She got it from me. I was the same way. I was hard to get along with, too. I exhibited flashes of irascibility and insensitivity, followed by waves of guilt and shame, and never any resolution."

Do I, too, have a sick heart? A blockage? Not enough blood getting in? Not enough blood getting out? Am I defective? Can a heart really just stop working?

Dad lasted sixty-one years before his finally quit on him for good. And it wasn't his fault. It just happens sometimes. Some people live happy, contented lives full of healthy, loving, satisfying relationships and die of natural causes when they are ninety-two years old. Others don't.

33

Demons

I was at Fort Apache Studios with the Blake Babies in 1988, working on our second album, *Earwig*. We had recently secured a record contract with the new North Carolina–based indie Mammoth Records, which was the one and only label that had made us an offer. Our friend Gary, who owned the studio and who also happened to be a talented record producer (and who would later become my manager), was producing the album. We were working on a song I had written called "Lament," a sonically bright and jangly portrait of an unnamed band who had sold out. We finished recording the basic tracks (bass and drums that we would keep) and scratch tracks (guitars and vocals that we would do over) and John and Freda and I went home for the night, satisfied that everything was sounding good so far, and excited that we were getting to make this album for a real label, with a real producer.

The next day we all returned to Fort Apache to work on overdubs. Gary, who was sitting in front of the sound board in the control room, pressed PLAY on the tape machine and we started listening to what we had done so far on "Lament." I immediately noticed that something wasn't right. It sounded to me as if Gary was playing the tape back at the wrong speed, like when you play a 45 record at 33⅓ on a turntable. Or maybe the tape machine was broken.

I looked at the others—John, Freda, Gary—questioningly, and was baffled when none of them appeared to be the least bit concerned about the slowed-down tape problem. I asked Gary, "Gary, did you slow down the tape?" (I knew his tape machine had the capability to do this.)

Gary said no, and why? Why would he do that?

"I don't know. That's what *I* wanted to know. Doesn't the song sound weird to you? Like it's in slow motion?"

He listened carefully for a few seconds without speaking and then he looked at me with a tentative, questioning smile on his face, like maybe I was joking, and said no, it sounded fine. Sounded exactly like it had yesterday. He hadn't changed anything. Then he turned to John and Freda, who were sitting on the couch against the wall in the back of the room, behind him, and asked them if the song speed sounded weird to them.

Freda said it sounded fine to her.

John said the same thing. Then he asked me if I was high.

I was confused, and a little angry, now, and I began to feel paranoid. Gary *had* to have slowed down the tape. (Who else could have done it? Gary was the only one of us who ever touched the tape machine.) And he was lying to me about it for some reason I couldn't comprehend. Was this a practical joke? Was Gary—and were John and Freda—messing with me? I continued to protest that the song was playing back much too slow and they all continued to assure me that no, it wasn't.

"Am I crazy?" I wondered. "Why doesn't anyone else hear how screwed-up this song is—how completely *altered* it is from yesterday? I would *swear* the song was faster yesterday."

None of them agreed. They thought I was nuts. I was frustrated and upset all day long, almost to the point of tears, at how sluggish the song had become overnight, not only because the sudden transformation didn't make any sense but because that wasn't the way it was supposed to be; the song was supposed to be perky and bubbly, driving along. It was like a dirge now, *not* the way we recorded it. Not the way I had envisioned my song sounding.

I felt like I was losing my mind. What was real: the current slowed-down speed or the faster speed from yesterday? And why didn't the others perceive any difference? Was my brain distorting reality? Why? How?

Things appearing to be slowed-down can be one of the symptoms of depression. I didn't know this at the time. I only knew that I had been in one of my funks, one of my really down moods, that day in the studio. I came back to Fort Apache two days later and "Lament" sounded fine again. I was back in sync with the others. I guess I must've been feeling better.

For most of my life I have suffered from chronic, mostly low- to medium-grade depression. Until I started paying attention to it and analyzing it, this condition was very much removed from my conscious understanding. I had no idea where all my sadness and hopelessness and dread and gloom and lethargy and apathy and self-hatred came from, or why. I only knew that these really bad moods of mine made every relationship, and every interaction, and everything I tried to do in my life more difficult than I imagine they would have been otherwise, and that I could count on the black cloud darkening my world on a regular basis.

When I was a child, I was absolutely convinced that the house I lived in was haunted, but I was the only one in the family who felt this way. I was terrified to turn out the lights and close my eyes at bedtime. After I did manage to fall asleep, if I woke up in the middle of the night I would immediately go and jump into my parents' bed in the room next to mine. But even nestled between my mother and father I was still petrified, with wide-open eyes unblinking in the darkness, watching, listening for approaching ghouls. I heard things no one else did. Unidentifiable bumps and scratchings in the night. I felt things. Evil, invisible presences skulking all around me, coming after me, hounding me, breathing heavily right up next to my ear.

I was always trying to convince my family that the house was haunted so that I wouldn't feel so alone in my fear. I once said to my father after a particularly terrifying night, "Dad, there are demons in this house. There *are*. Can't you feel them? They're even in your bedroom! And didn't you hear those weird noises downstairs last night? It was like something being dragged slowly across the floor."

Dad said, matter-of-factly, like it was the most obvious fact in the world, "Jule, there are no demons in this house. The demons are in you."

The Blake Babies played at the rock club CBGB's in NYC for the first time at the end of the 1980s, early on in our career. We were excited to play on the legendary stage that so many great, influential, respected New York bands had played when they were first starting out: Television, Talking Heads, the Ramones, Blondie, the Patti Smith Group. John and Freda and I hoped we could make our *own* mark; that the Blake Babies, too, would be known, and loved, someday. When we went on, after midnight, there was basically no one there—a few friends, Gary, two bartenders, the door guy, and Gary's friend, Bob, who was also our booking agent. Bob lived in the city and had offered to put us up for the night at his apartment.

We played through our set with our usual vim and vigor, Freda smiling behind her drum kit; John hunched over his Strat, attacking his strings with precision; and sweat dripping off me as I played my guitar and sang as hard as I could. And then it was over and we packed our stuff up. John and Freda went out into the city night with friends and I went back to Bob's tiny, cramped apartment with him and Gary. It was late. We were tired. I lay down on Bob's couch and Gary settled down into a sleeping bag on the floor while Bob said good-night and closed the door to the bedroom. As soon as my head hit the pillow I began to cry. I pulled my blanket over my head so Gary wouldn't hear me. I wept, as silently as I could, for about half an hour. I didn't know why, exactly, I was so sad. John and Freda hadn't seemed sad.

Even though the club had been empty, John and Freda knew it was part of paying our dues, and they were glad to be out on the road, and to play CBGB's. They were enjoying themselves and were hopeful that this would all amount to something eventually. Maybe to making a living. Maybe getting on a cool tour. Building up a fan base.

I didn't know if I was sad because playing to no one is sad or because I sensed, without consciously thinking it, that even if all my rock-and-roll dreams came true I would still probably never be content, because it was my nature to never be content. But John and Freda took

233

things as they came. They were smart, realistic, sane, fun, and always open to whatever might happen at any given time. They were neither overly optimistic nor easily discouraged. I had a hard time keeping things in perspective, like they did. This was our first gig at CB's and none of us had any reason to expect much of a response yet from New York, but this one poorly attended gig meant to me that we were probably doomed to obscurity.

I wanted our band to matter. I wanted it to mean something to the world. But it didn't mean anything to anybody but us, yet.

Throughout my many months and months of tours over the years, people in my bands and crews would often want to go out after gigs, to socialize, to have a few drinks, to listen to music, to see the town, to meet new people. But I would almost always beg off and go back to my hotel room. I didn't know how to enjoy the things everyone around me seemed to be enjoying effortlessly. I never knew if I was depressed because I wasn't able to let go and have fun or if I wasn't having fun because I was depressed; my mind went round and round the question.

If I did venture out with a group, I would spend the whole time in my head, worrying that I wasn't having a good time, wondering why I couldn't relax and why alcohol didn't dissolve the tension, why being drunk didn't make me any less self-conscious, didn't loosen me up at all. At every party, every bar I would sit or stand like a block of wood, petrified, a morose and befuddled spectator surrounded by carefree merrymakers who seemed like a completely different species—with a whole other set of instincts—than my mouselike self.

On one autumn tour of Europe, in Germany—cold, dreary, colorless, humorless old Germany—I was in a black mood on the Autobahn. My band and crew and I were in a minivan. Audis and VWs and BMWs were coming up behind us like race cars in the rearview mirror and whizzing by so fast that our van seemed to vibrate for a couple of seconds after each car passed. I would shudder, and brace myself each time, afraid that we would be slammed from behind, crushed and mangled.

We saw a Mercedes about a quarter mile ahead of us lose control and hit the left guardrail at about a hundred miles per hour, flip over, roll a few times, fast, across the highway, and land upright on the grass

234

slope on the side of the road. We slowed down and approached as the occupant opened his driver's side door and got out and stood on the grass, dazed. The Mercedes, and the man, looked to be remarkably undamaged. Not a scratch on either of them. So we sped up, passed by, and continued on our way. The Germans, with their solid engineering, their rollbars and steel cage construction, and their no-nonsense self-reliance, would be okay. But would I? I was sure this accident was a foreshadowing of some terrible disaster that would soon befall me.

On another road, in another town, traveling from one gray scene to another, from one dingy, sparsely populated dive to another, I fantasized about jumping out of the van, about escaping. From Germany/Holland/Canada/Ohio/South Carolina/wherever I was, and from my self and my head, and from the tour and all its demands to be confident, be assured, be fabulous, be great, be there, and there, and there, live, in person, available for all to see and criticize and judge.

I was in the backseat of the van, next to the door. My eyes kept going from the door handle to the speedometer, trying to gauge in advance how much physical damage I would do to myself if I opened the door and leapt out toward the side of the road at forty miles per hour, at fifty, at sixty. I imagined bracing myself for the blow of the hard ground and rolling. I might be able to walk away with just a couple of bruises, maybe a sprained ankle.

A person can't just up and quit for no real reason, can she? Because she's having a bad day, because she's feeling down? Because she doesn't have the energy to convince herself that she matters? That anything matters? No one loves every second of every minute of her job, I tried to tell myself. And: What right do I have to feel good all the time? What right does anyone?

So I stayed in the van, sucked it up, toughed it out, did my job, finished every tour.

It didn't matter where I was: on tour, in the studio, on hiatus or vacation. Even back at home, presumably safe and comfortable, my monster would find me, and pounce. And so, then, wherever I was, that was where I didn't want to be.

I once contemplated driving my car through a high wooden fence in front of a random house in my hometown. I drove past it and then I circled back a couple of times, turning the idea over in my mind.

Plowing my car fast through a big fence seemed a logical thing to do, given my state of mind at the time. It wasn't that I wanted to die, or even hurt myself; I just wanted to smash through something, to forcibly shake off the inexplicable anguish that was clinging to me like a leech.

But I am too sensible, in the end, to drive my car on purpose through a fence.

Depression is a recurrent subject in my lyrics. Emotional pain has always been my muse. Here's a partial list of songs about depression—or what it feels like to be depressed—in my repertoire: "Out There," "I'll Take Anything," "Alright" (and, well, practically the whole Blake Babies catalog), "Ugly," "No Outlet," "The Edge of Nowhere," "Universal Heart Beat," "Bottles and Flowers," "Waves," "This Is the Sound," "Feeling Massachusetts," "Running Out." Writing about it is a way to process it, or at least to do something productive with it.

34

August 20

San Diego

We checked out of the Hyatt at noon and drove to the Whole Foods on North Fairfax to get snacks before leaving town. I bought a pint carton of organic blueberries and went and sat in the van, eating my fruit and waiting for everyone else to finish their shopping.

Freda, Heidi, Brian, and Tim eventually ambled out, one at a time, each with his or her own biodegradable plastic bag of food, and we hit the road south to San Diego.

I decided to have a listen to my new Brian Eno CD. I'd never really heard any of his ambient stuff before, but I had always been curious about it because Eno's name was always popping up, and that meant that he was significant, somehow, or at least interesting. He'd clearly had an effect or an influence on many listeners. I needed to find out, once and for all, what this guy was all about so that I could have an opinion the next time his name came up in conversation.

After the first song, I was unimpressed. Same with the second and third songs. All Eno seemed to be doing on this record was to take a really simple, lethargic instrumental motif and beat it into the ground slowly.

By the fourth track, I was thoroughly bored.

Right about then, Freda interjected into the listening session from the backseat and asked, politely, "Juliana, do you think you could take this music off? Or maybe turn it down? There's some frequency that he keeps hitting on the keyboard that is hurting my ears."

"Yeah, sure," I answered.

I was more than happy to oblige at that point. I'd heard enough. I pressed EJECT.

"What's the big deal about this guy?" I wondered out loud. "Nothing happens in these songs. They go nowhere."

And all of them seemed to be in the exact same range, and hitting the same few piercing notes—like an irritating mantra—which produced the same excruciatingly trebly overtone (the one bothering Freda) over and over again.

"This stuff sounds just like the music they play when you're getting a massage," I said.

Was I not getting something? Was I too dim to understand certain revered artists' esoteric talents, or something?

Then a lightbulb slowly lit up over my head, and I thought, "Maybe Eno invented New Age! Maybe that's what all the fuss is about; he ushered in a whole movement, a whole modern genre of music. I mean, they call his music 'ambient' but isn't that really just another word for 'New Age,' or for 'hippie-crystal-massage music'? I get it, I think."

I took the CD out of the player, thinking, "Not my cup of tea at all." I held it in my hand and contemplated throwing it out the window of the moving van, but then I didn't do it.

The truth was, I had too much respect for the man for doing his own thing, for so long, outside the mainstream, to chuck *Music for Films* out the window, even if I didn't like it.

There was a bit of envy, too, because Eno had always been a critical favorite, one of those modern-day artists who, like Beck or the Beastie Boys or PJ Harvey, rock critics seem to think is important, no matter what he does or how she may trip up in the process of experimenting. One of those artists who, whenever he releases a new album, all of the critics, predictably, genuflect together in worship of the artist's genius and bravery. It's almost as if the critics' collective reaction had been decided upon beforehand, in a secret meeting, and put in writing and then signed, as a decree, by this exclusive community of rock reviewers: "We, the modern music arbiters, hereby declare that anything and everything Eno or Wilco or Radiohead or Cat Power ever does, from now until the end of time, will be lauded and applauded and given the maximum number of stars by us. Period."

But I just didn't get it. I thought *Music for Films* was incredibly boring. Am I stupid?

When I was ten years old I discovered, while casually, curiously exploring around the outside of my skull with my fingers one afternoon, that there was a large bump on the top. My skull was not completely uniformly round, and I had never before taken the time to notice. I somehow imagined that this lump on my skull was a tumor. A brain tumor. On the outside surface of my skull, where my hair grew. I asked my dad to feel my head one evening when he came home from work at the hospital. I guided his hand with mine to the spot where the lump was and I said, "See? Feel that? Is that a brain tumor?" Dad said, matter-of-factly and good-naturedly, "It might be." And so, without the definitive "No" I was looking for, I worried obsessively for months afterward, thinking, as I fingered my lump, that I was probably dying. Dad never set me straight, though I did eventually figure out that brain tumors reside underneath the skull, in the brain, and do not manifest as tactile lumps on the surface of the head.

After Eno, all was silent in the van for most of the rest of the way to San Diego. Tim, who was driving, had his eyes on the road and his thoughts somewhere unknown to me. I sat mute in the passenger seat. Freda was lying down, sleeping. And Brian and Heidi were in private worlds of their own, gazing out of their respective windows at the passing scenery.

We arrived in San Diego a couple of hours before our scheduled load-in time at the Casbah Club. We checked into our hotel, which was just off the highway and surrounded by malls and megastores: Circuit City, Borders, the Gap, Best Buy, Target, et cetera, et cetera, ad infinitum, in both directions up and down the highway. There were as many places to buy things as there were palm trees.

We all split up for a while, to do our own things: Freda went for a swim in the hotel pool, Tim set up his computer to do some work in his room, Heidi called a friend of hers who lived in town, and Brian went for a walk. I took the van down the highway to the nearby Borders bookstore. I wanted some periodicals to leaf through. At this point in the tour, my brain had just about shut down all of its nonessential functions. Thinking, or any type of concentration, was out. Too taxing. I'd given up on trying to read anything as substantial as even magazine articles; reading the captions underneath the celebrity photos in *People* was enough of a mental workout for me.

Approximately two hours later we were at the Casbah Club, right down the street from the airport. I hadn't been there since the late 1980s, when I'd played there with the Blake Babies. I remembered the club being very tiny then; almost, literally, a hole in a wall.

But this time, the place seemed bigger. I knew it was the same location because of the planes that were roaring in low over our heads, coming in to land just like they did thirteen or whatever years ago, but the club definitely seemed to have more space now—more square footage. I wondered, had the place actually been renovated? Or was it my mind; my worldview; my perspective that had expanded, making the Casbah appear larger?

While Tim set up his soundman stuff and Freda unpacked her drums, I explored the club. It was now a series of connected smallish spaces—more than the one little room in my memory that was now part of the front room where the bands played.

I went in the room in the back, farthest from the street, and discovered some old-school video games. I put fifty cents in the Ms. Pac Man machine. Nothing happened. I told the mustached, bald-headed guy drying glasses behind the bar, "Hey, the Pac Man is broken."

The bartender said, "Oh, okay. Do you want your fifty cents back?"

"No, that's okay."

Right then, I heard a cop car flying past the club, in hot pursuit. Its siren sounded just like the Pac Man would have, if it had been working: *wocka wocka wocka.*

Then I tried the Asteroids. It worked. I played for a while, then went back to the main room where the promoter had set out some hospitality for us. There was hummus and tabouli and pita bread and bananas. The tabouli was extremely oversalted, as if the cap had come off the salt shaker and it had all poured in, but I ate a bunch anyway. That was my dinner.

After soundcheck, Freda and Tim and I got in the van to go back to the hotel for a couple of hours before the show. Brian stayed behind to sell merch and Heidi waited for her friend who was coming to meet her.

Freda and Tim and I stopped at a Coffee Bean and Tea Leaf near the hotel. Tim needed a caffeine fix. I was feeling bored and lethargic and ordered a cappuccino to try to perk myself up, violating my "no stimulants other than tea" rule (which I had enforced upon myself at the start of the tour in hopes of making my insomnia go away). The cappuccino tasted weird; not like coffee or milk but like artificial sugar and liquid plastic and Styrofoam, with a strange chemical aftertaste. I wondered if this was how all cappuccinos tasted (fake) in California, where everything is plastic. I drank a few sips and threw the rest away when I got back to my hotel room. Technically, I had broken my "no stimulants" rule, but in effect, I was still on the wagon because I had imbibed such a negligible amount.

As soon as we arrived back at the club, I went straight to the tiny office that was doubling as a dressing room and tried on a bunch of different tops that I had brought with me from the hotel. In a confused rush, I decided on the red tube top. I was halfheartedly toying with the idea of trying to be a better performer—more of a crowd-pleaser—and showing off more of my body. Although this particular tube top was fairly demure, as far as tube tops go—there was no cleavage or stomach showing, at all (the only unexposed skin was arms/hands, neck, collarbone, shoulders, and of course, my face) and I knew that wearing it wasn't ultimately a big deal (I was even wearing a strapless bra underneath, so my breasts wouldn't bounce around) and couldn't possibly damage my reputation in the course of one night—I still felt like a hooker.

After the show I quickly changed back into my body-covering civilian clothes and went and sat by Brian at the merch table for a while and signed some stuff.

When most of the crowd had emptied out of the club and things had quieted down, my tourmates and I loaded our gear into the van and then hung out outside the entrance to the club watching planes roar in over our heads while Tim went to collect our guarantee. A few last stragglers and loyalists had me sign a few more CDs. One guy walked by, said, "Great show," to me with a smile ("Thanks," I said) and continued on his way. The scene was casual and pleasant. The night was winding down uneventfully. It was kind of a nice way for it to end. There were no weirdos, no creeps, no morons, no critics, no screaming crying hysterical teenage fans trying to tear my clothes off of me, no drama. It was just another day at the office, you know?

35

Windows

I was living in New York in the mid-1990s, gearing up for a short tour of mostly college venues in New England, to warm up for a series of European dates promoting my *Only Everything* album, after which there would be still more shows in North America. In the weeks leading up to the start of the college tour, I fell into one of my depressions, and with it some strange and disconcerting new sensations presented themselves: I would wake up every morning at 4 a.m.—regardless of when I had gone to bed the night before—suddenly wide awake, unable to sleep anymore. Once out of bed, facing the day, a pervasive inner agitation, like tiny wheels in my brain were moving way too fast, made it impossible for me to concentrate, on anything. Not on my writing, not on any book or even a magazine, not on any one continuous thought, not even on the most mindless TV show. So I had no way to distract myself from the awful, oppressive gloom I felt. At the same time, I had no physical energy. I felt weighted down and slow, and the air, inside and out, seemed thicker than normal, like a dense fog. My movements, my reactions, and even my speech were leaden.

I would sit on my couch looking out the window at the sky, grinding my teeth, too frozen in mute, silent terror to cry or even to move, really, and completely saturated with dread, worrying—*believing*—that the sun might not come up the next morning or that it would drop out of the sky and leave the world dark and cold and dead, like my spirit.

As usual, I didn't know where these feelings had come from and I didn't know how to make them go away. I was alone in New York. I had failed to make any real friends in the year I'd been living there. (I only ever left my apartment to buy food or to work out at my health club a few blocks away.) I didn't have any kind of therapist, nor was I in the habit of confiding in anyone in my family, which was scattered around the country. I had no one to talk to, really, and what was happening to me was worse and more frightening than any depression I had ever experienced before.

It felt like this time, unlike all the others, the cloud wasn't going to dissipate. This infernal woe had spread its poison all through my brain and body, as well as the city and sky, and I couldn't see any way out. And I had to go on tour. It was all planned and scheduled and arranged. I guessed going on the road would be no worse than sitting in my apartment waiting for the end of the world, alone.

It's so difficult to describe a bad depression. Even if one could capture it in all its blank, dead horror, she would know that there was not really any point in telling anyone else. Talking about how one's blood has run cold, or dry, or black, doesn't bring any relief. It's as tedious for the sufferer as for the listener. Telling someone is only burdening him with a big problem that doesn't appear to have any solution: It hurts to be awake. The morbidly depressed person's only hope is for unconsciousness; for the gift of sleep to free her for the requisite seven or eight hours each night. Even then, disrupted or stunted sleep is often part of the problem.

So I set out on tour promoting *Only Everything*, lugging my sluggish body from campus to campus, from stage to stage, from hotel to hotel, and so on, while consumed every waking second with the utter, definitive hopelessness and worthlessness of everything; of the future, of today, of the past. The ubiquitous, homely Wal-Marts and McDonalds and Taco Bells and Best Buys and Staples sprouting up out of every

244

roadside like poisonous, monster weeds seemed, in my funk, justifiable enough reason for anyone to shoot herself in the head.

The suicide note might read: "I did it because of all the Wal-Marts."

At the northeastern colleges I was visiting, I saw the inevitable death in every student's clean-scrubbed, innocent, smiling face. At NYU, the refreshments the student concert committee had set up for me and my band and crew—a bag of tortilla chips; a jar of salsa; a Saran-wrapped plastic supermarket deli platter of dried-out, precut broccoli florets, baby carrots, celery, et cetera, arranged in sections in cubbies around a centrally located foil-covered container of "dip"; a bunch of Budweiser bottles that had been shoved upright into the ice in a plastic tub to chill them—was the most tragic thing I had ever seen.

The way some of the curtains in some of the campus classrooms hung, powerlessly, like on the gallows, resigned to their eternal hanging fates, broke my heart. And the fluorescent lighting throughout many of the public rooms seemed to bring into harsh, stark relief all the sadness and ugliness and barbarism and pain that ever was, in the millions of years of the history of civilization.

I would hold myself together during soundcheck, and then afterward I would saunter off to some quiet, relatively hidden space— behind one of the tall, thick, floor-skimming industrial curtains shading the big long glass windows behind the stage in the auditorium at Brandeis, for example, or lying down under the table in the small class-room being used as a dressing room at Amherst—and just sob. Chest-heaving, face-drenching, hourlong uncontrollable epic bawl-fests. I would wait until my guys were off exploring the campus or going to find dinner so I could do my crying in private in the dressing room. Or if I happened to be in the auditorium, I would make sure, before I cried, that no ticket holders had been let in yet and couldn't catch me in the act, with splotchy cheeks and snot dripping off my chin.

Once in a while one of my guys from the tour would find me and would rub my back for a minute or ask if I needed anything, and offer unspoken sympathy. I wanted to explain what I was going through, but I couldn't explain and I felt there was nothing anyone could do to help me, anyway.

At Amherst, I went outside and had a walk around the campus after load-in. The air seemed heavy, pressing on me from all sides, like I was under deep ocean water. My mind kept repeating, "The world is a dark and lonely place. The world is a dark and lonely place." I found a wooden bench along a brick walkway among some bushes and under a tree. I sat down, looking out over a grassy hill that led down to a soccer field.

I felt as if I was made of very thin glass. I was afraid that the breeze rustling the leaves in the trees might knock me off my bench and send me falling to the bricks, shattering into a million tiny shards.

A twig landed on my pant leg. A spider scurried up its web between two bushes next to me to check on the bug it had snared. A grackle squawked and I winced. Nature's sounds and stirrings went on harmonizing discordantly at full force, broadcasting their harsh indifference to my wretchedness.

It was very clear to me at that moment: the night falls and the day breaks and they don't stop for anyone. And sometimes a baby bird falls from its nest before its little wings ever have a chance to fly, and it's dragged away to some shaded spot where, before long, its bones and feathers and black sunken eye-holes are covered in leaves, and forgotten, as if it had never even existed.

How could I get up onstage and sing "Spin the Bottle" knowing all this?

I became fixated on windows. There was a lot of downtime spent waiting, hanging around before and after soundcheck and before and after the show, while equipment was being set up and broken down, and while opening bands were playing. I began spending all of my spare time studying the windows in the campus buildings we were stationed in each night. The first thing I would do as soon as I came upon a new window was to see if it opened, and if it did, how and how far. Some didn't open at all. And some opened wide enough for a person to fit through. I would nestle myself as comfortably as I could right up next to the glass and gaze out, pondering what would happen if I jumped and hit the ground below. I envisioned the blow knocking me unconscious, and thought how wonderful that would be. How wonderful it would be to sleep, I mean, and to not wake up for an extended period of time, until my depression had lifted.

"I'm gonna do it. Now, tonight. I'm gonna," I thought, every night after the show, as the others were packing up the gear and I waited in the dressing room, looking from my chosen window out at the ground. But every night I would lose my nerve. I would worry: I could break my neck or my back and then wake up paralyzed, *if* I woke up. What if I died? I didn't want to die. There was no question about that. I just wanted to feel better, and in my severely depressed, muddled head I honestly believed that the only way for me to make this happen was to jump out of a window.

Every night I got up in front of a room packed full of enthusiastic, clapping, cheering college kids, not knowing how I would summon the energy to get through the show when, because of my diseased state of mind, I had no faith in what I was doing anymore. That was the worst part. All of a sudden my music felt hollow and worthless. I was singing without any love or conviction. Without the belief that what I was doing was meaningful and necessary, there really was no reason for me to be here, to be anywhere. There was nothing else to hold on to. My faith in my music was my one reason for getting out of bed in the morning. It had always been my lifeboat and now it was sinking, fast.

I somehow managed to get through each show and then, later, after I'd chickened out and not jumped out any window, I would go back to my hotel room and pray to God, every night before bed, for the courage to follow through on my plan the next day, to jump out the *next* window, the next night, on the next campus. Just thinking that it was finally going to happen—to really happen—tomorrow would make me feel almost happy, late at night, for a little while, like a bit of weight was lifting from me; I knew I would soon be lying blissfully unconscious, somewhere safe, out of the swamp in my brain, and away from everything and everyone; from the pressure and the business and the people at the label watching the charts and counting the days until they could drop the ball on me, on my album, on my future. And people would finally understand how much I was suffering, and that I wasn't sullen and antisocial by choice, and that I hated that I was that way, and they would understand how hard it was for me to navigate the world of people.

But every morning when I woke up, the terrible crushing malaise would be upon me, full force, and I would cry upon opening my eyes, cry because I was awake, cry because I didn't know how I was going to get through the day and the show.

This went on for the rest of the college tour until the last night, at NYU, where I had an epiphany. I realized in a moment of clarity that this depression of mine had become so unbearable that I was going to *jump out of a window* to get away from it, and that this was completely insane. I was sick in the head and something had to be done about it, immediately. I needed to cancel the European tour. My problem wasn't a simple problem, with a simple solution and a quick turnaround, like flu or a headache or food poisoning or a sprained ankle, and I couldn't manage it on my own anymore. I needed to check myself into some kind of psychiatric treatment facility where trained professionals could help me to fix my broken psyche.

Before the show at NYU, I called my manager and told him that I wanted to cancel the European tour (which was scheduled to begin in a few days). I explained the situation and told him that if I didn't do something about it I feared I might end up hurting myself. And then I said, "Gary, I am not well."

I found it hard to admit that something seriously bad and out of my control was happening to me, and even harder to make the decision to actually try to find someone to help me. I was always reminding myself that everybody gets blue sometimes. "It could be worse" was my mantra. But "worse," for me, now, might mean a broken back or a coma or two shattered legs.

I knew that my guys and my audiences and the European promoters would recover from my canceling. But I also knew there would be repercussions. Record companies don't like it when artists shirk their promotional duties, for whatever reason.

For example, I was once in the middle of a tour when my bass player received word that his beloved grandmother had passed away. He wanted to take two days off to fly home and attend the funeral, and then rejoin the tour. It would mean a canceled show. When we informed my record company about the situation, their reaction was, "Does he really need to go to the funeral?"

I knew that my decision to cancel a whole tour of a whole continent, which was meant to launch the release of my newest album over there, would quite likely hurt the album's success and sales. If I didn't continue working, pushing my new product, working the momentum I had built up from my last big attention-getting album, I could screw up my whole career and future by failing to capitalize on whatever fleeting buzz I'd managed to acquire, temporarily.

And on top of that, my musicians and crew had been counting on paychecks and had planned their lives around going to Europe and working for the next two months. A couple of them had sublet or given up their apartments and so had no place to go back to until two months later. And now they were going to be all of a sudden out of work in New York City.

Just before showtime at NYU, I gathered my band and crew in the dressing room and told them what I had told Gary: I was canceling the European tour. The guys had seen that I was struggling with something pretty badly, and most of them, when I announced the cancelation of Europe, were either sympathetic or graciously hid their displeasure from me. My merch guy, Dale, however, said without blinking an eye that he wanted to be paid for the canceled dates, and wasn't shy about letting me know that he was annoyed, angry, and unsympathetic.

"I'm really sorry, Dale," I said. "I'll still pay you, okay? But I just can't go to Europe right now. I really cannot do it. I'm not well. I need to see a doctor." And then, addressing all of them, I said, "It wasn't an easy decision to make, but I have to do it. I waited 'til the last minute to cancel because I was hoping I could just keep it together but I can't. At this point I really feel like I don't have a choice. This thing I'm dealing with has gotten kind of out of control."

I had never canceled anything before. How could I explain to my guys that if I didn't quit right now, I was probably going to end up mangled on the ground under a second-story or possibly even third-story window? Would they understand?

I didn't understand it myself. That was why I needed to try to get on some kind of path to figuring it all out. In the meantime I needed medicine. I had read all the books on the newly popular SSRIs and I thought I'd be the perfect candidate. When my mood had been stabilized, my plan was to move out of the city and back to Massachusetts, where it was a bit more low-key and comfortable for me; get a puppy; find a good analyst; maybe try yoga. Anything and everything I could think of to help get me on my feet, and get better, and stay that way so I never had to go through this again and so I could do my job. I had to take charge of my mental health and well-being rather than continue to react to my feelings and to life with harmful, self-destructive thoughts. If I'd ruined my career by opting out (albeit temporarily) in the middle of it, then so be it. I wasn't enjoying myself anyway. This way, maybe I could figure out *why* I wasn't having a good time, and how I could in the future, if I still had a future.

It was reported in the music press that I canceled my tour due to "nervous exhaustion." I wondered why my publicist hadn't simply told everyone the plain truth—that I was suffering from a spell of severe depression and had sought medical help and was currently undergoing treatment—instead of issuing such a vague, all-purpose "nervous exhaustion" line, which doesn't really mean anything and as far as I know isn't even a real diagnosis. "Nervous exhaustion" made it sound as if I had collapsed, but in fact I had done the opposite: I had deliberately walked off and away from the stage, and the road, and my career, for a little while, in order to *avoid* an impending collapse—to nip it in the bud. I had taken necessary action to save myself. And this was seen by some as a bad move (and not in everyone's best interest). In the eyes of the music business and media Machine, it's better—saner—for a girl to work, work, work, and promote, promote, promote until she breaks down or blows out and is hauled away on a stretcher than for her to walk away on purpose when she still has some power to decide for herself what is right.

Severe depression was my problem. I had no reason to hide it from the world. I *couldn't* hide it anymore. Why couldn't they have called it what it was? People would have understood. Besides, "severe depression" sounds so much more badass than "nervous exhaustion."

36

August 21

Tucson

It took us about seven hours to get to Tucson from San Diego. The drive was uneventful. Lots of cactus. No one talked. I slept, on and off, and half-dreamed/half-fantasized about going home, and not having to carry my bags and guitars into and out of a new hotel every morning and night, and not having to talk or perform or impress anyone, and just staying in one quiet place.

It was the final leg of the tour and I was spent. I felt half-dead, like a zombie, unable to sustain a thought for more than a couple of seconds, unable to maintain a conversation unless it was at about a third-grade level of intelligence, and barely able to even squeeze out more than a grunt in answer to any of the simplest yes or no questions. All I wanted was to lie down and close my eyes.

We had become one big, multilevered, ticking, humming, rocking and rolling machine, programmed to Do the Show. That, and the other few essentials, was all any of us knew or cared about at this point: Eat, Drink, Do the Show. Then shut down, unplug, and pass out. And drag ourselves out to the van again the following day and aim for the next destination so we could do it again: Eat, Drink, Do the Show, Sleep. And so on.

We checked into the Congress Hotel at five o'clock. At least we thought it was five. The big clock in the lobby said four o'clock. None of us had realized until that moment that we had passed over from Pacific Time into Mountain Time during the drive. Which meant that now we had a whole extra hour to relax and do nothing, which was all I wanted to do.

The hotel and the Club Congress, where we were to play, were in the same building. The rooms were right upstairs from the club and that meant we wouldn't have to leave the premises at all, all night long, if we didn't want to.

My room was small and suspended in time, somewhere in the past, when there were no TVs or air conditioners or cordless digital devices. There was a hefty black rotary telephone connected to the switchboard at the front desk. The operator would get you an outside line if you needed to make a call. A simple white chenille bedspread covered a high iron bed, and an old-fashioned wooden radio with one big tuning knob and a built-in speaker sat on a big bureau.

After I'd dropped my bags, I turned on the ceiling fan, which generated surprisingly voluminous amounts of lovely cooling air, and lay down on the bed. I was almost asleep when the really loud old phone rang, I mean really RANG, a few minutes later. It was the man at the front desk telling me that Hank, my old friend, whom I hadn't seen in a few years, was downstairs in the lobby. I got up and went down to see him. We sat down for a cup of tea and caught up. He and his beautiful Swedish wife, Lena, had just had a baby girl two months ago. Delilah. That made two with Lena (Delilah plus Luke, aged five) and one (Sandy) from a previous marriage.

"How's Sandy doing?" I asked.

"She's really tall," said Hank. "She's fifteen now."

"Wow! Sandy's already fifteen? I always think of her as a little girl."

"Yeah. She just dyed her hair black. And she's on the verge of having a boyfriend."

"Oh my God. Wow. She's a teenager. How did that happen?"

I started playing in my first band when I was Sandy's age. I couldn't believe how fast all the time since then had gone by. My high school cover band, the Blake Babies, and the Atlantic years all seemed to have happened in a different lifetime, so long ago, but only yesterday. And now here I was in Tucson, again, with my old friend Hank, and he had gray hair now, and three kids, and was pushing fifty.

I met him when he was thirty-three and I'd thought, at the time, that thirty-three was so old and that it was kind of exotic to have a real grown-up for a friend. And then, later, when we became a little more than friends, and started collaborating on some music, I could have probably chosen to make a life with Hank. I could be living in Tucson now, with kids and stepkids with whom I could share my record collection. But I had opted to be alone and to pursue my own music at the expense of love and family and home and Hank and everything—*everyone*—else.

Hank had to go do some errands but said he would be back to see the show. Tim and Brian and I and the girls ate dinner at the restaurant in the hotel. Then we walked through the lobby, into the club, and did a soundcheck. Afterward, fatigue was like an anvil strapped to my back as I climbed the stairs up to my room.

"What I really need is a pipe cleaner–like thing," I thought. "To clear the fuzz out of my brain. Or I need like an oil change for the brain. Or like a leaf blower or snowblower but for the inside of the head. A mindblower."

I got to my room and lay down on the bed and talked to myself some more:

"Oh God, I so don't want to play tonight. It feels so good to be lying down. I'm so ready to go home. I want to eat ice cream and watch TV and do nothing. But I have to maintain. I have to keep it together for four more shows.

"Four more shows? That's nothing. It'll be over before I know it. And then I'll miss it, and wish it was still happening.

"I'm just tired. A little burned-out. I love my job, I really do. How can I complain? This is a wonderful life. It is. I'm lying on a bed in Tucson. It could be so much worse. I'm just tired."

When showtime approached, I went down and started setting up my pedals onstage alongside Freda and Heidi, in front of the crowd, as usual. A young man with untamed frizzy blond hair came right up to me, pushing others aside, like a heat-seeking missile, with an unrolled poster of me and it was instantly obvious that he was not quite right, mentally. (He didn't say hello; that's always a sign.) He radiated a jittery, threatening energy that seemed about ready to fly off from its tether at any second into incoherence or possibly rage. He muttered, "The Blake Babies rock," and smirked inappropriately as he thrust his poster at me, for me to sign. Then he made the devil horns with his index finger and pinkie.

I signed the poster with a Sharpie from out of my toolbox and tried not to make eye contact. Then I turned and went right back to setting up my equipment and tried to look busy. But the guy with the Einstein hair remained standing in front of the stage, mumbling dementedly toward me.

Soon Tim, ever watchful and sensing possible impending danger, arrived on the scene and placed himself between me and my strange fan and said to me, loud and clear enough for the guy to hear, that if I had, you know, a problem, to just let Tim know and he would fetch the security guy who would take care of the situation for me.

I said, "Thanks," and Tim went back to his mixing board.

It was a fairly explicit warning directed toward the weird guy, but at the same time Tim was leaving it in my hands and making it seem as if I could take care of myself so that I didn't come across as a diva. Tim is sensitive to the fact that I don't like to be coddled and that I am fully capable of defending myself in minor skirmishes, but he knows when to intervene discreetly, to let me know that I'm not on my own if I don't want to be.

My demented fan now appeared even more agitated than before and said to me, or rather, spat at me, "Hey, man, tell that fucking faggot that he needs to get his dick sucked."

Right about then, the security guard Tim had mentioned intervened and grabbed the lunatic, gently, and removed him from my immediate vicinity.

"Fine with me," I thought.

This way, being rescued, I didn't have to try to reason with a crazy person. I really didn't think the guy would have complied if I had told him myself to please settle down. I didn't think he was necessarily a bad person, or that he deserved to be treated unkindly. I just thought he maybe needed some psychopharmalogical assistance. And I couldn't help him with that. So the next best thing was for us to be separated from each other.

When I was about seven years old, I overheard my mother and father talking in low voices about an acquaintance of theirs who had just been sent to "the funny farm." I interrupted them and asked, "Dad, what's the 'funny farm'?"

"It's where they plant people," Dad answered, with only the tiniest hint, I think, of a smile.

From then on—for years—I had an image in my mind of live human heads, sticking out of the ground in neat little rows, like crops. I didn't know why they did this to these people, or where these funny farms were; I just knew that they existed and that people were living out there, in the country, stuck in the dirt up to their necks.

That night, it felt just right onstage, playing the songs. Everything was in place—words, melody, harmony, voice, guitar, drums, bass, flow, rhythm—chugging and humming along, continuously regenerating itself. The crowd was warm and accepting and generous with their positive energy and applause. I saw Tim smiling and dancing in place in time to the music at his perch behind the sound board, so I knew we must have been sounding pretty good.

It's funny how, as a tour progresses and the band gets tighter and sharper as a musical unit, everything else seems to kind of disintegrate—the body wears down, people start to get on one another's nerves, the brain goes all fuzzy. In fact I've often wondered if focusing so intently on playing music for hours every night doesn't damage other, nonmusical parts of my brain. Could it be that strengthening one area (the musical area) takes away from other areas? Like it creates a right side/left side imbalance? Is that why, upon returning home from

255

a long tour, I always feel as if I have killed or at least lost a whole lot of brain cells, even though I haven't been drugging and drinking?

Immediately following the show, I signed some CDs and ticket stubs and posters from the stage. While I interacted with my public, I overheard Hank telling Tim that tonight's show was the best-sounding show, in terms of sound quality, that he had ever heard there at the Club Congress. And he'd been to a lot of shows there.

I glanced over at Tim to see his reaction. He was beaming, looking simultaneously proud and grateful.

Tim doesn't often receive feedback or appreciation for the work he does. Sound engineers generally don't. People in the crowd reserve all their praise for the band and they take it for granted that the sound quality is tolerable. They only notice the soundman's work when the sound is messed up.

It was nice to see Tim get some notice.

After the club had cleared out and I was finished with my social duties, I sipped a tequila on ice at the bar with Hank. He liked the show a lot—said it was the best show he'd ever seen me do. That felt good. Hank was an honest man and he'd been around for a long time, and seen a lot, and wouldn't say anything he didn't mean.

After Hank had gone, I went up to my room feeling the satisfaction of a job well done. Freda and Heidi and I were all into the rhythm of the tour and though tired, we were sounding good and as a result I wasn't so worried about whether or not I could pull this trio thing off. I knew at last that I could—we could—do it. We were doing it. It had all come together, at the end. Finally.

And I could sleep. Man, could I sleep. My insomnia from the first half of the tour was nothing but a memory, and now I had the opposite problem; now I was practically narcoleptic.

"I want to write tonight," I said to myself. "I'll write until I fall asleep."

I pulled my pen and my notebook out of my backpack and got into bed with the pillow propped up behind my back. Five minutes later, I put the pen and notebook down on the nightstand beside the bed and laid my head down and fell asleep.

In the morning the weird frizzy-haired guy from the night before showed up with a video camera as were loading our equipment into the van outside the club/hotel and started filming. No one seemed to mind but me. I stayed inside until Tim made him go away.

"Can you believe that guy?" I said after he had gone. "Filming us, first thing in the morning? When we don't have any makeup on or anything? Before caffeine? Doesn't he realize how fucked up that is? That guy really is mental."

37

Begging to Be Dropped

In *Moby-Dick*, when young Pip falls overboard, he sees a vision underwater of "God's foot upon the treadle of the loom." His vision, or maybe the trauma of having almost drowned, transforms him. After Pip is rescued, it is clear that he has lost his mind and will never be the same again. He has had a transcendent, illuminating experience that he can't make others understand—to them, Pip just seems crazy.

I decided to call my next album—my third for Atlantic—*God's Foot*.

I felt God, or fate, or whatever you want to call it, always working on the loom of my life, and it was futile for me to struggle against it. I had always gone obediently where it led me, knowing it would lead me to where I needed to go. Although I sometimes found myself disgruntled, discontented, and aghast at my circumstances, I always knew that compared to lots of people, I was really lucky. Making music, and making a living at it—having an audience to listen to it—was a great gift. And I was always afraid that if I complained too much, it might all be taken away from me as punishment for not appreciating it enough, and I would have to get an actual job. A real job.

I started working on *God's Foot* in 1996. My record company had given me the go-ahead to produce it myself. Either someone at the label still had faith in me, or they had already written me off and didn't care what I did. At any rate, I went ahead and booked a few weeks at Dreamland, a studio in an old church in Woodstock, New York, and I hired a great engineer named Dave Cook, who knew the studio well.

My Atlantic A&R guy, Barry, would visit the studio from time to time to check on my progress. A&R stands for "artists and repertoire." The A&R guy (or gal) is a sort of liaison between the record company and the artists or bands to whom he or she has been assigned, or has chosen, to work with. The A&R person is there to help guide artists through the songwriting and recording process if they need guidance—and sometimes even if they don't—and to help choose which songs to focus on as the potential hits. Another part of the A&R person's job is to scout for good or promising new artists to sign to the label.

Every time Barry would leave the studio after one of his visits he would say something vague and mildly encouraging to me, like, "Sounds great. Keep at it." But then he would report back to my label, who would tell Gary, my manager, that Barry had said, "I don't hear a single. She needs to keep writing. There's no hit."

So I kept writing songs—more and more songs—and then recording them, in batches. It was fun, actually, and a good exercise in discipline and perseverance. Though I'd never worked like this before: writing on cue, crafting a song with mass appeal in mind. I knew that it was part of the process for many artists, so I went along with it, feeling energized by the fact that the label even cared at all. Barry would come back in to listen to the newest stuff and he would report, again, "I still don't hear a single." This went on for a while.

Barry didn't tell me how, exactly, I was supposed to write a hit; he never gave me any constructive criticism, or insight into what constituted his idea of a hit or how to go about composing it. He just told me that I hadn't yet composed it, and that he would let me know once I had.

That's the problem with hits—no one really knows for sure how to make one; there is no surefire hit-assembling blueprint. That is why if someone is fortunate enough to find himself with a hit on his hands, he cannot count on ever having one again. And this is why the music industry is, at the end of the day, a great equalizer, and why so many artists thank their creator on awards shows and in their album's liner notes; why many of us are eternally humble, and hopeful. We're grateful for our hits, because they're all essentially gifts, given to us by the fickle gods of song. Any one of us could have a hit fall into our lap one day.

Big hits are often surprises, accidents, songs that no one thought would become hits. Radiohead's first big song, "Creep," was a throw-away that the band started playing around with in the studio as a kind of a lark when the "real," serious album tracks were not coming together as well as they should have been. "Creep" featured an almost ridiculously loud guitar coming in like a sledgehammer just before the chorus. (It was, incidentally, produced at Fort Apache by the loud guitar specialists—Paul Kolderie and Sean Slade—who produced my *Only Everything*.) The song was an anomaly and didn't really sound like any of the band's other songs. It was more jarring, more radical, but it had that special ineffable something that makes a hit a hit. The band only recorded one take—only played it through once—and it was perfect. It was their biggest hit.

The record company rep will not hesitate to take at least partial credit for every hit that happens with every artist on his roster, but he will oftentimes have not had, really, any hand in the creation of the hit. Only in the recognition of its brilliance and its hitness, once it has been written and recorded.

Hits create themselves. They come out of nowhere, surprising the record label and even the artist when some perfect chemical reaction in the song's elements, or in the atmosphere, or between instruments and voice, hits everyone in the sweet spot. No one can ever repeat the process on purpose. Well, hardly ever.

I knew this, and so I'd never consciously tried to write a hit before, and the label had never asked me to. They'd allowed me to just do my thing. I'd write my songs, make my albums the way I wanted to, and deliver them to the label and then they'd release them. My most popular song, "My Sister," certainly wasn't crafted to be a hit. It didn't even have a chorus. (If I had been trying to make a hit for the radio, I probably would have written in a big singalong chorus.) "My Sister" was simply chosen, and then marketed, as the first single, and it caught on.

My second most famous song was "Spin the Bottle." The song is in an odd time signature—five beats per measure—so I was surprised when it was chosen to be used in the Winona Ryder–Ben Stiller movie *Reality Bites* and included on its soundtrack album, which eventually sold half a million copies.

Most pop and rock songs and almost all hits are in a more even, danceable meter, like four beats per measure, which is pleasurable to the ear and to the body; it's easy listening, in every sense of the word. Think of army cadets walking together in formation: Hup! two, three, four. Hup! two three, four. A round count of four is a soothing, natural repetition. You don't even have to think about what you are doing, and it's easy to fall back in line if you step out for a second.

A count of five, on the other hand, is more difficult. It demands something of the listener; namely, that he not be so passive, comfortable, and unthinking in his listening. The listener must count along in order to understand what is happening or else, expecting each measure to turn around after four beats, he risks losing the thread of the piece, the whole thing running away from him. If your mind isn't tapped into the *five* feeling, you'll be lost, scratching your head like a dancer who misses a few steps and then finds herself hopelessly behind the others in the routine, unable to catch up.

A song in five can smack of a kind of smugness and arrogance and elitism in the composer: he may be showing off his compositional prowess by self-consciously crafting a challenging, mind-stimulating piece of music, almost as if the whole thing was designed solely to impress his learned colleagues.

Five, or seven, or thirteen—odd meters—can feel awkward and disjointed, as if the songs are lurching. Some musicians I have worked with—drummers, in particular (even good drummers)—have had a difficult time picking up and getting into the groove of songs I've written in these weird time signatures. The musicians usually eventually figured it out, though for some of them, these songs continued to be a problem. Playing them never became second nature, like playing the songs in four were. In more arty and cerebral genres like progressive rock and modern jazz and speed metal, odd time signatures don't seem so odd, because the art-rock/jazz fusion/death metal player wants a mathematical challenge. And the fan is primed for a prickly listening experience. But in pop music uncommon time signatures are not necessarily welcomed or appreciated.

Led Zeppelin's "The Ocean," from *Houses of the Holy*, is one of the more well known examples of a song with a strange, disjointed feel. The lines of the song alternate between eight beats and seven beats. Also, you might know Dave Brubeck's "Take Five," possibly the most famous of all songs written in five. The song's title is a reference to its own meter.

"Spin the Bottle" was the last song I wrote before I went in to record my Atlantic debut, *Become What You Are*. I thought the album needed one more song—something out of the ordinary—that would give the album some variety, to shake it up a little and to break the potential monotony of an album full of songs in the usual four/four pattern.

Before I went in to make *BWYA* I had been obsessively listening to PJ Harvey's first album, *Dry*, which was new. I loved it, loved her unique approach, loved what she was doing. One of the fascinating things Harvey had done on the album was to utilize five/four time in a really compelling way. *Dry* was a cool, raw, sexy, slinky rock record and, like the rest of the album, the couple of songs in five/four time were cool, raw, sexy, and slinky. They weren't prog-sounding or slick or music-school geeky, and neither did they come across as haughty or condescending; it wasn't an intellectual experience, listening to *Dry*. The songs in five—"Water" and "Hair"—were groovy and catchy, without the listener having to count along in order to get into the groove, and this was fascinating, and quite an achievement.

With my "Spin the Bottle," I challenged myself to do what PJ Harvey had: to write a catchy, driving, danceable pop song in a weird, unpopular time signature. I wanted people to dance and sing along even though the song was in five. Moreover, I wanted my song to be relatable, with respect to the subject matter—more relatable than Harvey's kind of tortured, goth damsel-in-distress lyrics (which I loved, and which, more than any female artist in a long time, spoke to and of my experience as a young woman).

The song was a fictional account of playing the game with an unnamed movie star. I thought people would be able to relate to it because spin the bottle is a game that almost everyone has played. It's a universal experience, and it's a part of most listeners' life stories. I, however, had and still have never played spin the bottle. I was writing about an experience that I could only imagine.

By counting the song off at the top on the recording ("One, two, three, four, five") I was calling attention to the fact that it was kind of absurd and obnoxious of me to have written this poppy, bouncy, adolescent song in a very serious, sophisticated, grown-up meter. I wanted everyone to be in on the joke. But then I wanted them to dance and sing along.

The song did surprisingly well. It got a lot of attention and, like I said, it ended up in *Reality Bites*. I even made a video for the song, directed by Ben Stiller (who also directed *Reality Bites*), featuring a handful of the actors who appeared in the movie: Ethan Hawke, Janeane Garofalo, Steve Zahn.

One of the songs I wrote during one of my last *God's Foot* rewrite periods was called "Number One." It was a literal reaction to being told, yet again, by the record company that I needed to deliver a chart-topping smash. The first verse went like this:

"I wrote this song for you/Because you asked me to/You said you don't hear a hit/So here it is/You asked for it."

The chorus went on to say:

"This is the number one song in the universe/Though radio may lie and say I'm never heard/You know it's really good and if they had some taste/They'd put this record on and keep it on all day."

I was getting frustrated, with the rewrite process and with my new struggle to be seen as relevant in a world that was in the process of turning its back on me, and I wanted to finish my album. I thought all of my songs were hits (in the perfect world in my head) and if the record company couldn't convince millions of people of this, it was the company's problem, not mine. I was beginning to realize that *God's Foot* was not going to be very well promoted and that not many people were going to clamor for it, or hear it. The song "Number One" was preemptively giving the finger to the record company—specifically, the new regime at my record company—and to the music business in general, and to all the people who weren't going to listen, all at the same time.

I wanted to send a message to Barry ("Back off, already") and to express the difficulty of trying to write real, honest, heartfelt songs under the gun.

With "Number One" I also wanted to celebrate the joy that I felt in writing and playing and listening to music. What I was trying to say was that what makes a song a great song isn't the fact that it's a hit on the radio but the fact that it's a great song. And I wanted the song to embody that truth; I wanted it to be a great song, and I thought it was a great song. (After I left Atlantic, I almost got signed to another major, largely on the basis of my song "Number One." The new label really loved it and thought it could be a kind of a hit, but they ultimately passed on signing me.)

The fact was, I really was trying to write a hit when I wrote "Number One." I had tried to write an effervescent, catchy, fun, uplifting-sounding song for people to enjoy and for myself be proud of. Apart from the unconventional subject matter, I'd succeeded. I came up with a sweet, simple acoustic guitar riff, played over a perky drum machine beat, and then I overdubbed a bouncy, melodic bass part. Next I added a cool-sounding clavichord part that played off the acoustic guitar riff, and finally, I brought in my friend Mike (who had played second guitar in a late, touring version of the Blake Babies) to play some beautiful swirly Television-esque electric guitar. With my faithful engineer Dave Cook by my side, I built something sunny and bittersweet from nothing and it was exciting. It was pretty and bratty and sad and tough and naive and vulnerable; it was real and it was true, to me. And it was funny, too.

Barry wasn't amused. I don't think he thought the song was as clever as I did. I was obviously running out of things to write about, by then.

At some point—I think it was after Barry had listened to "Number One" and realized that I was never going to give him the "Every Breath You Take" or the "Like a Virgin" or "I Will Always Love You" or "Smells Like Teen Spirit" or whatever it was that he wanted—I made the decision to get off the Kafka-esque merry-go-round of writing more songs, recording them, Barry rejecting them; writing more songs, recording them, Barry rejecting them; writing more songs, recording them, Barry rejecting them, et cetera, ad nauseum, ad infinitum. I decided that *God's Foot* was finished, and that it was great.

When I delivered the completed album to Atlantic, I was hopeful they would come around to my side and fall in love with it. I believed that the album's merits would eventually pull us all through this rough patch. Even if it didn't sell a ton, it would sell some; some people would really like it. I was intensely proud of the work I had done and I looked forward to the world—or at least a small part of the world—hearing it. The label would put it out, I thought, and it would find its own little niche in the universe, its own comfortable patch on the huge lawn of history.

A few weeks went by, during which I listened obsessively on headphones to my mixes. I was enthralled, as if I were an outside observer, with this enigma of musical creation, and by all the nuances of each song and the myriad ways all the instruments weaved in and out and through and around each other, all blended like a delicious, nourishing stew. Listening, it was as if I were looking into the eyes of my newborn baby; I could take partial credit for what I had conceived, but mostly I was in awe, and in love, and feeling very protective of my baby.

God's Foot was no radical departure from what I had been doing from the start with the Blake Babies. I wasn't reinventing the wheel or anything. Still, it was a testament to my slow and steady progression, evolution, and improvement; it was a solid collection of personal, thoughtful, melodic, depressive guitar pop songs personalized with my distinctive youthful vocal signature. (I say "depressive" because there was even a song, "Takin' It E-Z," about a man who begins a Prozac regimen at his girlfriend's insistence. It was inspired by my own recent experience taking an antidepressant, post–wanting to jump out of a window.) The album was more layered, lush, and pretty than my last album, *Only Everything*. More accessible, too, I thought, and easier on the ears. I had branched out a bit from my usual guitar/bass/drums (and sometimes keyboards) and brought in a pedal steel player and a violinist to add some fresh texture. I had tried my hardest to do my best and to give the record company an album that people would like, an album that wouldn't be too difficult to sell.

I heard nothing from anyone at the label for a couple of weeks after the master tapes had been turned in to them. The album was sent to be mastered (a sort of last sonic polishing tweak in the process before manufacturing) but still, no word from Gary, my manager, who'd been calling Barry to get his take on how the album might be set up for marketing and promotion.

After multiple worried, beseeching phone calls to Gary ("What does the label think? What did they say? Did they pick a single? When's the release date?"), he finally delivered some really shocking news: the powers that be at Atlantic had officially decided that they weren't going to release my album. They didn't think it was commercial enough and didn't think it was worth the effort and additional expense (on top of the recording costs) that they would have to put into the manufacturing, marketing, and promotion of it. They wanted to cut their losses now and not get any deeper into the hole with me with this project, since I wasn't the type of artist who could be relied on to dependably move a lot of units out of the box every time I released an album. I was an artist who hadn't lived up to their expectations, who had never paid off in the big way that they had gambled on. I wasn't worth the risk at this point. I was wasting their resources.

In my naivete, and blinded by my love for my new album, I hadn't even considered that Atlantic might not release *God's Foot*. I knew it happened to other people—I had heard of albums that were made and never released—but I never thought it would happen to me, and I was blindsided when it did.

Atlantic wasn't dropping me from the label, at least not yet. They were, in effect, putting me (and my music) on the back burner, but not going so far as to kick me off the Atlantic roster. It was possible that someone at the label still believed I had potential as a moneymaking entity, down the line, or maybe they were just waiting for the biannual "Who should we drop?" meeting (if there was such a thing) to roll around, or for their legal department to get the pink slip paperwork together before they could officially kick me to the curb. I didn't know. All I knew was that keeping busy, working, producing, releasing songs out into the world, and playing them in front of audiences, religiously, regularly, was essential to my sanity.

I had always had a plan, and a schedule: write, record, tour. And then start all over again with the next cycle. Now I didn't know how long it would be until I could make another album. I was under exclusive contract and wasn't legally allowed to release music under my name if it wasn't on the Atlantic label. I had no idea how long they would keep me on the shelf, waiting, smoldering, rotting as who knew how many fruitful creative years passed me by. I had nightmare visions of a bitter old hag, once young and beautiful and talented and full of hope and potential, now sputtering angrily and raging against the evil conspirators and persecutors who waylaid her career and snuffed out her fire and kept her enslaved and took the best years of her life—the artistically fertile years. I had seen women like that. I didn't want to end up like that. Beaten down and broken by something—some power or influence—outside of me. I wouldn't end up like that.

I had made a good album. I had always done consistently good work for Atlantic, and I continued to do so. It wasn't as if I was in a creative slump. And I hadn't been a total failure, commercially—I had done pretty well, in fact. Not bad at all for an emerging artist. In my eyes, the way I had conducted myself in my dealings with the big bad music industry was almost admirable; I had not done anything outrageously immoral or mercenary or crass. All the things I had done were done in order to further the cause and range of my music. I had tried to do things with some integrity and dignity.

Atlantic knew what they were getting when they signed me. I wasn't ever going to be competing for slots on the top-10 charts with the likes of Madonna and Janet Jackson and superstars like that, because I wasn't that kind of an artist. I'd thought that was always understood. If Atlantic suddenly couldn't accept this, and if they didn't appreciate me, anymore, then it made sense to me that I should leave the label.

But Atlantic hadn't granted me a divorce; they had only gone so far as to banish me to sleeping on the couch.

I hatched a plan: I would have Gary schedule a meeting with me and Val Azzoli, the new president of Atlantic. The purpose of this meeting would ostensibly be to discuss my future at the label, to see what their long-term intentions were for me, now that it had been decided that my latest album was going to be shelved indefinitely. And once in Val's office, I would beg him to set me free, to release me from my contract and let me go and take my album somewhere else, somewhere it might have a chance.

Val and his staff had plenty of other signees to attend to now, anyway. There was, for example, Jewel, my labelmate, who had been signed around the same time I had been, as a voluptuous teenage hippie-folkie from Alaska and who was starting to break out commercially in a big way and who was proving to be much more universally palatable and marketable and easy to swallow than I on the radio and with the record-buying public.

Part of my plan was to go in to my meeting in Val's office looking really terrible. That would make them want to drop me. I would look as unattractive as I could and act kind of deranged. Maybe I would remind Val of my recent spell of "nervous exhaustion" that had led me to cancel a big European tour—that would definitely strengthen my case. Why would they want to keep me on, knowing I was a flight risk, and a nutcase, and a dirty, badly groomed one at that? How could they possibly say no to letting me go? What major label wants to put their energy and resources into promoting someone like that—a pretty young singer who doesn't seem to care about cultivating or capitalizing on her prettiness, or about presenting an appealing package to her public?

I stopped bathing about a week before the scheduled meeting. And stopped brushing my hair. I stayed out of the sun and put a halt to my normal everyday exercise routine in order to eliminate any traces of a healthful facial glow, and replace it with a sickly pallor.

Atlantic had their eager, willing, ambitious, smiling, dewy-skinned, super-accessible Jewel. They didn't need me. It would be a cakewalk to convince them of this.

Val wanted this meeting to happen. I probably could have just as easily begged for my freedom over the phone or had Gary do it for me, but Val wanted to see me in person, to hear from my mouth what I wanted to say. It was conceivable that he would try to convince me to stay. And that was why I had to be very prepared (ugly, crazy, dirty) to convince him otherwise. Because I could see the writing on the wall, and it said: "You, Juliana, are no longer needed at Atlantic Records." God's foot was nudging me in the ass.

My tall, brainy, kick-ass lawyer, Sage, accompanied me and Gary to the Atlantic offices in New York City. Sage and Gary both agreed that it was effectively over for me at Atlantic and that I would be better off trying to find a new record company. The three of us waited in the foyer outside Val's office for a couple of minutes until the receptionist told us we could go in. Val came to meet us at the door to his office, welcomed us, shook hands with Gary and then Sage and then me. We all sat down and with Val back behind his desk, I jumped right into my anti-pitch.

It went something like this: Will you please release me from my contract, please? You'd be better off without me. You and I both know it. So why don't you let me go and try to pitch my album to other labels and then you can at least make your investment back on it?

Val put up a good front, listening to me all the way through and pretending that he was disappointed that I wasn't happy at Atlantic; pretending that he hadn't already written me off, that I wasn't only trying to expedite the inevitable.

The meeting was more for Val to go through the charade of hearing me out rather than for him to make an on-the-spot decision or give an immediate answer, and as such, Val was noncommittal and formally friendly; pleasant all the way to the end. As we shook hands on my way out of his office, I wondered why we had bothered with the meeting at all. It was a farce, played out as much for my benefit as for Val's. Now he could drop me from the label and he wouldn't have to be the bad guy who had axed me, because I had asked to be axed. And I could leave the label and I wouldn't have to tell people that I had been dropped, since I had begged to be let go.

On the elevator down from the Atlantic offices, I felt confident, in the way that someone waiting for her soon-to-be-ex-husband to sign the divorce papers is confident: thinking the impending split is all for the best—in everyone's best interest—and anticipating a new freedom but maybe in a little bit of denial about how much it really is going to hurt, and how much it will affect her future.

Atlantic did agree to release me from my contract.

I had either "won my freedom" or I had been "dropped," depending how you looked at it. Six of one, a half-dozen of the other. Now I could take my album out onto the open market and shop it to all the other labels, and sell it to someone else.

Unfortunately, I never did find a buyer for *God's Foot*. I thought for sure someone would cough up the cash to take it off Atlantic's hands and release it, and support my future music-making endeavors, but I was wrong. It took a long time for me to recover from the shock of this new reality wherein certain music is never heard, never loved, never sung. I was always determined to make sure that all the music I recorded found an audience—some small audience, at least—and *God's Foot* never did. It never had the chance because it was never released.

I initially made the album—like I do all of them—to quiet some nagging compulsion inside of me. Though that is the main motivation, the next stage requires an appreciative audience so I can be sure what I've done really means something. If none of it means anything to anyone other than me, does it even really exist? Do I? Or is it like the proverbial tree falling in the forest? The hard part wasn't knowing that I was so easily and quickly let go. It was that my work might not be heard.

I would have found a way to release the album myself but I couldn't afford to buy it back from Atlantic. It wasn't a spectacularly expensive album as far as major label records go, but it wasn't cheap, either. I wasn't wasteful. I wasn't having bottles of Dom Perignon delivered to the studio every night. I didn't slack off. I was always working when the time clock was running in the studio. Still, I had taken full advantage of my major label budget, flying in various musicians from out of state and using as much studio time as I felt I needed to do it right, and in the end it amounted to tens of thousands of dollars. And Atlantic Records declined to transfer ownership of the album to me for anything other than the full amount they had spent on preproduction, recording, mixing, and mastering. Once in a while, in this situation, a record company will opt to give the record back to the artist for nothing and write the whole thing off as a loss at the end of the year. But I wasn't so lucky. Atlantic wanted to hold on to my album in hopes of some record company eventually paying full price for it. Unfortunately, none of the other big labels who could've afforded to buy it wanted it, and the cost was prohibitively high for most of the smaller, independent labels who might've been interested in it.

If I took Atlantic's accounting department's view into account, I could see that their holding on to *God's Foot* was an understandable position. Why should Atlantic eat tens of thousands of dollars if there was a chance someone might decide to cough it up one day?

God's Foot, the master tapes, languishes still in a vault somewhere, gathering dust.

When I was a child, whenever I whined my dad would say to me, "Bitch, bitch, bitch," as if to say, "Yeah, yeah, yeah, whatever, I'm not listening, you take yourself way too seriously." He wouldn't indulge me even one little bit. I guess I learned not to complain. Or at least to feel bad about it when I do. How could I complain now, when it was such a privilege to have ever had a record deal, and an audience, in the first place? When my whole existence, making music and making a living at it, was such a charmed one?

So I picked myself up and I went back underground, whence I came. It was supposed to have been a triumph, extricating myself from that tired, stale marriage with Atlantic, but I felt like I'd eaten a whole humble pie. And I was scared. I felt like I was starting all over again. I steeled myself for an uncertain future, checked to see that my savings could carry me for a while, and made some adjustments to my thinking, to my goals. I lowered my sights. There would be no more major label budgets and no more flying musicians in from L.A. and putting them up in hotels and no more big-time producers producing my records. The only thing I could think to do next was to write and record a brand-new album. Put *God's Foot* in the past, because there was nothing else I could do. Record the new one on my own dime, inexpensively, quickly. Then I could figure out a way to release it myself, independently, if I had to. The Blake Babies put out our first album, *Nicely, Nicely*, on our own self-created record label. I had done it once, I could do it again. And I would if I had to.

Or I could try to license the new album as a one-off to an outside independent label for a little chunk of money (enough, hopefully, to pay back what I would have spent recording it, and then a little extra, to help pay my living expenses). This label would own the masters and have exploitation rights for a set term of a few years, at which point ownership would revert back to me. This seemed like a good business plan for the immediate future.

The more I thought about it, the more I realized that it was a good thing that no major labels had made me any offers after I left Atlantic. I was better off this way. I realized that I didn't want a new long-term record deal, even with an indie; my experience with Atlantic (and Mammoth, who had sold my contract to Atlantic) had left me commitment-phobic. Now that I was no longer entangled with Atlantic, I wanted to enjoy my freedom. I wanted to get back to a more self-sufficient, self-run way of working, on the fringes of the recording industry, where I wouldn't be under any pressure to be glamorous or to sell a lot of records.

I never understood how an artist, after an album sells poorly, or is unfavorably received, quits. Or disappears. Or switches careers. As if her drive to create, or sing, or play, suddenly left her when faced with a little resistance. For me, there was never any thought of quitting. I wasn't ready to surrender. I wasn't done. I was just as unflinchingly, single-mindedly focused as ever on writing and singing and playing guitar and churning out recordings. I would find a way.

My next album, *Bed*, was recorded and mixed in six days. I produced it myself and played all the guitars, with my friend Mikey Welsh on bass and my old drummer from the "My Sister" era, Todd Philips, on drums and John Williams (who was in the great late-eighties Boston band Volcano Suns) at the board. We all hunkered down in an old firehouse that had been converted into a studio in Providence, Rhode Island (providence=timely preparation for future eventualities). Todd and Mikey and I had rehearsed for a few days prior to recording so that we wouldn't be wasting time (and money) working out song arrangements in the studio.

The studio had bedrooms upstairs and the four of us—band and engineer—slept there every night that week. Gary gave me some old, used reels of two-inch analog tape from Fort Apache (his studio) that weren't needed anymore and I brought those to the firehouse and recorded the *Bed* tracks over the old stuff on the tapes. John, the engineer, also spliced together bits of empty spots between songs on various reels to make more clean tape space onto which we would record. If you listen carefully to "I Want to Want You" (track number two on *Bed*) you can hear the sound of a splice—a tiny hiccup in the tape, where it had been cut with a razor blade and then taped carefully back together at a different spot on the tape—on the first "I want" in the third chorus of the song. Another time- (and money-) saving trick was to leave multiple vocal takes in the final mixes of the songs, all piled on there together, so that I didn't have to nail any lead vocal perfectly from start to finish (which can take time, if it's a hard song to sing), nor did I have to comp any vocals (vocal comping: choosing the best bits from each of the four or five or so passes of each lead vocal I had sung and then putting them together to form one master lead vocal track, for each song).

Bed was my "I hate the music biz" album. There were no softening, warming effects and no EQ used on any of the instruments to even them out; I wanted it dry and raw. The songs were full of hurt but also determination to stay strong and rise above and suck it up and keep going and make the most of the new situation I found myself in. I was now free to do whatever I wanted. Any financial or logistical constraints I now faced forced me to be resourceful, which was good for a person. Being dropped was a blessing. I wanted to believe it. "Setback" was just another word for "opportunity." I wanted to prove it. Being out of the public eye suited me. I wanted to enjoy it.

I had faith that this would all make sense someday, that I would look back and see that things had unfolded in exactly the right way.

38

August 22

Albuquerque

We arrived in Albuquerque at five in the evening after driving eight hours from Tucson. All I'd had to eat all day was a Clif Bar, a cup of tea, and a banana. I was very hungry. The club looked just like it had the last time I was there two years ago. I poked my head inside the dressing room, hoping to find a little something to spike my blood sugar, but there was nothing. I dropped my backpack on a chair and went back outside to help load in.

"Hey, Freda," I said to Freda. "Guess what? The rider's not here. Can you believe that?"

Freda frowned and said, "Really? That sucks. I'm so hungry." She went back to unloading her drums from the van.

Hauling my gear from the back of the van onto the high stage on a completely empty stomach was a painful yet familiar exercise in self-flagellation. I knew the others would have picked up my slack and done my share for me if I had told them I wasn't feeling up to the task, but I wanted to suffer; I wanted to be punished, for complaining (again) about the rider not being here on time, and for my incorrigible ill humor.

After loading in, Tim, who had noticed me peek in the dressing room earlier, asked me if the food and drinks were there yet.

"*No,*" I said. I tried to direct my indignation toward the club rather than Tim, adding, "It would be nice if *some*one, for *once,* could have it here when it's supp*osed* to be here. I'm *star*ving."

Tim, looking and sounding genuinely peeved, said, "Are you kidding me? It's not here?"

"No."

"I called them ahead of time to make sure it was here at load-in. Man, that really pisses me off."

"It's not your fault," I said, not very convincingly, and stormed off to the dressing room to sulk. In a few minutes, Freda joined me in the cramped space.

When I used to tour Europe, the rock clubs would often put together an artfully arranged spread for the band, with freshly washed and cut vegetables and good grainy bread and local chocolates and cheeses and other delicious morsels. Even in the tiniest, skankiest, gnarliest dive bar in deepest, most rural Bavaria, they almost always welcomed us in this warm way. And it would set the tone for the whole night, getting us off to a good start well in advance of the actual gig.

But there was no crunchy sliced English cucumber or Camembert or Toblerone for us backstage tonight in Albuquerque. There was nothing at all until a guy in a baseball cap walked in on me and Freda in the dressing room, said nothing, made no eye contact with either of us, and put a plastic Shaw's bag down on the table before exiting the room and letting the door slam behind him.

"Here's your goddamn rider," he may as well have said, as he plunked it down on the table.

Freda opened the bag and took out a small container of hummus, a few green apples with the stickers still on them, a few green bananas (too unripe to even think of eating), six hard, whitish-pink strawberries, and a plastic bag of pita bread.

Where were the vegetables? The Clif bars? The rice cakes?

After a wan soundcheck, we were pointed down the street by the bartender to the restaurant that had an ongoing arrangement with the club to give bands playing there free dinners. Once there, we were given the special "band menu." It was special in that it had fewer choices than the regular menu and the handful of options it did present consisted of the cheapest and easiest-to-prepare items that they had to offer.

I selected the one option that had no animal products in it, and at the same time wasn't fried: a bowl of vegetarian chili, which had no beans in it, which made me wonder, "Is it chili if there are no beans in it?" No, it's not, in fact, chili. What they brought me was vegetable soup. Thin, bland, vegetable soup. Which is not chili.

When Tim ordered the super-duper hot wings, the super-duper hottest-ever code-red hurt-yourself wings, the waitress's eyes opened wide and she asked, "Are you sure you want them?"

Tim nodded and smiled as she continued: "They're really hot. I've never seen anyone be able to eat more than a couple of them. They're really hot."

Tim likes to test the limits of his mouth's endurance in extreme trials of spiciness. When he eats sushi, he dumps the whole wad of wasabi—all of it, all at once—into his little saucer of soy sauce, turning the whole thing green and thick and mushy and, one would think, inedible. But Tim seems to like it like that. It's not that the heat doesn't hurt him. You can see he's in a bit of pain when he's eating wasabi-drenched sushi. But when he is in a bit of pain, most of us would be screaming for water.

When his wings arrived, Tim was still, and silent. He appeared to go into a sort of meditative trance state, like an actress before her big scene or a quarterback before an important game, focusing his mind and energy on shutting out the world around him, in preparation for the intimidating challenge before him.

The waitress issued one last warning before she turned and went away: "Be sure not to rub your eyes after eating these. It'll burn."

I could smell the peppery scotch bonnet glaze from the other side of the table. It curled my nose hairs. I worried for Tim's safety.

Tim picked up a chicken wing. He proceeded to eat the meat off the bones, slowly and deliberately. Tiny beads of sweat materialized on his forehead as he finished and quietly put the bone down on his plate.

My curiosity could not be contained. I burst out with, "Is it hot? How hot is it? Is it as hot as she said?"

Tim, finally breaking out of his trance, smiled and said, his eyes glassy, simply, "Yeah. It's hot."

He had never before, in all the time I'd known him, admitted that any hot thing he'd eaten was truly hot. It was always, "Nah, it's not that hot," or, "It could be hotter," or, "This is nothing." That meat must have really been scorching his mouth.

Tim took a break from his wings and drank from his bottle of beer while the rest of us shoveled our food into our mouths like we hadn't eaten in days. Tim, who fancies himself kind of a gastronome, and a beer and wine (and wings) connoisseur, likes to linger over his meal and savor the flavors. The rest of us are like animals at mealtimes. Dinner for us on the road is not a time for idle conversation or reflection. It is a time to feed—nothing more, nothing less. We want the food to be good, of course, and healthy, if possible, but we want to scarf it down, because we haven't had a real meal all day and besides, there's a show to think about, to prepare for, to play.

Between bites, RJ called me. I took the phone to the back of the restaurant, in a quiet spot near the restrooms, where I could have some privacy. RJ sounded groggy, his voice low and serious. He was in a hotel in Cambridge, on a tour stop. He recounted to me how he had taken a bunch of pills—a dangerous amount—the night before and slept until four the next afternoon (today), at which point he rolled out of bed and stood up, somehow, and promptly vomited.

"You shouldn't do that, RJ," I said. "You could die, you know," was all I could think to say.

"Yeah, I know," he said. "But I'm in your town and you're not here."

I felt, suddenly, overwhelmed, and almost sick, myself. RJ was explaining to me that he had almost killed himself, and that, somehow, it had something to do with me. He was leaning on me and it was heavy. Too heavy. I didn't want to be drawn into this frightening drama with someone whom I only saw once a year, at most. It was too much to ask of me, wasn't it?

"Get a grip, man," I wanted to tell him, but I knew he already knew. He was perfectly aware that he was an anxious, depressed, and occasionally self-destructive guy, prone to overmedicating when times were tough, and that he needed to pull himself together.

"He's just down," I thought. He thinks he wants me, he thinks he needs me, but he doesn't need me. He needs a nurse. He's like an

277

invalid when he's back on the pills and the drink. Besides, I don't think I could handle taking care of him when he's like this. I don't want to take care of him. Of anyone. I can barely take care of myself.

RJ was just going through a rough patch. It happened from time to time. And he'd reached out to me, because he was in my town, and thinking of me, knowing I'd understand. But self-destruction is such a personal, private pursuit; no one can really help someone who's hell-bent on it. All one can do is to say, "Be careful," and hope for the best. Only the one who is self-destructing can pull himself out of his down-ward spiral. And I knew from RJ's historical pattern of self-abuse/self-preservation that he would pull out of this one. He always did.

I decided right then and there that I wasn't going to mess around with RJ anymore. He was too fragile and so was I. I made him promise not to take so many pills again—not to be so stupid—and then, satisfied that he was okay, I said good-bye gently, hung up, and went back to the table.

"Is everything all right?" Tim asked.

"Yeah," I said.

Brian was the first to finish his dinner. He threw a couple of dollars down on the table as a tip, stood up, and announced, "I'm gonna go back. Doors open in a minute."

Freda smiled and said, "Okay. See you soon."

About five minutes later, when I was done with my watery veg-etable soup, I said, "I'm going to go back to the club, too. I want to check out the opening band. Do you guys want to come?"

Tim, who was only about a third of the way through his plate of food, said, "No. I think I'll stay here and work on these wings."

"All right. I'll see you back there."

"Yup."

I turned to Freda and Heidi. "You guys?"

Heidi nodded and Freda said, "Yeah. I'll come with you."

Each of us threw some money down for the waitress and left Tim alone with his pain.

Back at the club, the young opening act was onstage, already play-ing. "Oh my God it's really loud," I yelled to Freda, who nodded in agreement.

"Am I this loud when I play?" I wondered as I fished through my backpack for a pair of earplugs. "Why do soundmen always blast bands through the PA like this? Why does it have to hurt? Do they think it's fun for the listener when his ears are bleeding? I just don't get it. Is it like a macho thing—like, the louder they can blast it, the more manly they are?"

I found my earplugs and stuck one in each ear and then sighed wistfully, thinking, "Going to see bands play would be so much nicer of an experience, not to mention much less potentially damaging to the ears, if the volume was turned down a notch, or five."

As a matter of fact, I had already lost some of my hearing in my right ear. The only reason my hearing wasn't thoroughly shot, and I didn't have tinnitus (permanent ringing in the ears), was that I had started wearing earplugs during gigs around the time of my second album, in the early 1990s. That had, I believed, saved my ears from further damage.

The opening band was awful, but compelling. Watching them play was like rubbernecking at a car wreck. There were a girl and a guy singing. The guy was playing guitar and the girl was playing bass. Both had thin, reedy voices and they were out of tune with each other. There was also a cello player. She was out of tune, too, both with the singers and with the guitar. The drummer was all over the place, alternately speeding up and slowing down. It was terrible.

But there was an innocent earnestness to their terribleness, which made them kind of endearing, and beautiful. Because isn't it beautiful whenever anyone has the courage to get up on a stage and present his heartfelt creations to a bunch of potentially judgmental strangers?

When it was my time to take the stage, I noticed a striking young guy of twenty or twenty-one—tall, olive skin, dark wavy hair, skinny— standing one or two people back from the front, directly in my line of vision, watching me closely. He wasn't exactly handsome, but he had an interesting gaunt face—the kind of face I find beguiling—and seeing him watching me was discombobulating. Every time we made eye contact I could feel myself blush. I could see myself flubbing lines and chords if I didn't get a handle on the situation right away. So I set myself straight, thinking, "Pull yourself together, you loser. He's practically a teenager, for Christ's sake. And he's not even handsome, really," and did the rest of the show without another glance in his direction.

After the show, the guy was hanging out by the side of the stage with the opening band and a few additional people. They all looked really young. As I packed up my things on my part of the stage, the interesting-looking guy said to me, "You guys were awesome."

I said, "Thanks," and tried to play it cool, and not betray my little crush.

Then I held up my one remaining unused drink ticket (good for a free drink at the bar) and, directing my question to all of the kids gathered around me by the stage, asked, teasingly, "Are you guys over twenty-one?"

The singer of the opening band said, "Yeah," speaking, apparently, for all of them.

Then I said, "Does anyone want this drink ticket?"

The singer said, "Yeah, sure," and took it.

Then I asked, addressing the whole group of friends, "Are you sure you guys aren't in high school?"

They said a collective, insulted, "No."

I said, "College?"

The drummer of the band frowned, and said, "We graduated from college," clearly vexed by my stupid and offensive question.

I said, "Sorry," and chuckled.

It was strange to feel like I was almost a whole generation older than the one represented here by the support band and their friends. They reminded me so much of myself at their age: cocky, eager, shy, self-conscious, desperate to connect, excited by everything, proud, uncertain about a lot of things but one hundred percent sure that what I had to offer the world was what the world wanted and needed, more than anything else.

Now that I had settled into this life, the life of a touring musician with a small following, working outside of the mainstream, the reality was: this is it. This is life. The world keeps turning and things don't really change. You reach a pinnacle and then what? You either jump off or stumble off or you're pushed—you come down—and you go on living. You continue. Because what else is there to do?

I make music, that's all. I used to think it was magic. Sometimes I still do. But it's actually much simpler than that, and easier to understand: I do this because this is what I do.

When we were all loaded up and ready to go, I waved good-bye to the new generation and took my leave, okay (for the moment) with my place in the universe.

39

August 23

Albuquerque to Oklahoma City

We hit the road at about 10 a.m. A couple of hours east of Albuquerque bright yellow billboards began to sprout up intermittently next to the highway, like weeds. There was one every few minutes, for miles and miles, advertising something called "The Thing," over and over again. "Stop and see The Thing!" "The Thing! Only 20 miles!" The signs didn't say what The Thing was, just that It was on display at an upcoming service area.

When we reached The Thing's exit ("Stop Now and See The Thing!") we needed gas so we pulled off. Tim filled up the tank and the rest of us—Freda, Heidi, Brian, and I—went inside. There was a Dairy Queen and a gift shop filled with southwestern-themed junk: sombreros, Mexican jumping beans, copper bracelets, belt buckles, string ties, feather mobiles crafted by Native Americans, and ashtrays and shot glasses and coffee mugs, all with "New Mexico" painted on them. I picked out a couple of essential things—a pair of orange maracas and a T-shirt with a painting of a wolf's head printed on it—and went to pay for them.

Up near the cash register was a doorway that led to The Thing. For a dollar, you could go in and have a look. We all kind of half-assedly dared each other to venture in, but none of us took the chance. It wasn't that we were cheap and didn't want to pay the dollar. It was more that we were all a little afraid of what The Thing might turn out to be. Was it something alive? A mutant creature of some sort, like a three-legged lizard? A deformed fetus in a jar? We envisioned the grotesque but were also open to the possibility that it might be something disappointing and anticlimactic like maybe just a weirdly shaped cactus. Whatever The Thing was, it was probably better left to the imagination.

Back behind the wheel, I put on the Talking Heads' *Fear of Music* and after that we listened to Al Green's *Let's Stay Together*. It felt good to be on the road. Just driving. Moving through space at a safe, steady speed with one friend beside me and three others resting peacefully with their own thoughts in the back. There's nothing at stake during these suspended moments, traveling; the only thing necessary was for us to get where we were going, and that was easily done. Right then, in the van, all I knew was: the white broken line and the music and the air rushing past and the purring engine and the darkness closing in on the distance. The unknown, out there, was the possible. I was getting there and the miles were something tangible that I had accomplished. I was content, if temporarily. "This is why I go on the road," I thought. "For this feeling."

But why am I comfortable only when I'm en route? Why is it only in the opening between a starting point and a destination that I am at ease? Why can't I take this feeling back home with me?

We arrived in Oklahoma City at about 8:30 p.m. We checked into a disgusting (more on that later) Red Roof Inn by Interstate 40 on the outskirts of the city limits. Out front they had put FREE "HOT" BREAK-FAST on a sign. Did that mean the eggs would be lukewarm? We dumped our bags in our rooms and then went to eat dinner at a Cracker Barrel down the street.

Cracker Barrel is a chain of restaurant-stores with an Americana theme. They're all over the country, but concentrated mainly in the south, usually by the highway. Each Cracker Barrel is laid out exactly the same and each has the same menu and sells the same stock merchandise in its gift shop section. I have, more than once, walked into a Cracker Barrel and totally forgotten what state I was in.

283

This is what it's like, every time: You first encounter a row of wooden rocking chairs out front. The rocking chairs are meant, I guess, to evoke porches and verandas in the lazy summer days of yore in the south, or maybe the heartland, where there are farms and gingham and fresh lemonade and stuff like that. The chairs all have price tags hanging off them, so if you want, you can buy some of this nostalgia.

Next, you walk through the store, which is packed wall to wall with knickknacks (refrigerator magnets, Christmas tree ornaments, wooden wall hangings with devotional messages painted on them) and gift foods (preserves, nuts, saltwater taffy) and all manner of little toys and games (jacks, cards, Mad Libs) for the kids.

Once through the tacky bric-a-brac overload of the store, you're greeted by the host or hostess and you follow him or her into the restaurant, past the big stone fireplace. Your eyes are immediately drawn to the walls, which are covered with a mix of old-time American kitsch and quasi-authentic historical artifacts like, for example, turn-of-the-century black-and-white portraits of dour unsmiling country folk, washboards, faded and yellowed old Coca-Cola advertisements from the 1950s.

The food is mostly southern-style—catfish, chicken-fried steak, black-eyed peas and collard greens, sweet potato pie—in keeping with the "Aw, shucks, we're just country folk" theme.

In the summertime, it is always freezing cold in Cracker Barrel. The AC is kept on high for all the well-insulated hordes who come in to load up on meat and potatoes and cobbler in the hot humid months. On this particular night it was about eighty-five degrees outside and we were prepared. We had, the scrawny lot of us, gotten our jackets out of our bags in the back of the van before going inside.

With my jean jacket on, I was still shivering in the restaurant's icy artificial chill. When she came around, I asked the waitress if the air-conditioning could be turned down. At first she looked at me funny, like I'd asked the question in a foreign language or said a dirty word. (Apparently no one had ever asked her this before.). When she'd processed what I'd said, she replied, "Oh, sorry, no, I can't turn it down. And, well, there are fans and there's not even a fan here."

I did a quick scan of the room and I noticed many ceiling fans going full blast in addition to the arctic air conditioning, but when I looked up

I saw no fan above us here at the round table in the corner of the room. I gathered that what the waitress meant was that the best I could do, as a cold person, was to be where I already was—at one of the tables without a fan whirring above it—so I should stop complaining.

Then the waitress added, "We don't control the air." In her Oklahoma accent it sounded like, "Way downt kintrahl thuh eye-er." And with that, she was off to attend to another table.

After dinner, at about ten o'clock, we wanted to get a bottle of tequila or wine to wind down after the long day in the van. The first liquor store we came to was closed. Tim went into the convenience store next door to ask where a person might buy a bottle of something around here, and the clerk inside informed him that all the package stores closed at nine in OK City.

We went back to our hotel and split off to our separate rooms, booze cravings unsatisfied. When I crossed my threshold, an offensive moldy smell assaulted my sinuses. I quickly deduced that this stench was due to the visibly damp carpeting beneath my feet, near the door. It squished when I took a step into the room. The wetness had probably attracted the flies. The room was infested with them—it seemed to be a breeding ground—and they immediately began dive-bombing me and accosting me about the ears with their damnable buzzing. I kept the door open so they could fly outside and be free, but they wouldn't go. They liked it there inside my room, where they could amuse themselves by torturing me all night long.

Normally I don't like to kill things, but the satanic little motherfuckers had completely taken over my personal space. Or I theirs. Either way, one of us had to go. And I had nowhere else to go. So it had to be them.

After a bunch of futile attempts in which I only slapped myself, I succeeded in assassinating one fly. I whacked a couple more and then gave up. There were too many of them. I was helplessly outnumbered. As soon as I flattened one, another would materialize and take its place.

I resolved to try to coexist with my annoying roommates. I went to sit down to write in my journal and as I did I happened to notice that the desk was sticky and there were stains on the chair.

I considered for a second switching to a different room, but then in the next second I remembered the NO VACANCY sign at the front desk;

all the other rooms were occupied. Besides, all of the other rooms were probably just as nasty as this one. This was a nasty motel. Period. There was nothing I could do about it.

So I stayed where I was. I did my best to ignore my surroundings and continued writing for a while.

The last thing I did before getting into bed was go into the bathroom to run a bath. I pulled back the shower curtain and to my dismay but not surprise, I spotted three pubic hairs, at first glance, sitting in the tub. It made me think of that old Naughty by Nature chestnut, "OPP." Other people's pubes. (I'm definitely not down with that.) One pubic hair, I could almost let slide, but multiple pubic hairs was too much for me to take. A bath was out of the question.

"Fuck," I said, and changed into my pajamas.

I leapt from the bathroom tiles onto the bed, doing my best not to let my feet touch the dank carpeting. I put my socks on and then got in and lay down on my back and pulled the covers up just to my chest, not wanting to leave any part of my face or neck or head vulnerable to infection by whatever germs and substances and bacterial microbes were living in the sheets and blanket.

"I wish I had my sleeping bag," I said to myself. Sometimes I bring it on the road so that at times like these, I can sleep on it, on top of the bed, and not have to worry about incurring any diseases or rashes.

I closed my eyes.

"It could be worse," I thought. "I could be homeless and sleeping on a sidewalk in the middle of winter. I could have cancer. I could be wasting my days away at a desk job that I hated."

And I was asleep.

40

August 24

Lawrence

We pulled up in front of the Bottleneck and a bunch of young guys in T-shirts and jeans filed out of the club to help us. These tattooed worker bees instantaneously transported all of our equipment from the back of our van and into the club. I didn't have to lift a finger. For a minute, I felt pampered, like a princess, or Beyoncé.

I had about an hour before Tim would be set up and ready for me and the girls to soundcheck, so I walked across the street and down about a hundred yards to the big new Borders bookstore that had sprouted up since the last time I'd been in Lawrence. I picked out some magazines (*Nylon*, the *New Yorker*, *Martha Stewart Living*) and a *New York Times*. Then I handed my credit card to the guy at the cash register. It went through and then he tilted his head and asked shyly, "Are you *the* Juliana Hatfield?"

I wanted to say, "No, I'm a different one," or to flee. I never know how to respond to this particular question—not that I get it that often. An affirmative connotes a pride or cockiness that I do not possess. A negative answer is an outright fib. And unfortunately for me, I'm a terrible liar.

And so, wishing I'd paid with cash, I answered, witlessly, "Uh, yeah, I guess so." I blushed and suddenly felt much too warm.

In my discomfort, I feared I was in danger of dissolving into a puddle on the floor, before I could escape, done in by the hot eyes of the guy behind the cash register burning into me. I was wilting, crumpling—and fast. Sweat was dripping down from my armpits. I had to get out of there.

As I signed the bill, I tried my hardest to act normal, like a normal person, having a normal conversation, and said, "I'm playing over at the Bottleneck tonight."

"Oh yeah? What time?" cash register guy asked.

"Around ten."

"Oh, too bad. I'm working 'til midnight."

"Oh well," I concluded, and as he handed me my mags and receipt, I told the guy, "Thanks. Bye. See you."

"Bye. Have a good show."

"Thanks," and I was out the door.

Inside the club, the opening band was unpacking their gear from its roadcases. I introduced myself. They were a healthy-looking young trio; two guys and a girl in their early- to-mid-twenties. The most gregarious one was the drummer. He seemed to be the natural leader of the band, the always networking alpha dog. In the course of our short conversation, he came across as outwardly but good-naturedly ambitious about their music and so confident that I couldn't help but look forward to checking out their set.

The drummer soon made himself right at home in the one backstage room, inquiring straightaway if he and his bandmates could have some of our food and wine. I was surprised and impressed by his forwardness and self-assurance. Opening bands in small clubs like this often stay deferentially away from the backstage area. There is no rulebook mandating that it be so; it's more an unspoken and widely held assumption that if there is only one dressing room, it belongs to the headliner. It's the top-billed band's private haven to hide out in. Alone. And this unwritten law goes on to stipulate that the rider is there for the headliner. Not the support. The support band is lucky to have the gig at all, the common thinking goes.

So when the opening band's drummer came right on in and asked if he could have a glass of our wine, some people in my position might have been offended. Or angry, even. But these kids were all right. They seemed pretty normal and nice enough and neither ingratiating nor overbearing. So we welcomed them in. (Not that they weren't hanging out in the dressing room already.)

When they went onstage a couple of hours later, I watched them play for a while. All of the songs were very slow and serious, with an overstylized sense of drama and arrangement. They were not much fun. And not at all what I'd been expecting. I would expect that kind of gothy darkness from a band of sullen, greasy-haired social outcasts, but these people had seemed so well-adjusted when I'd chatted with them earlier; so amiable, so well-spoken, so clean. Why weren't they playing power pop, or indie rock?

Were they poseurs? Were they faking it? I felt betrayed, in a way; betrayed by my own assumptions, I guess. Or was it possible that they were in fact seething, under a "normal" facade, with the psychic agony that their music suggested? Just as some people imagined me to be a bubbly, friendly, engaging gal because of the energetic, effervescent sound of my voice, had I read the opening band incorrectly due to superficial reasons?

Freda, Heidi, and I played an uneventful show. The crowd seemed to like it okay but I felt it was nothing special.

Immediately following our encore, just after we'd gone through the door into the dressing room, a young man, who had followed us, entered. He didn't say anything. He just stood there smiling dumbly, as if he couldn't remember why he had come. I stared at him and waited for him to speak first and explain himself. I was mildly outraged at the boldness of this intrusion. The man had invaded our space. He had penetrated our backstage bubble.

Freda broke the silence. "Can I help you?" she asked him diplomatically.

"Can I get a picture?" he said finally, holding up his little camera.

I responded, "You can't just come in here. This is private."

He went on, still smiling, not discouraged in the least. "Oh, no, my girlfriend said it was okay. She said that you said it was okay to come in."

I shot back, "No. No, I didn't say that. I didn't tell anyone that. Your girlfriend's lying. Go tell her I said that no, you can't come in here. You can't just barge in like that. Do you understand? This is our dressing room. We just got off stage five seconds ago and we need a few minutes to ourselves. Okay? Can you give us five minutes?"

He disappeared, and about one minute later a buxom blond amazon, about six inches taller than the man who had just left, came in with a big smile on her face.

I wondered if these people were moonies, or born-agains. They had that impenetrable, lobotomized glaze of annoyingly relentless positivity.

"Hi!" she exclaimed. "I was just wondering if we could get a picture with you."

I said, "Are you with the guy that was just in here?"

"Yeah!"

"Well, I told him to go away 'cause we want some privacy right now, and we don't want to pose for pictures right this second. Okay? We'd appreciate it if you'd give us some time alone. You're not really supposed to just walk in here. I told that to your boyfriend. Didn't he tell you what I told him to tell you?"

"Oh, no, yeah, but we just wanted to get a picture with you."

The boyfriend appeared again, peeking out from behind the girl.

I was completely awestruck by this couple. I kind of almost had to respect them for not giving up, no matter what I said. I thought it made perfect sense that (A) I wanted them to leave, so (B) they should leave. But my logic wasn't working on them.

I tried one last time to forcibly inject some common sense into these people's heads.

"Please leave," I said. "*You can't have a photo right now.* Maybe later. Come back later. Maybe we can do it then. Just give us a few minutes, okay?"

They still weren't moving.

So I kept going. I wasn't going to give in. It was a matter of principle.

"You're not even supposed to be allowed in here. That door is supposed to be locked. There's supposed to be a security guard out there in front of it, stopping people from coming in here. And you know, right now, of all the times you could have chosen to come busting in back here, right now is probably the worst time. We just got offstage. You know? I'm all covered in sweat. I need to change my clothes. So I need a little privacy. Just, please go away. Please. Please leave us alone for a little while?"

And with that they finally got the message and went away. But I didn't feel good about it. I hated having to give the postshow etiquette lecture.

In about ten minutes, Tim knocked on the door and then came into the room holding a paper bag. He handed it to me and said, "It's a gift from a girl out there."

I looked inside and there was a big bottle of Ketel One vodka with a bow on it. I was puzzled. "Why vodka?" I wondered.

When I was finally ready to meet my public, I opened the dressing room door. There was a short line of people waiting for me and Freda and Heidi. A line of people who'd had the sense and the manners to wait *outside* the dressing room. I signed a few people's CDs and was given demos by a few more people and then a young woman, about twenty-one, with short dark hair and a pleasant gentle face approached and said quietly to me, "I was the one who gave you the vodka."

"Oh. Thank you," I said. "What's the significance of the vodka?"

The girl said, "You said in an interview once that your favorite drink was Ketel One and orange Slice. Remember?"

"Oh, yeah! Oh, that was so sweet of you, really sweet. Thanks. What's your name?"

We talked briefly, about inconsequential things. I didn't tell her that I wasn't into vodka anymore. The Vodka Slice was a brief phase I went through. But I wanted to give her something back, a part of me, at least some of my attention in response to the thoughtfulness of her gift. But I quickly ran out of things to say. "Thank you" probably would have been enough, but I'd stretched it out until it felt forced and ungenuine. Maybe, I couldn't help thinking, as I looked around, I would be doing these people a favor if I stayed in the dressing room and never came out. I could spare them the disappointment of meeting me.

The vodka girl and I said good-bye. The next guy in line said to me, "Hey, I met your friend Hunter."

Hunter is a friend of mine from Alabama.

"Oh. Yeah?" I replied, trying to sound interested.

"Yeah. I met him at a show I was working at. I work at a club in Birmingham. My friend's band was playing and Hunter was there and he was really nice and he said you two knew each other."

I wasn't sure how to respond to this information. My first reaction was, Why is Hunter going around telling strangers that he knows me? My next instinct was to stare blankly. And then to look at the ground. I wanted to be friendly and excited, to honor this guy's noble attempt to find a common ground between us, but I just didn't seem to care very much that we had a mutual acquaintance. Why didn't I care? Why did I only feel numb?

I looked over at Freda and she too was engaged in meeting fans and signing autographs. Unlike me, though, she had a big warm welcoming smile on her face. A big warm welcoming and, most amazingly, sincere smile. Freda has this ability to make strangers feel that she is truly glad to meet them. Because she is glad to meet them. She glows like a fire in a fireplace and her warmth radiates to those around her, making every one feel special, important, liked, appreciated. People love Freda. I love Freda. Freda is love.

I, on the other hand, am not love. I am something else. I am the cold gray ashes the morning after. I am the wet kindling that won't burn. I alienate everyone with whom I come into contact. I can see it in their faces. I squirm so they squirm. I must remind them of what they don't like about themselves. Their insecurity, their dissatisfaction, their frustration, their loneliness, selfishness, dread, petulance, impatience, hurt.

Watching Freda make people feel good makes me yearn to be more like her. I wish I could be nice. I wish I had a smile for everyone.

Lately I'd been pursing my lips in front of fans' cameras in what I was hoping resembled a funny party face, puckering up exaggeratedly, as if to kiss. It was an alternative to the sour, surly frown I usually project naturally.

Another recent tactic was for me to say, as the photographer pointed the camera and got ready to shoot, "Say something funny." That sometimes worked. The person with the camera would, about one time out of three, come up with something on the spot, like "caca" or "I just farted" that would make me smile, for real. Or I tried to do a sense memory of something really hilarious, something that had made

292

me laugh in the past. I tried to visualize Chris Farley as Matt Foley, the motivational speaker on *Saturday Night Live*, hiking up his chinos and then falling onto the coffee table and breaking it. Sometimes that's effective.

A smile really shouldn't be such hard work.

41

Hunger

The demons you live with at home will follow you out on tour. And without the carefully built armor you normally have to protect you from your fears, touring can exacerbate your worst impulses. Whatever your particular issue is, any tour is a long and bumpy enough road that it can easily push you off the wagon. My struggle was with food.

I used to be hungry all the time. Being hungry all the time was exhausting and painful. Physically painful. It made me even more irritable and antisocial than I was to begin with, but I felt like I had to keep a lid on my appetites so that they didn't get out of control. Having known, and loved, and worked with quite a few drug addicts and alcoholics (this was the music business, after all) I was aware of the sometimes deadly consequences of overindulgence. Food could be abused just like any drug. And there's such a fine line between too much and not enough—it's a line I was always trying to find, and walk, and balance, and when I couldn't, I erred on the side of caution.

I had had, since high school, a tendency to want to eat too much—way too much—when I was anxious, or sad, or angry, or lonely, or confused, which was much of the time. Stuffing myself with food numbed me and dulled my feelings, temporarily, like heroin numbs the heroin addict and alcohol numbs the alcoholic. Then I would compensate by starving myself after every gluttonous episode. I felt that if I didn't correct myself like this—if I didn't forcibly rein myself back in— the binge would never stop. I would eat everything; I would eat the kitchen, and the whole house, and the entire city, and I would have a heart attack, or burst a blood vessel in my brain, or simply explode because my stomach couldn't contain the gargantuan volume of food I had jammed into it. These were scary thoughts.

Once, while a student at Berklee, I went without food for five days, drinking only water and the occasional glass of tomato juice. It seemed, at the time, like the right thing to do, even though it made me feel like I was dying. Eating was just so dangerous; such a slippery slope.

I would have terrible stomachaches sometimes when I did eat, after a fast. The pain was sometimes so intense that I couldn't stand up; only lying on my back would calm the shooting, knifelike spasms in my gut. I knew that I had brought this on myself and it frightened me to think of all the violent abuse (bingeing, starving, bingeing, starving) I had, over the years, imposed upon my poor gastrointestinal system. I would moan, my arms wrapped around my middle, and think, "I'm sorry, I'm so sorry, I'll never hurt you again, I promise."

But then I would.

I never talked to anyone about my eating problem because I thought that compared to other people's really serious problems mine was a stupid, immature, selfish one and that I should just get over it. I kept it hidden, never mentioned it, tried not to act weird around food when there were other people present. I didn't want anyone to think that I had a problem with food, of all things. I was embarrassed, struggling with what was generally assumed to be an adolescent concern, well past adolescence.

I often thought, "Why couldn't I have developed a drug problem like everyone else? That way, I could just quit, quit doing the damn drugs. Quitting is doable. I quit smoking, and it wasn't so hard. I got myself addicted to sleeping pills for a spell once, and I quit them, too. I suffered withdrawal pangs for a few days, maybe a week, and then I moved on. But I can't quit food."

And I felt guilty, guilty that I was making myself feel sick when there were people out there dealing with cruel, randomly occurring diseases such as cancer and schizophrenia and multiple sclerosis. And what about all the malnourished children in the world who weren't getting enough to eat? I had a hell of a lot of nerve, eating so much more food than I needed and then starving myself on purpose, knowing those children were out there somewhere, on the streets, scrounging for scraps. So I hesitated to admit to anyone what I was going through, and I struggled on my own, every day, to find a balance, to right the seesaw of my perpetual back-and-forth between the extremes of too much and not enough. Some days, some weeks, I did well, and felt good.

Around the turn of the millennium, after *Bed*, I started tilting heavily toward the "not eating enough" side of the pendulum. I was feeling scared and unappreciated and unsure of my place in the world, and of my future, feeling a bit battered and beaten. My wounds weren't healing right, or fast enough. It was starting to sink in that my career was on the downswing and might never recover. I might have to think about finding some other way to make a living, but I didn't think I could do anything else. It stung, having failed to live up to expectations with my last album (*Only Everything*) and with my major label career, and having my last project (*God's Foot*) taken away from me, banished to the realm of silence and invisibility.

I pretended that I didn't care that *God's Foot* was never released. I pretended I didn't care that *Bed*, my first post-Atlantic album, sold only about one-tenth what *Only Everything* had sold. I claimed I was free and in charge of my career again and loving my new old-school DIY independence. And part of me was. I was dedicated to continuing to make music on my own terms, as I always had, only now with little interference or pressure. (With *Bed*, I hadn't sold my soul or my master tapes to the Man. Instead I had licensed the album to Zoe/Rounder records, a large independent label, for a $25,000 advance, for a seven-year period, after which ownership of *Bed* would revert back to me.)

But I worried, Could I sustain a career? Would I have to get a job to support myself and my music? Would people continue to care if I kept making records?

Anorexia starts as a coping mechanism that kicks in when you feel like the world is falling apart. In the short term, not eating is a way to fool yourself into believing you have some control, over something. A girl can control what she puts into her body, at least.

Like I said, I had no authority over the fate of *God's Foot*. And I could never control critics' reactions or radio programmers' choices. I couldn't force people to buy my records or to come to my gigs or, if they did, to enjoy them. I couldn't control my commercial success or failure and I couldn't even control my performance half the time. My ability to play well, and to enjoy myself, seemed to be at the mercy of a host of conditions outside my command.

Even my personal safety seemed precarious out on the road. Once in a while an overzealous fan would try to kiss me, brusquely, without warning, wantonly intruding into my cherished personal space, or jump onstage and run toward me and try to grab me in the middle of a song, and these things always shook me up whenever they happened. I was a small girl to begin with, not very physically strong, with no sure way to defend myself if someone crossed the line and became threatening or dangerous. My music had always attracted quite a few lonely outsiders, people whose social skills were more hopeless than even mine; ones whose imaginary lives were probably more vivid than the lives they were actually living; even people who had maybe spent a little time on a psych ward—some of whom, since their release, were obviously not taking their meds.

Other bands, when I would tour with them, would tell me, after a few days on the road with me, "Man, you have some weird fans." Although after I left the major label world my crowds had gotten smaller and I was selling fewer records, I still seemed to have an equally large and fervid contingent, proportionally, of the reality-challenged following my career. And there were usually few if any security people on staff to look out for me now, in these small rock clubs. I had to be watchful and wary of every stranger until they proved to me that they were harmless.

Once a man followed my tour bus from the venue to my hotel, and as I got in the elevator to go up to my room, he tried to jump in the elevator with me as the doors were closing, a deranged look in his eyes. My big strong tour manager at the time, who was in the lobby, managed to grab the guy and pull him out of the elevator, and I flew up to my room and locked myself in safely. But who knew what the crazy-eyed guy might have done had he gotten into the elevator alone with me? Was he another Mark David Chapman? I had no way of knowing.

I am five-foot-seven. On tour, I kept my weight under a hundred and ten pounds. Even without a scale I could gauge what I weighed by the relative prominence or obscurity of the sternum bone between my breasts, and by the fit of my pants (were they hanging off me?), and by the amount of empty space between my thighs when I stood with my feet together.

To maintain this low weight I would usually eat a Clif Bar for breakfast and a handful of trail mix or a small plastic bag of peanuts, the single-serving kind, for lunch. At dinnertime, when I was really starving after a whole day of being hungry, I would allow (or force) myself to have a slightly more balanced meal, even if it was sometimes small; a healthy, vegetarian meal to give me strength to play the show. Like if we were at a Japanese restaurant, I might have two or three vegetable maki. Avocado rolls and cucumber rolls were my favorites. I would have one drink at night, if I was in the mood. (If I had more than that, in my hollow-stomached state, it would leave me nauseous and unpleasantly drunk, with nothing in my system to absorb the alcohol.) Snacks were generally verboten unless it was to suck on a cough drop or a lollipop to ward off the ever present bad taste in my mouth. Or if I was on the verge of fainting and dinner was still hours away, I might allow myself to eat part of an apple or maybe a rice cake or two. Dessert was only a concept, a long-forgotten memory.

Sometimes I would go jogging or lift weights while hungry, when I had little physical strength, knowing it was hard on my heart, knowing that my father and grandfather had died of heart attacks, but also knowing that I couldn't not do the exercise. I was feeling so trapped in my anorexic mind that I pushed myself—dragged myself around and around the track—even though I knew it could be harmful. When I happened to be at the extreme low end of the weight spectrum and I looked in the mirror or stepped on a scale, and saw that I had lost a few more pounds, it was always with a mixture of horror and pride. I knew I was in dangerous, potentially health-damaging territory, but at the same time I wanted desperately to succeed at keeping my weight down. Losing weight was something I had the power to do— something I had become good at—and I had to prove this to myself, over and over again. I couldn't make the world buy five million, or five hundred thousand, or fifty thousand, or even five thousand copies of my latest album, or to love it—I couldn't even get *God's Foot* released— but I could lose five pounds.

Anorexia nervosa is a pathological emotional disorder. The weight loss is a manifestation of emotional disturbance and diseased thinking. I knew this; I'd even written a research paper on the topic for a high school biology class, and I'd read all the anorexia literature. I was an expert on the subject. I knew, intellectually, that it wasn't right, or healthy, or smart, or sane to force myself not to eat, and I knew it could be dangerous if my weight went too low. That is why when I did eat, I tried to at least eat things that were relatively healthy and had some nutrition in them. But I felt trapped by my unconscious impulses, like I was a puppet. Just like an alcoholic who, upon waking, hungover, in the morning, vows never to drink again, but then goes back to the bottle that very day, and hates herself for doing it. I was a broken record.

All of my neuroses and fears and worries about the world and myself and my career were subsumed into the fear of losing control of my body and appetites and of getting fat. I panicked whenever the scale hit a hundred and ten. I really believed that if my weight went above this mark, I would be powerless to stop its continuing upward ascent and then I would have lost control of the one thing I had control over (or thought I did), and of the world, the only world I knew, the world I inhabited—my world. That's how the anorexic mind thinks.

I came home from the Blake Babies reunion tour in 2001 weighing a hundred pounds, my lowest ever. One of my brothers said I looked like a concentration camp victim. I knew, when I stepped on a scale upon my return home and saw that my weight was lower than it had ever been in my entire adult life, that this was bad. I had started out thinking that losing weight would help me get my life under control, but now I was starting to lose control of the weight loss. I hadn't meant, hadn't expected, to go that low. And my friends' and family's reactions, upon my return, shocked me just like my bony appearance shocked them. The situation had taken on a dangerous life of its own.

Some time after this Some Girls tour, I noticed a nagging numbness in my lower left leg. The numbness persisted and after a few weeks I began to worry that maybe this was the first stage of multiple sclerosis. I called my doctor and she had me come in to see her the next day. I was diagnosed with a vitamin deficiency which, left untreated, could cause permanent damage to my nervous system.

My self-mothering instinct finally kicked in. I took large doses of a supplements for a couple of weeks, to get my levels back up into a healthy range, and then, rather than continuing to take a bunch of pills every day (vitamins in food absorb better than vitamins in supplements, the doctor told me) for the rest of my life, I started to eat a bit more and to put on a few pounds, carefully, deliberately, sensibly. I was too scared not to. With the help of Carl Jung, and behavioral therapy, and discipline, and regular exercise, and constant vigilance, and self-forgiveness when I messed up, I gradually taught myself how to eat right.

Truth was, the world wasn't going to end if I gained five or ten pounds and kept them on. I could see that now. It had taken me such a long time to believe that I could be healthy and actually feel good about it. My problems weren't going to be eliminated by starving them to death.

42

August 25
St. Louis

S t. Louis. The last stand. We arrived at the club, Blueberry Hill, at
about four in the afternoon, and I was in a bad mood for no particular reason. It was probably partly due to hunger. There was some time
to kill because we were early; the house soundman wasn't due for
another hour and Tim couldn't set up the system without him. So I
slipped out, silently, to the street while everyone else began unpacking
and setting up their stuff. I didn't want to hang around bad-vibing
everyone. I walked down busy Delmar Boulevard to the Starbucks on
the corner.

I try to avoid Starbucks when I am at home, for the usual reasons:
Starbucks is a monolithic corporate chain playing a great part in the
homogenization of American (and global) culture. But on tour, with
my body and mind in a weakened state, I succumb much more easily
to the green and white sign's insidious pull. Out on the lonely road,
Starbucks is something comforting and familiar, like a night-light or a
beacon shining in a strange, dark landscape where so much is alien and
out of my control.

I always know what I'm going to get when I walk into a Starbucks. Because it's always the same. And out here, it's a relief to find something I can rely on to be what it always is. A decent cup of something hot, on a trying day in a strange town, can be the difference between a nervous breakdown and blissful contentment. This is how they rope me in, so easily led, like a cow to the trough. I hate it but it's true. I ordered a cup of tea and I grabbed some sections of the Sunday *New York Times* from the magazine bin in the corner. I sat down in a big purple velvet armchair stained with coffee splotches and dried milk spots.

I was reading a piece in the arts section when Tim walked in the door. I quickly pulled the newspaper up so that it covered my face and didn't lower it until I saw Tim, out of the corner of my eye, exit with his to-go coffee. I was still in a funk and didn't want to talk to anyone.

After decompressing with my tea, I was refreshed and ready to rejoin society. I left my quiet faux-living-room corner and walked back to the club and did a soundcheck with the band.

When we were done, I needed to get something out of the van, which was parked behind the club. I pushed on the back EXIT door's bar on which was printed, in red, "Warning: Alarm Will Sound," thinking, "The alarm won't sound. The alarm never sounds." But of course the alarm went off, blaring. And then I felt dumb and was effusively apologetic when the guy with the special key to shut off the noise came running with the special key to shut off the noise. I saw the busty brunette bartendress in the red "Che" T-shirt look over at me from behind the bar and roll her eyes, as if to say, "That is so typical. They're all the same, those stupid, irresponsible, self-absorbed musicians."

I was outside for not two seconds when Beatle Bob accosted me. "Hi, Juliana. I'm Beatle Bob. Remember me? Think I could get on the guest list tonight? I have some stuff here. Do you think you could sign it? Blah, blah, blah," a mile a minute. Apparently he had been waiting outside the back door for me to come out, figuring, wisely, that I had to come out eventually.

I remembered Beatle Bob from the last time and all the other times I'd played in St. Louis. He's a local character known to touring bands as the eccentric middle-aged guy in the bowl-cut hairdo and the mod suit, dancing idiosyncratically in front of the stage. I guess you could call him a professional superfan. He was usually clutching an assortment of records and posters and other memorabilia pertaining to the band at hand, for them to sign.

A guy working at the club—the man who had come to my rescue and shut off the alarm—told me later that Beatle Bob had been banned from certain local record stores for allegedly stealing stuff. Which seemed plausible when I considered the rare and out-of-print collectibles that always seemed to materialize from between his nervous hands. But he had always seemed completely benign to me.

Upon hearing the news about Beatle Bob's supposed kleptomania, Tim said to me, "Hey, isn't he the guy that tried to steal your pedals from the stage after the last St. Louis show?"

I had a vague memory of my tube screamer going missing directly following my encore a couple of years ago, at another rock club across town, and a shadowy figure hurrying in a blur toward the side door, but to my recollection the supposed perpetrator was never identified or apprehended. I wanted to believe Beatle Bob was a harmlessly enthusiastic supporter of live music. Innocent until proven guilty. I put him on the guest list.

All day long and for weeks leading up to this gig, people had been telling us that Blueberry Hill was "Chuck Berry's club," whenever we mentioned that we were going to play there. There were pictures of him all over the place.

The room we were playing downstairs was called "The Duck Room," presumably after Berry's signature "duck walk" move across the stage. The space had been conceived with a generalized duck motif in mind. There were duck references everywhere you looked. Old framed comic strips featuring cartoons of, yes, ducks peppered the walls, and a row of wooden decoy ducks was displayed on a lit-up Lucite shelf on the back wall behind the bar opposite the stage. Stuff like that. The whole thing was kind of confusing. I mean, the duck room? And if this was Chuck Berry's place, why was it named after a Fats Domino hit?

Upstairs in the sprawling, multiroomed, rock and roll–themed restaurant, framed copies of old *Rolling Stone* magazine covers and other general popular music relics decorated the walls. In addition, there were framed photographs of a middle-aged man I didn't recognize with his arm around seemingly all of the famous people who had ever eaten there or played there, from Keith Richards to Mandy Moore to Dan Fogelberg to Dave Grohl.

It turned out that the place was owned by a guy named Joe. Not Chuck Berry. Joe was the man in all of these photos. He came down to the duck room to have a photo taken with me after our soundcheck.

I wondered, "Why does he want a photo with me? I'm not a celebrity. I only kind of sort of almost was, once. He must just be one of those all-purpose 'music fans.' One of those people who just 'loves music.' All music. Or maybe he is a compulsive collector and obsessively thorough and ritualistic about having his photo taken, without fail, with *every person who plays in his club*, for his archives—not only every legitimate star but also every fringe artist with questionable credentials and a diminishing fan base."

We ate dinner in the restaurant upstairs. Bands playing downstairs ate for free. The menu looked extremely dicey so I ordered just a salad.

It consisted of wilted, brown-edged iceberg lettuce with two hard flavorless tomato wedges and a few desiccated radish slices. When I picked up the piece of bread that had come with the salad, my fingers were slimed by warm, soft, abnormally bright yellow butter that I hadn't known was there. My bread had been prebuttered, and copiously.

When I was done, I announced to everyone at the table, "That was, I think, the worst salad I have ever had. Worse than Denny's, even."

I added, "There's no love in this food at all."

"And I think there might actually be some hate in it," said Freda, referring to her homely half-finished spaghetti with marinara, pushing it aside.

This is the price you pay when you eat for free. It was our own fault. We shouldn't have ever attempted to eat here in the first place. Freda and I should have taken a cab to someplace else and spent our money on a good meal. Because here at Blueberry Hill, all signs led to the food being dodgy at best, especially to a sensitive-stomached, recovering-anorexic, vegetarian health nut like me: lots of meat, lots of fried stuff. What did I expect? The place was a theme restaurant, like Hard Rock Cafe and Planet Hollywood. The food at those kinds of places is never very good. It's not about the food; the food is an afterthought, incidental to the "fun."

It seemed everyone at the other tables was happy with their food. They looked cheerful, digging into their heaping mounds of fried stuff and attacking their fat burgers with both hands grabbing onto the sides and their mouths wide open. No problems at all with their dinners.

"What's wrong with me?" I thought. "Can't I enjoy anything?"

We tried not to make a big deal out of the fact that this was our last show. We're a fairly unsentimental bunch and we treated tonight like it was just another gig. I did put on a dress, though, which hardly ever happens. It was my version of a festive and celebratory gesture. (Either that or I just wanted to wear it once so I knew that it hadn't been taking up space in my bag all that time for nothing.)

The crowd was very attentive and appreciative in a smart, informed, indie-rock fan kind of way; they seemed thoughtful, studious, sane. Young adults and grown-ups alike watched and listened, smiling, eyes pleasantly aglow, moving from me to Freda to Heidi, taking it all in curiously, hungrily, as if this thing of which they previously had only a vague understanding was now becoming, right in front of them, fully illuminated, for the first time. And then there was Beatle Bob, bopping around up front, doing his thing. (He didn't try to steal anything.)

At the end of "Choose Drugs" I usually sing, "I say it's me or drugs, you choose drugs," and then a melodic refrain of "drugs, drugs, druuuuugs." But tonight, right at this climactic moment in the song, I happened to notice the lit-up row of duck decoys facing me, on the back wall, and "drugs" became "ducks." "Ducks, ducks, duuuuucks," I sang.

If my eyes aren't closed, which they usually are, I'm easily distracted by the things around me. And besides, when I'm singing my songs in front of an audience I'm so detached, at that point, from the lyrical content and the specific events that inspired the song (having written the songs in some cases years ago) that "drugs" can become "ducks" just like that. I'm not thinking about the words. The words have become strictly a phonetic means of transmitting feeling, or unconscious gray matter—unarticulatable invisibilities—via melody. The facts, like memories, have blurred. Drugs or ducks? It doesn't really matter.

From my point of view, strings of sung lyrics are pure emotive sound coming from the heart without thought. I write them, and then I don't ever really contemplate them again; I just use them to carry my melodies, which are more eloquent than my rhymes and metaphors ever are. Memorization is a means of getting to a place where articulation, on the spot, of truths (melodic, harmonic truths) having to do with the pain and joy of existence—truths larger and more wide-ranging than the sordid little facts specific to my one little life—is effortless. Music is a universally understood mode of transport out of oneself and one's incessant, chattering thoughts, and out of the everyday world, into something deeper and more unconscious, and thus, more authentic and undeniable; something more penetrating than any spoken words, filtered through the censors of the brain, can express.

When I listen to music, the sound—the melody and the harmony—hits me first. (It is only later that I engage my intellect, if I ever do at all, in trying to figure out what is being deliberately said.) And it often hits me hard, without my even realizing what it is, exactly, that is affecting me so strongly, or why.

It's enchanting in the way that the sight of the person you are in love with sends instant jolts of electricity to your neurons. Goose bumps. Butterflies. I hear a certain song on the radio or coming out of a passing car's open window or during the end credits of a film or even on a TV commercial, and suddenly I feel drunk with inexplicable physical and emotional well-being. I feel like an animal, but wonderfully, fully human, at the same time: I want to screech and jump around like a monkey and I want to grab someone's hand and squeeze it and I want to wrap my arms around the whole world. Random, disparate bands and singers have made me feel this way at one time or another. Made me feel like screaming, like breaking windows. Made me feel weak, in love; dreamily, delectably helpless, like I was melting, but also strong, superhumanly strong, like my heart was alchemizing into gold because of a joy that was much too powerful to be contained in blood and flesh.

After the show, Brian was being goofy and making me laugh. He kept referring to Beatle Bob as "Dick Beatle" and to Stryker, the drummer from the opening band, as "Zephyr." Brian may have been slightly tipsy. It was our last show together and most of us ended up a little buzzed on drinks, in celebration of making it to the finish line. I think even I may have gone over my limit of one and had one and a half or maybe even one and three quarters.

We loaded up the van and said our good-byes to the opening band. Tim, the only fully sober one of us, got behind the wheel. It was about midnight. We were going to drive a couple of hours to take a chunk out of the long way home. I took an internal self-measure of my intoxication level and determined it was low. Then I calculated that I would need about half an hour and about half a liter of water, guzzled, to sober up.

"Tim, I can take over in a while," I said. "I just need about half an hour and then I should be fine to drive."

"Great," said Tim. "But I think I can go all the way."

We drove out of the city past the majestically illuminated arch and already I was feeling nostalgic, leaving it all behind. I am always conscious of the moments slipping away, even as they are happening, in real time. Even when I am having a bad time, like I was at certain times during this tour, I am always aware that whatever I am doing is something irrecoverable, so it should be remembered. In some ways, the remembering is sweeter than the doing. I like missing things and people and places; it makes them seem like they were more perfect than they were. And I always have such high hopes. I don't talk about them much, but they are why I am so easily discouraged.

I went on this tour because that's what musicians do. They tour. I'm a musician. Maybe that sounds like this doesn't mean enough to me. Like I'm not sufficiently grateful. Like I take it all for granted. I think that maybe it all means a little too much; that I see my musical life as a sacred duty and so when it doesn't measure up, when it all fails to be as spectacular as I'd originally intended, it is disappointing.

Maybe I was born disillusioned. The public part of my career has been a constant source of much inner conflict. I can't remember ever feeling truly, lastingly satisfied or content; only when I am immersed in the spasmodic act of writing do I feel free and clear and unencumbered by doubt; when the songs are first coming to life, I feel like a fierce, proud, blissful, new mother, ready to defend to the death what I've created. But writing is such a private, personal thing. Bringing my songs on the road has never been easy or simple for me. I lose my nerve, and my confidence, and the will to try to convince others that I have anything worthwhile to offer them. I want them to figure it out for themselves. Or to convince me that it's true.

I never particularly wanted to be in the spotlight. I just wanted a little illumination in my life. I wanted what writing songs gives me, again and again, and what live performance gives me less frequently, when all the variables that are out of my control happen to be in sync.

I wanted elevation, and escape, if only temporary, from the loneliness and confusion that were always threatening to consume me. I wanted to transform sadness into the joy of singing a melody over some electric chords. I wanted to express that pain can be made beautiful and, thus transformed, can even be a comfort to someone else.

I wanted to say things—things that I couldn't ever say—without having to actually say them; things that I knew other people were feeling, too. And people would hear me and feel connected to something for a little while, and with their positive reaction, my existence would be acknowledged, and validated, and I would feel that I had done something worthwhile. And I have. I know that, thanks to the people who have come to see me play, over and over again.

Music was the only place I ever felt I belonged. I just don't know, anymore, if I belong on the road, out there, in the rock world. It seems that the road somehow draws me away from what is most important to me: the music. All the little things that I complain about—fatigue, bad food, rude people, excessive heat and cold, windows that don't open, faulty wiring—only annoy me so much because they distract me from the Music, which was, originally, a distraction from all the things that got me down about normal everyday life in the first place.

I envisioned a perfect world, my own willed, self-created environment filled with Perfect Songs and the people who loved them. All of my dreams came true, in a way. I did create that world, and there were people there with me—people who'd followed me there, believing in what I was doing even after I'd disappeared from the radio and TV and magazines. And there were people—Freda, Heidi, Tim, Brian, and all the others who have played with me over the years—who traveled the road along with me.

So why was I still frustrated? Because touring wasn't simply a way to sell records; it was a way for me to try to connect to people and to elaborate, in a different context, on what I was trying to say in my writing. And I had failed, continuously, in this. I hadn't been able to get any sort of point successfully across, consistently. I was always too damned conflicted to believe in anything I was saying. Or maybe I just never really knew what it was I was trying to say. I'd been trying to articulate a Self that was not yet fully formed. How could I expect an audience to rally behind such doubt?

Some people think rock and roll, or pop music, or whatever it is that you call what I do, is just mindless fun or lighthearted diversion from more important things like money or love or politics or religion or whatever. For me, it was always much more serious—more holy— than a merely good time. Music was—still is—a way to obliterate all the shit and the ugliness, in me and out there and all around me, and it was something to put my faith into. (I didn't ever need to go to church to hear a preacher tell me what I already understood every time I wrote a song.) It was a reason for being alive, for getting out of bed in the morning, for not jumping out a window. A reason to go to Columbus, Reno, and North Bergen, New Jersey (the only reason, I think, to go to North Bergen, New Jersey). Music wasn't something I decided to do, one day, for kicks. Music kept me company when I thought I had no one. It brought me friends. It drew kindred spirits out of their garrets and mouseholes. It made some people happy. It made my days and nights purposeful. And that was why I would continue to carry on. I felt obligated to the thing that made life worth living.

Two hours later we were at a hotel somewhere in Illinois and we all said good-night and went to our rooms to rest up for the long drive back to our everyday lives.

309

43

The Last Leg

After the tour ended I continued to write, record, produce, and release albums at the rate of about one a year. Following my release from Atlantic in 1997 I had done an EP for Bar/None Records called *Please Do Not Disturb*, and then there was the *Bed* album. Since I was no longer hindered by slow major label production schedules, I worked at a brisk pace. After *Bed* there was *Beautiful Creature* and *Juliana's Pony: Total System Failure*—two albums (one pop, one rock) released simultaneously on Rounder Records in the year 2000. In 2001 came *God Bless the Blake Babies*, the reunion album, also on Rounder. In 2002 there was *Gold Stars*, a solo career-spanning compilation of songs—highlights—plus a handful of new, previously unreleased tracks. In 2003, soon after the tour in this book, the first Some Girls album, *Feel It*, came out on Koch Records, and 2004 saw the release of my *In Exile Deo*, which was named one of the year's top-10 albums by the *New York Times*. In 2005 I started my own label, Ye Olde Records, and put out my debut solo self-release, *Made in China*. In 2006 Koch handled the second Some Girls album, *Crushing Love*; and in that same year a live album—*The White Broken Line* (named after the stripes in

310

the middle of the pavement I had slogged over day after day, month after month, year after year, logging thousands and thousand of miles)—also came out on Ye Olde. In 2007 there was a six-song EP titled *Sittin' in a Tree . . .* I never stopped working.

The *Made in China* tour, in the fall of 2005, was my last extended series of U.S. dates and it was more brief than any tour I'd done in the past. I'd traveled all around the country to promote every album up until *M.I.C.*, but this time I scaled it down and stuck to the East Coast—and then I decided I'd had enough of the road. I was burned out. I'd been on this schedule for years, since the Blake Babies: write, record, tour; write, record, tour; but after the turn of the millennium, the schedule had started to become a grind.

But that consistent, repetitive work cycle was all I had ever known. If I stopped, what would happen? Would life—real life—come crashing down onto me? Or would my life be over? Would I cease to exist without an audience acknowledging my existence? Could I adjust to the life of a regular person or would I think something was missing? Could I get a real job?

A job like mine—any job without specific hours, really—can start to make you question whether you are working hard enough, or working enough; whether you are even really *working* at all. Without a clear schedule, every minute you spend not working is one you later worry you should have spent working.

Lately, I had begun to envy people who went to an office every day. That sort of lifestyle seemed so exotic, so foreign, so desirable to me, after all the constant moving around I had done. How calming it must be to go to the same clean, well-lighted place every day and to see the same familiar coworkers' faces. I secretly wanted to be one of them— to be a "normal" person with a "normal" job. Having a place to go every morning—a place you knew you belonged—and a clear-cut, doable job to do and then to be able to go home at the end of the day and have the night to yourself, away from work, and do nothing if you wished; to not have to be consumed by the job twenty-four/seven, sounded pretty good to me. Was touring a kind of addiction and would quitting cold turkey be a shock to my system? Would I miss the attention? Would I be forced to confront my fears and my feelings, which touring had pushed aside so effectively and for so long? I needed to find out.

I had no idea what I would do next. I hadn't realized until now that I had a choice. I'd set off running out of the gate when I met John and Freda, as if my music, and getting it out there, were a race. And now I was tired of running. I'd driven myself and my career like I had that first van on the first Blake Babies tour around the country—until it broke down; until it had nothing left.

People in the business (managers, publicists and the media, record label staff, even other musicians) were always telling me, "You have to sustain your moment in the sun—keep your name out there in the public consciousness; keep touring, or people will forget about you." Well, I'd been banging it out out there unceasingly and the majority of people had still forgotten me. My audience was shrinking. The more shows I played, the more the numbers dropped. Maybe they were bored. Maybe they sensed my lack of excitement. My burnout. For once, for the first time, I questioned the logic of staying on the road. Maybe I'd saturated the indie chanteuse market. Maybe being gone would create a new demand for me. (If not, it couldn't really hurt much. My audience couldn't get a whole lot smaller than it already was.)

I wasn't very inspired or excited anymore when I played live shows, and I wasn't bringing in much money, so what was the point of doing it? In interviews I gave along the way, I found myself increasingly mute, and bereft of opinions and witticisms and sound bites. All my interviewers sounded as bored on the phone talking to me as I was. They rarely had anything new to ask. They already knew everything about me that they cared to know. I had less and less to say until finally, at the end of the last tour, there was only air coming out of my mouth. I'd said it all. Or it had all been said. By someone or other. There was nothing left to discuss, nothing for me to comment on, nothing to promote, no convincing arguments I needed to make to anyone. Hardly anyone cared anymore, and neither did I. It was time for me to finally shut my mouth and disappear, at least for a while.

I was cheating the fans and demeaning myself. It was time to give it all a rest and to reevaluate what I was doing, and why I was doing it, for the first time in my life. Like every important decision I ever made, it was scary but it felt inevitable.

But first, I did two last weeks on the East Coast of the United States supporting the Los Angeles band X—the last leg of the *Made in China* tour. I'd been all set to quit and put my guitars in mothballs when I got the call: did I want to be X's supporting act on one last blast before Christmas? Over the years I had gotten to know John Doe (his solo project, the John Doe Thing, opened for me once on a tour in the 1990s) who, along with Exene Cervenka made up one of the great male-female singing/songwriting duos of the modern rock era.

X had a reputation as one of the coolest, most original and creative American bands to emerge from the febrile underbelly of the L.A. punk rock scene and they were one of my all-time favorites. I'd fallen in love with them—specifically their 1982 and 1983 albums *Under the Big Black Sun* and *More Fun in the New World*—as an impressionable teenager, when Maggie brought them into my house via one of her milk crates full of music.

Exene didn't look or sound like anyone else. Before her, the female singers I liked to listen to were Olivia Newton-John, Marie Osmond, Joni Mitchell, Aimee Mann in her 'Til Tuesday days—women like that. All sweet-sounding, nicely groomed, vulnerable-seeming, with a clean, pleasing sheen and songs that were easy to understand. Exene was vulnerable, too, but also tough and raw, with an obvious dark side and many apparent levels of depth to explore. She wore glamorous goth makeup, old dresses, and scuffed black shoes, and she had artfully unbrushed hair (which sometimes turned into white-girl quasi-dreadlocks). She had a tattoo on one shoulder of a question mark and a tattoo on the other of a string of codified expletives (something like this: #*%@!). She came across as an uncompromising, independent, self-aware, sexy, intelligent, pretty, kind of scary, supercool art-school rock-and-roll witch poet who wouldn't take any shit from anyone. She sang in an untrained, vibrato-less sort of monotone wail that was some-how both emotionally expressive and tonally flat, and dry, with a trace of a smirk in it. Her voice, blending incomprehensibly with John Doe's sweet, melting croon, was a totally original sound.

I don't know why I connected to X's songs. They seemed to come from a completely different world than the one I was living in in high school, when I discovered X's music. The world of their songs was gritty, dark, crime-ridden, and fraught with all kinds of betrayals. Mine wasn't. Their characters were urban, street-smart, hard-drinking, married, tattooed. I wasn't any of these things. They sang of poverty,

Catholicism, disillusionment, adultery, death, bitterness—stuff I didn't yet know much about as a young middle-class girl in a small coastal Massachusetts town. My darkness was inside me and my house—not so much in the world around me, or in the lifestyle I was living. But something in Exene's voice, and her bearing—some life force—connected with me. Something sad and defiant and unapologetically honest and temperamentally dissatisfied, which was in me, too.

And when X came knocking, I jumped up and ran to answer their call. Although I was all set to go into indefinite retirement from the road, I got my *Made in China* band together—me, Ed Valauskas on bass, and Pete Caldes on drums—one last time. I also got Tim, my soundman, to bring his recording gear on the tour so that we could get good twenty-four-track concert documentation. I was already thinking ahead to my coming seclusion and hibernation—having good quality live recordings in the bag would be like someone in the olden days pickling beets or making jam out of strawberries, and storing them for use in the winter when there were no fruits or vegetables to be had. I could compile the live tracks sometime down the line and release them as a live album on Ye Olde and bring in a little money that way, if and when I needed it. A live album could also work as a substitute for my regular in-person appearances.

X and I played some of the big-ish places I had headlined in the 1990s: Roseland Ballroom in New York, Masquerade in Atlanta, Avalon in Boston (where I'd done two nights with Jeff Buckley on one part of the *Only Everything* tour). It was bittersweet, going back to revisit old fields of glory, but it was also very much a relief to be back in venues with good sound systems with big, powerful vocal monitors that I could actually hear myself in, and relatively clean and spacious dressing rooms, and friendly, accommodating club staff looking out for me and taking care of the rider and getting our gear off the stage for us. And it was nice to not feel any of the old pressure—as the opening act, I could do my short set with my small band, and then relax and watch X play, from the side of the stage.

Toward the end of the tour, John Doe asked me if I wanted to come up and sing with X on their song "Motel Room in My Bed." John knew that the song was one of my X favorites. It was special to me because it was the first X song I ever heard—the one Maggie put on her record player one day, and which perked up my ears and drew me in and made me ask, "What the hell is this? This is amazing. I've never heard anything like it."

I knew the song backward and forward and upside down and sideways. I'd spent hour after hour listening over and over to *Under the Big Back Sun*, the album on which the song appeared. I'd probably heard the song hundreds of times and I knew all the words and every nuance of every vocal phrase and inflection, so when I got up to sing on John's mike with him, and with Exene a few feet to my right on her mike, it was almost like singing my own song, I knew it so well.

For three or four nights I got up and sang this song with them, and on my last night of the tour, in Northampton, Massachusetts, before I came up Exene introduced me. Usually John, my friend, would say something—a brief welcome summoning me from the wings where I was waiting eagerly. But tonight Exene wanted to do it. She let the crowd know I was going to come out and sing with them and there was some applause, and I expected that to be the end of the intro so I took a step forward, but then Exene went on to say that she really respected me and my music.

I was completely surprised. I hadn't really known what Exene thought of me. She hadn't said much to me so far on the tour, as I hadn't said much to her—although pleasant, our interactions had been brief. My reticence was partly due to the intimidation factor. Exene had been an exalted, iconic figure to me during my most impressionable years, and because of the powerful and lasting effect her voice had had on me during my development as a person and as a singer/musician/songwriter, she still seemed an important, larger-than-life presence and I was a bit dumb and tongue-tied around her. Exene seemed like a woman who didn't waste her time with small talk and who only said something when that something really needed to be said. Maybe she was a little shy, too, like me.

Her words, in my introduction, seemed characteristically deliberate, like this was a necessary, important thing to say, like she'd thought about it. It seemed a kind of an admonishment, to those in the audience who maybe didn't respect me; who hadn't paid attention during my opening set or who had disregarded me or written me off a long time ago as a flash in the "alternative rock" pan, or because of the

315

girlish, unserious sound of my singing voice. Exene had just put her seal of approval on me and all I had tried to do over the years. She'd spoken out on my behalf, in front of the audience, and I was proud and glad.

John, at his microphone, looked over at me behind the monitor board by the dark side of the stage, waiting to make my entrance, to see my reaction to Exene's words. He knew in what high regard I held Exene, and how much I respected her, and X, and what they had done. John was smiling. I was smiling, too, and I put my hand over my heart. As a teenager I had fantasized about maybe meeting Exene one day, and now I had not only met her and shared a tour with her but had won her respect. It was a wonderful feeling. It was the perfect ending to the tour. And it would be the perfect ending to my career, if this was the end.

Made in China was a sonic white flag. In its songs I surrendered to the fact that my time in the spotlight—my season of cultural relevance— had come and gone and there was nothing I could do to change this. I was on my own, releasing my albums on my own label (which was just me—filling orders, stuffing CDs into envelopes—in my apartment) and that meant a small audience or, rather, an even yet smaller audience. From my vantage point, to continue to slog it out in the clubs would be masochistic.

M.I.C. was recorded fast and cheap. It was an abrasive, resigned collection that paid homage to my limitations and my frustrations.

"It's a miracle I'm even here," I sang in the chorus of one song, imagining I was gazing out over a crowd who had come to see me play—my small but loyal group of fans who kept returning to my gigs and buying my records and caring about my music after all these years. I was trying to count my blessings, in those choruses.

"I'll sing to the clock because no one came," from the *M.I.C.* song "Oh" was a reference to a 2003 gig in Eugene, Oregon. It was on the first official Some Girls national tour, after our album *Feel It* had come out. There were only a handful of people in the all-ages community space's rec-hall-like auditorium when we went on. It's hard to get up in front of almost nobody. You have to ask, Why bother? You have to seriously contemplate canceling the gig at the last minute because playing would be so pointless, thankless, and depressing. Who do you sing to?

How do you sing your heart out if there is not really anyone to receive it and to reflect back to you some of its warmth and compassion and understanding? But you go on. Maybe you cry a few tears first, in the dressing room, and then you take a few breaths and dry your eyes and put on your professional face and push the pain away—you go on because you have to play a full set in order to be paid your guarantee. And you need the money.

In Eugene that night, I focused my eyes on the big clock hanging up high on the wall opposite me, all the way across the room, over the heads of the five people there to see the show, because it was too hard, too sad, too heartbreaking to look at those people standing awkwardly in their conspicuousness, out in the open, with empty space all around them in the big old wooden hall. So I sang to the clock. As if the clock might care what I had to say. Trying to telekinetically will its hands around the dial, faster than time, so that my set could be over and done and put behind me and forgotten, quickly.

It was like the Blake Babies first CBGB's show all over again, except this time, I had hundreds—maybe thousands—of gigs, all over the world, under my belt, and I'd put out multiple albums and been on TV and in magazines and on the radio. And I'd come full circle. I was right where I started. And now, unlike in the beginning, I didn't have the energy or the faith or the determination to fight to convince people I was worth listening to.

I'd already done that.

44

The Year of No Music

After the X tour, I stopped. Not only did I retire, indefinitely, from touring, but I vowed not to write another song for a year. I felt stale, used up, drained, and empty. (The X tour had been great, and gratifying, but mainly because I was watching one of my favorite bands play every night, not because my own performances were especially good or satisfying.)

I stopped to protect and preserve whatever creative spark I had left flickering weakly inside of me.

I also wanted to explore other possibilities, or other ways of thinking about my life after music. I had never, until now, even contemplated the possibility of the end of my music career, but now I had to confront it. Maybe there was something else I could do if I was no longer able to support myself financially with my music. If I could find a new focus—a new cause to which to dedicate myself—I could transition into that: a new life with new work.

I moved out of the tiny, cramped apartment in the run-down building—full of poor, struggling musicians—in Inman Square in Cambridge that I had been living in, and feeling trapped in, for six years. I lost contact with people. Friends slipped away. I retreated, from everything and everyone associated with the rock world, and found that away from that scene there wasn't really anyone left. I would have to meet new people.

I loved not having to prove anything to anybody: that I could sing, play, write; that I was authentic, that I had integrity, that I was a legitimate artist—something I had struggled to prove, throughout my career. It was just me and myself, getting to know each other really well, learning how to coexist. And what I found was that I liked myself a lot. And I didn't really need anyone, nor did I need anyone's approval. I just needed to be alone, to sit with my feelings and see if I could handle them. And I could. I wasn't lost without an audience clapping and propping me up. In fact, I found myself, away from the crowds. I saw the real me, clearly, without confusion, and it turns out I am a pretty normal, likable girl, after all. I did what normal people do. I ate three meals a day, went to the movies with my new friends, worried about my future, my finances. Same as everyone else.

The attention given to popular young musical artists often focuses on their struggles and addictions and weaknesses, and to some extent this attention reinforces and prolongs the artists' negative, damaging traits. The most fascinating artists are often the ones who are the most screwed-up. A good smash-up can be very entertaining. And if what an audience wants is a train wreck, well, you want to give them what they want. I always fought this. I tried to keep all my problems hidden. I was determined not to play that game of public self-destruction. It was a too-easy shortcut to winning attention. I wanted my work to be noticed for its own value as music, and not because I was a depressed, antisocial, anorexic freak. I thought of those problems of mine as obstacles to be overcome, in private. I never wanted to exploit them to boost my record sales or my public profile. But being in the public eye—being scrutinized and critiqued—amplified my insecurities.

I loved the quiet out of the clubs, away from the bands and the crowds and the scene. I didn't realize how very sick of it all I really was (and how much it cluttered up my mind) until I had some real distance from it. After a few months, I couldn't go within a half mile of a rock club or I would start to feel almost nauseated. The thought of going inside made me shudder.

319

I was like a snake in a hole shedding its skin. Even Gary—my old friend, the only manager I'd ever had, my sometime producer, my fellow malcontent, the one who discovered the Blake Babies and took us under his wing—bought a farm and moved to the country. He was just as burned-out as I was on the music business and he wanted to get away from it permanently. For the first time in fourteen years, I didn't have a manager, an advocate, a trusted comrade behind the front lines with me, but it was fitting because I wasn't on the front lines anymore. I'd surrendered. But I was okay.

I was relieved to take a break from singing, because singing was difficult. Singing was a constant struggle for me. I was always having to practice my vocal exercises. I had a binder notebook of staff paper full of written drills that I would break open and work from, regularly, to keep my naturally weak voice muscles in shape. It was physically strenuous, and tedious, like any prolonged repetitive exercise, and there never seemed to be any end to it, so it was wonderful to take a whole yearlong break from it, for the very first time since I was a student at Berklee.

I took a memoir-writing workshop and I worked on this book. I took a couple of art classes. I rediscovered my love for writing prose and for drawing and painting, all of which I had abandoned when I started writing songs and making records. I even contemplated a career in journalism, or in illustration, and though both things seemed almost ridiculously far out of reach, the fact that I could see a way past playing the rock club circuit filled me with excitement. I read a lot. I stuck to my self-imposed one-year exile from writing any music. I embraced the quiet, and the solitude. I didn't fall apart and I didn't miss the road.

Ironically, touring can become a way to avoid experiencing life fully. It's a shutting out of the real world, escaping it; escaping into the bubble of your music, your crew, the dark clubs and dressing rooms. Off the road, I finally opened my eyes and began to see the world anew.

I started noticing people. Some of them seemed familiar, as if I sort of knew they had always been there, as part of the natural environment, or the background, but I only half-recognized them as shapes I had only ever seen in my peripheral vision. I was reintroduced to people who had been living within a five-mile radius of me, and who had traveled in the same circles, and who had gone to all of the same places in town, and whom I had maybe seen around or had even met but couldn't fully remember. They knew me but I didn't know them. I had been walking around in a haze and now it was clearing. I made an effort to get to know them, now. Years later. And no one held it against me that I had been so not-there for so long, and didn't recognize anyone or anything. I felt like a coma patient who had just regained consciousness.

The same old town that I had been asleep in, and that I had escaped from, over and over again, was now new to me, as if I was seeing it with a new pair of eyes. I realized there were plenty of cool, interesting, smart, good people right near me, whom I had overlooked for many years when I was out traveling around the world trying to make myself heard. I'd always wanted to get away, get out of Boston, make a mark nationally and maybe even internationally. As far as I was concerned Boston represented my own limitations; it was something to break through, and past. But now as I gradually started to reacquaint myself with Boston—specifically Cambridge, where I lived—and its people, I realized that maybe everything I needed was all here. Maybe it didn't matter where I was. If I felt bad, I'd feel bad anywhere. What mattered was my perception of things. If I was confident I'd made the right choices, I wouldn't need an audience to tell me I'd done the right thing.

Almost a year to the date after I'd made my vow, I wrote a song. I had become friends with a guy in a local Boston band called the Dead Trees, whose music I loved. Mike was the main songwriter. He and I were getting into my car one night at the end of November—the first really cold night of the season—and Mike shivered. It was one of those brief, whole-body-stiffening tremors, and Mike said, out loud but kind of to himself, "Ooh, the first shiver of the year."

That gave me an idea. I said to Mike, "Hey, Mike, let's each write each other a song for Christmas. We'll exchange songs instead of gifts." Mike was game. My song was called "The First Shiver." Mike's didn't have a title and in it he sang about "the queen of the scene" and "no entropy." We recorded them in our respective homes and presented them to each other just before Christmas.

After that, the floodgates opened and songs started pouring out of me. My plan had worked! Forcing myself not to write any music for a year had indeed recharged my creative batteries, and I was off and running again, as excited as ever at what was streaming out of me and onto the page and into my tape recorder, with no worry of eventually having to go on the road with the new songs and prove myself, again. This time I wrote and sang for and to only myself. My music came back to me. It was part of me. It had nothing to do with a career or with rewards or with acclaim. It was, simply, who I was. And I had to let go of my career, and I had to put a halt to the relentless pursuit of applause in order to understand, once and for all, that no commercial success— no outside affirmation of my talents and my self—will ever be enough, on its own, to make me happy.

I wrote and wrote like the house was on fire, like words and chords and melodies were going to burn up and disintegrate into the air if I didn't capture them fast enough. It was like being on a drug binge—or what I imagine a drug binge might feel like. It was a wonderful holiday from pain and troubles, and from time and space, being fully present in the series of moments that make up the act of creation. But, unlike a person on a drug binge, I wasn't escaping from myself. When writing, I was myself. My best self. The songs were bursting to get out, bursting with life. I let go, let it happen, let my body and soul do what they were born to do, wired to do; born to want to do: to write. To make songs.

45

How to Walk Away

I made plans to record an album in New York City with Andy Chase, a producer I had done some exploratory demos with in the past. I received a surprisingly large, totally unexpected royalty check from my publishing company the week before I went in to the studio. It was just large enough to cover, almost to the penny, the whole budgeted cost of the recording project—a serendipitous godsend. Up until I received the surprise check, I had been worrying about the big chunk I was about to take from my savings to pay for the album.

I didn't want to cut corners and motor through these sessions to save time and money like I had on the majority of my recent albums. I wanted to give these new songs what they needed to shine their brightest. Because I really loved and cared about them. And I felt like maybe this was my last chance to give people something to remember me by; my last chance to muster all my will to try before I gave up for good. It just seemed that it was getting harder and harder to do what I did and to sustain my career, the way it had been going for the past few years.

The songs reflected that: almost all of them explored the idea of leaving; of getting out of bad situations or ones that were no longer worthwhile, learning from past mistakes and moving on, alone.

There were a couple of songs that I was really worried were going to be tough to nail: "This Lonely Love" and "Remember November." Both reached to the high and low extremes of my vocal range. I needed to deliver dynamism, subtlety, and power within their snaky roller-coaster melodies. I put off singing these two songs until the end of the recording sessions. When I finally went in to record my vocals I was very nervous, and was thinking it would take all night to get it right, but to my surprise and delight the voice that came out of me was powerful and assured and able to reach all the lows and the highs without much struggle. There was a new strength and confidence, even a playfulness, in my vocal instrument, which mirrored my own emerging maturity, decisiveness, and will to feel better in my life. I broke through some wall—some wall I had always been slamming against—and over a plateau I'd been stuck on, for years, as a singer. Somehow I'd opened up a door for my voice to come through, and I kind of stood back and watched, happy.

Andy Chase's production was lush and pretty and layered with lots of piano and acoustic guitars and violins. It was beautiful-sounding. Polished but not overly so, with just enough of my natural rawness still intact.

I had no idea when or if or how the album would come out but I believed, maybe for the first time ever, that what I was making deserved an audience. I needed to believe it. Not that it would have a big audience—but that it was as good as any popular bunch of songs. That's what I needed in order to summon the strength, the will, and the energy to get through the complicated recording process; to believe that it would matter to people other than myself, if they heard it. Should matter, because the songs, full of pain and joy and sadness and hope and humor and strength and vulnerability—human things, universal things—were good and my voice was in top form. But would that count for anything? Now that I was finally at the top of my game—now that my brain and body had finally caught up to my potential—was it too late? Would anyone care?

I had always thought that I was just really lucky to get to make records, and that every little bit of good fortune or success or praise that came my way was a fluke, or that it was the law of averages dictating that once in a while I would be lauded by somebody out there simply because I was always there, putting out records, playing shows, refusing to go away, and someone had to like me. But now I allowed myself to believe that maybe I deserved it, as much as anybody else.

The new album was made without guarantees, without a safety net, without any outside encouragement. If no one cared, if no one heard it or bought it, if I never made my investment back and subsequently ran out of money, if this latest and possibly last best effort had no effect on anyone, at least I would have the satisfaction of knowing that I had tried as hard as I could to make a good album. Part of me felt that it would be a tragedy if this album never found an audience. The songs and production were more accessible and pleasing to the ear than anything I had ever recorded. Still, I had to accept that maybe no one would hear it. Maybe my day in the sun had come and gone, period.

I had to be okay with that. I had to love the new album for myself and maybe love it on my own in a vacuum because I had no other choice. That was all I could do. I was powerless to affect the reactions of other people. And without a big, well-endowed record company or any investors backing me, I had very limited funds with which to promote and publicize my new album. Maybe people would find their way unexpectedly, unsuspectingly, happily, to the album, like a person comes upon a twenty-dollar bill in the street. I had to let it be. Let it exist without hoping for or needing an audience.

I'd done it for me and for no one else. Not for any record company. Not for fame or money. Not for the love of beautiful boys. No matter what anyone said or failed to say about it, I would know I had finally made a great album. And I could retreat, into a new, postmusic career life, whatever that might comprise, with my head held high; with no embarrassment or shame or regret. I decided to call the new album *How to Walk Away*.

While I was in New York working on the album, I met somebody. It was the first time in a long time—years, in fact—that I had even given anyone a second look. I'd almost forgotten it could happen. I'd become pretty reclusive and I really believed it was my fate to be alone, for better or for worse. After Sam ("The Darkness") I had stopped

325

bothering to try to make any connections with anyone. I figured it was for my own good, since rock guys were what I was attracted to, and all I ever did with them was get into trouble. The only alternative to rock guys was to be alone.

But Bill wasn't a rock guy. And he wasn't young and confused. He was older than I was, and he had a realistic view of himself and the world around him. He wasn't penniless or lost or fragile or moody or addicted to drugs or alcohol and he didn't have stars in his eyes. He was the opposite of all that. He was grown-up in all the right ways: responsible, kind, smart, funny, hardworking, reserved, calm, patient, thoughtful, gentle, modest, reasonable, conscious that actions and words have consequences. Above all, Bill was sane, refreshingly so. (For once in my life, that wasn't a bad thing in a guy; his sanity didn't make him less interesting.) He had nothing to prove and no show to put on for anyone. He was different from anyone I had been involved with in the past. He wasn't my type, I didn't think; he was mature and responsible.

As we spent time together in New York, something wonderful and unexpected began to happen. Bill and I found ourselves finishing each other's sentences, and speaking the same words at the same time. We seemed to be always thinking the same thoughts, and having the exact same reactions to things. There was an ease with Bill. Silences were never uncomfortable and I felt no need to fill up space with chatter or fidgeting or worry. Whenever Bill and I made eye contact, there was tenderness and understanding. Never in my life had I felt so strongly connected to someone for reasons that had nothing to do with music. And I wasn't afraid, or nervous, and I didn't feel that Bill and I were doomed. It felt good, and it felt real, not like a fantasy—not like all the others.

With Bill, I didn't feel that I needed to change, or that I wasn't good enough or fabulous enough or talented enough or that there was something wrong with me. I didn't have to be anything but what and who I already was. Knowing that someone smart and reasonable and sane liked me made me feel that maybe I was all right. Even just right. All at once, I felt comfortable in my skin.

This, I thought, is how it should be. All of life should be so effortless. If only everything made sense like this!

I'd never known that caring about somebody could be so pain-free.

All my past failed relationships, and often the relationship I had to myself, had been so fraught with tension and strife and difficulty and ache, but it wasn't like that with Bill. With Bill, it was easy.

One night Bill cooked me dinner at his place. It was just a simple dinner, nothing fancy, but it meant a lot to me because no man had ever made me dinner before. I know that must sound crazy but it's true. None of my previous boyfriends ever made me dinner.

Bill and I ate that dinner together and it was such a normal thing for two people who liked each other to do (and no doubt hundreds of thousands of people were doing the same thing at the same time that night, in New York City) but for me it was a really special, significant moment. It was a refreshingly, wonderfully nice, simple way to enjoy each other's company. A good hour without ego or insecurity or arguing or doubt or worry or performance anxiety.

All this was a revelation to me.

Maybe I could have a regular life after all, and it wouldn't seem to be lacking, as I always feared a "normal" existence would. Maybe I could take pleasure in simple things and a simple, quiet life, rather than needing the approval and the applause of large numbers of total strangers.

Bill lived in New York and I lived in Boston so I knew that when the album was finished I'd go back to Boston and he'd stay in New York and he would be a great memory—but also a great friend forever. This isn't a fairy-tale ending. Bill and I didn't walk off into the sunset together. But my time with him left me feeling very hopeful because I never knew normalcy could feel so great. Maybe I could be normal, too?

Maybe my life could be more than just music. I could love an adult, I could love like an adult. I could find love on solid ground instead of jumping onto a ship that we both knew was sinking.

Love was now something to look forward to.

The great thing about art is that, as an artist, you can always come back with another album, another painting, another book, another movie, another play, another ballet. You have the chance to prove yourself, again and again. I have always operated under the "Field of Dreams" assumption: If I build it, they will come. And they did, and I know they will again. Someday. I have to believe it. And why shouldn't I?

Art—pop music, literature, painting, design, acting—needs an audience. If the art can't be seen or heard or read, and felt, and contemplated, what is the point of its existing at all? The artist won't stop working if there is no audience. The true artist's art isn't a hobby. It's a necessity. But he will always hope—for recognition, for respect, for love, for accolades, maybe for money and rewards—even if he doesn't admit it.

I have been lucky. From early on, I had an audience. My audience has been scattered around the country, around pockets of the world, and it has swelled and shrunk according to the seasons of my career and the whims of popular culture, but it has never left me completely. For this I am grateful. Even if I stay away from the rock clubs, even if my audience is unseen, I will know it's out there because my music is out there. People have always found it, even when it wasn't being shoved in their faces by MTV and all the magazines. I went out looking for an audience and I found them, just as they found me. Now I am by myself, and I can feel it: it is as it should be.

When—*if*—I decide to come back, they will come, too.

Epilogue

I threw the last pair of socks into the washing machine and then I reached into my duffel bag and pulled out my Levi's—the one remaining dirty item of tour clothing, none of which had been cleaned since before leaving home a month ago. I checked each of the two front pockets, to make sure there weren't any bills in there that were about to be laundered, and there weren't. But then in the left back pocket I felt something. I pulled out a small square of folded-up paper. "Hmmm. What could this be?" I wondered as I threw my jeans into the washer and closed the lid. I held the paper in one hand and with the other I put my six quarters in the slots, one by one, and watched the machine's WASH light turn red and heard the water start sloshing in. Then I walked over to the row of plastic chairs in front of the dryers, unfolding my note. I sat down and read what I'd found in my pocket:

Dear Juliana,

Just a quick note to say thank you for sharing your songs with us. Your music has been a real inspiration to me over the years, as I'm sure it has to many people. I'm looking forward to hearing the next album and hope there'll be plenty more over the coming years. I really hope it brings as much happiness to you as it does to us.

Alex

It was the note I'd been handed by a fan in San Francisco, I remembered, as I made my way from the stage to the dressing room right after the show. I'd stuffed the piece of paper in my back pocket and forgotten about it. Reading it now, when I was calm and relaxed, back at home, and on my own, and free, and utterly without pressure or duties, I was able to see things clearly and I thought, as if realizing it for the very first time, with amazement, "It *does*, Alex! It does make me happy. And I *will* make more albums. Maybe I'll dedicate one to you. I don't need to sell millions of them and I don't need to see my face in magazines and I don't have to be perfect and I don't have to put on the best show anyone has ever seen in their entire lives to feel okay about what I'm doing; I just have to keep going, keep trying. Thank you, Alex, for reminding me."